Men of

The Second World War

*'Arm yourselves,
and be ye men of valour.'*

Winston Churchill, May 1940

Other books by Brian Hodgkinson

Men of Valour

The Second World War

Poetry by Brian Hodgkinson

Illustrations by George Murray

SHEPHEARD
WALWYN
PUBLISHERS

© Brian James Hodgkinson 2021

First published in 2021 by
Shepheard-Walwyn (Publishers) Ltd
107 Parkway House, Sheen Lane,
London SW14 8LS
www.shepheardwalwyn.com
www.ethicaleconomics.org.uk

British Library Cataloguing in Publication Data
A catalogue record of this book is available from the British Library

ISBN: 978-0-8568-547-6

Printed on FSC accredited paper

Cover design by Eleanor Russell-Jones

Typeset by Catherine Hodgkinson

Printed and bound by 4edge Limited

Contents

In Memory of George Murray

artist and friend

*'That is the gods' work, spinning threads of death
through the lives of mortal men,
and all to make a song for those to come.'*

The Odyssey, trans. Robert Fagles,
Book Eight, lines 649-651

1 The Approach of War

Once more the light of Christian Europe shone,
Its source undimmed, on nations stunned by war,
As silence fell at last on every front
Where dreadful carnage for so long had raged.
And yet, by those oblivious of law,
In Russia first, in Rome and then Berlin,
The old authority of king or State
Was cast aside; illegal violence ruled
Those populous lands. Enfeebled by distress,
The mass of people were too soon deceived
By raucous speeches blaming every ill
On traitors, foreign enemies and Jews.

The greatest evil lay in Germany,
For there, at Europe's heart, a poison spread
Throughout the State, infecting every limb -
Government, law and Church, workplace and home -
Founded on hatred, fostered by belief
In gross betrayal at the Treaty made
To seal the Great War's final armistice.
No promise by the Allies had been made
As to the form of any settlement,
But Germany mistook the high ideals
Of Woodrow Wilson for a proffered peace,
And cried 'betrayal' when it found itself
Deprived of land and blamed for causing war.
Their fleet beneath the waves at Scapa Flow,
Denied a powerful army, forced to pay
Six billion pounds in reparation claims,
Some dreamed of vengeance, and rebirth of pride,
And welcomed those who spoke again of war.

Others, like Stresemann, chose another way,
Of compromise and sound diplomacy;
But when depression came, and millions lost
The chance to work, and saw their homes beset
With hunger, sickness, fear and apathy,
They turned to wrathful leaders, those who spoke
Of enemies within, of 'Reds' and Jews,
And stirred the pot of xenophobic hate.
Then civil strife erupted in the streets,
Fuelled by despair and led by violent men,
By nationalists and barons of the press,
By Communists, and those who stood to gain
From manufacture of great armaments.

The new Republic could not long sustain
Such brawls and beatings, marches, riots, plots,
Inspired by men devoid of liberal thought,
Who sought to end Weimar democracy.
Both Communists and National Socialists,
Though bitter foes, grew strong upon the fears
That each induced of losing what was owned
Of life and land and personal property
By Bolshevist revolt or Nazi putsch.
Moderate parties lost hard-won support
To these fanatics of opposing wings,
Who undermined the rule of law at home
And vilified the hope of peace abroad.

Above this turmoil rose one strident voice,
Compelling, harsh, adulterate with hate,
The cry of Adolf Hitler, one possessed,
Resentful, homeless, lonely, insecure,
Whose overriding love was brutal war,
Where he had found companions under arms,
Facing with them the rattle-death of guns,
And choking mustard gas and live grenade
In fearful dug-outs on the western front.
Germany's plight he blamed on foreign powers,
On Jews, and on those hapless few who'd signed,
In their distress, the Treaty of Versailles.
He looked for glory in a Greater Reich,
Which would embrace all those of German blood,
A nation pure in race, a Herrenvolk,
Devoid of all miscegenated stock,
Contemptuous of other breeds and tongues,
Insistent on the justice of the strong.

To this obscure and cruel, irrational end,
Hitler advanced by bold and cunning steps.
Selected by the aged Hindenburg -
A senile hero of the former war -
As German Chancellor, he soon removed
All opposition from the seats of power,
Replacing them with National Socialists -
Frick and Goering, Himmler, Goebbels, Hess
And thousands more throughout the German Reich.
Then Nazi principles of race and State
Were introduced in every sphere of life.
All fair debate and freedom of the press,
The right of legal trial, the right to work,
Independent churches, unions, schools,
Respect for learning, literature and art,
Philosophy, and all that was profound
In centuries of German national life
Were now denied in favour of one aim:
The power to dominate, and to that end
To re-ignite horrendous fires of war.

Elsewhere in Europe men once more recalled
Those battlefields where Germany had marched:
Soldiers impaled on wire, blinded by gas,
Blasted by shell or mortar, thousands dead,
Buried in alien lands, in nameless graves.
So many then had died that it was said
That never more would such a war be fought.
Now in the mind of Europe lay the fear
That once again great armies would enlist,
And warships put to sea, and, worst of all,

That new-created bombers would release
Their tons of death on undefended streets.

Then German columns marched across the Rhine,
Defying what the Treaty had prescribed,
To leave the western bank without defence;
And Italy, avenging past defeat,
Was led by Mussolini to expel
The Ethiopian emperor from his land
And thus extend her Afric colonies.
Then Austria was forced within the Reich
By Hitler's threats, and in Sudetenland,
Where Germans dwelt, though governed by the Czechs,
The local Nazis clamoured to secede
And join with the Fuhrer's 'Fatherland'.
Therefore, at Munich, Anglo-French accord,
Fearing aggression, bowed to Hitler's greed.
The Czechs were left without security;
And 'Peace with honour', Chamberlain proclaimed,
Upholding, like a victor, to the skies,
A piece of paper bearing Hitler's name.
Winston Churchill was not so deceived,
And warned again that war could not be stemmed
By feeding the aggressor's appetite.

When, six months later, Prague was occupied,
The world could see the Führer's real intent,
For this was not an Anschluss as before
Of German-speaking subjects in the Reich.
Britain and France now tardily were moved
To give the Poles and Greeks their guarantees
Against invasion by the Fascist powers.

Then, finally, despite what he'd proclaimed
Of anti-Bolshevism and Teutonic pride,
The Führer signed a Nazi-Soviet pact
Partitioning again the Polish State,
To make secure the Prussian borderlands
Against the threat of Communist attack.
All dreams of peace were utterly dispelled.
The ancient port of Danzig now became
The German *casus belli* with the Poles;
But '*Mort pour Danzig?*' Why should Frenchmen fight?
Would Britain go to war for Polish pride?
The Führer gambled on their lack of will,
Forgetting others' words were honoured still.

2 Blitzkrieg

Inflammatory stories, spread abroad
Of how in Poland Germans were abused,
Made propaganda for the Nazi claim
On Danzig and the Polish Corridor.
Dressed up as Polish soldiers, detainees
Were shot attacking Gleiwitz border post:
A facile plot contrived to brand the Poles
As first to look to arms for settlement.
The world was not convinced by this device;
But tanks rolled forward, followed by the mass
Of field-grey soldiers, young adventurers,
Whose families did not share their lust for war,
But watched in silence as they marched away.

Vainglorious Poland, ill-equipped to fight
Against the *blitzkrieg* which the Germans brought,
Faced four attacks when dire invasion came -
From Eastern Prussia, Pomerania,

Silesia and from the Slovak hills,
Across a border lengthened since the time
When Czechoslovaks bloodlessly succumbed.
For now, at last, the Wehrmacht could unleash
Its modern army, well prepared to fight
On eastern plains still dry from Summer drought,
Where tanks and mobile infantry advanced
Past fearful peasants, fleeing from their homes.
On Polish airfields fighter planes were wrecked
By shrieking Stukas' catastrophic dives,
While desperate armies struggled to deploy,
As railways and communications burned
From bombs that fell on troops and towns alike.
Upon the flat and ripening fields of rye
The untried *Panzers* briefly were delayed
By gallant Polish horsemen, charging guns
That soon destroyed their futile panoply.

Ancient Cracow fell, and pincers closed
Upon Warsaw, where Polish troops withdrew.
Along the Bzura river one attempt
Was made to halt the enemy advance,
But German reinforcements quickly doused
This final flame of Polish chivalry.
Warsaw, besieged, fought on for many days,
Bombed by Heinkels, shelled by heavy guns.
In smoke and dust, with smell of burning flesh,
Its people stayed defiant, till there came
A lack of food and water, then of hope,
As Poland's government fled towards Lublin,
And Soviet armies entered from the east.
The ruined city bowed its blooded head,

And Poland was divided once again.
For twenty years the Poles had been released
From Russian bondage. Now they were condemned
To witness new atrocities of war.
Chelmno, Treblinka, Auschwitz, Majdanek:
An odious fame would gather round such names.

No spirit of offence stirred France to strike
As she was wont to do in former wars.
Three bridges on the Rhine were blown up,
But nothing threatened Hitler's Siegfried Line,
And German guns traversed the autobahns
To reinforce the Polish enterprise.
Conscripted soldiers slowly filled the ranks
That stood in France to guard the sacred land
Against a third assault of Teuton arms.
Britain could only send a token force
To build again another western front,
In hope to dam the furious flood of war
That Allied soldiers knew from fathers' tales
Might rise again in Artois and Champagne.
But through the Winter months and early Spring
The 'phoney war' prevailed, the '*drole de guerre*',
Whilst on the farms of France new crops were sown,
And Englishmen commuted to their work,
But practised army drill on village greens.

Meanwhile, the Russians, fearing Leningrad
Was vulnerable to any hostile power,
Demanded from the Finns exchange of land,
Especially on the Gulf of Finland coast.
The Finns refused, and so a war began

In Winter forests, hanging deep with snow,
Where Finnish soldiers, uniformed in white,
Outfought on skis, amongst their trees and lakes,
The ponderous mass of Russian infantry,
Who grew to fear the 'White Death' unforeseen.
From Soviet Karelia they came,
By Lake Ladoga's frozen emptiness,
And on the narrow isthmus, where the Finns
Had built in depth a strong defensive line.
They dare not turn to face their commissars,
But died in thousands, falling hand in hand,
Immured by nature to their wintry end.

This check on Russian arms appeared to prove
To all observers that the recent purge
Of Soviet generals, caused by Stalin's doubts
Of loyalty to his sole authority,
Had gravely weakened Russia's own defence.
Amongst the Allies other hopes were raised.
Could French and British troops relieve the Finns,
Whose courage *in extremis* was admired?
Would such a step enable them to seize
The Swedish iron ore sent to Germany?
For Narvik port would serve two purposes:
To help the Finns, and reach the Swedish ore.
Decision was deferred; uncertainties
Beset the Allies when they understood
That war with Russia strengthened Hitlers' hand.
Nor did they want to breach neutrality
At Narvik and the Gallivare mines.

But Hitler was aware that Allied eyes
Were turned on Norway. Nor was he surprised
When British sailors, in the Josenfjord,
Boarded the German 'Altmark', and released
The British prisoners held below its decks.
Accordingly the Fuhrer authorised
A ruthless strike against neutrality:
By 'Operation Weser' Wehrmacht troops
Would land at Norway's capital and ports,
Forestalling any Allied enterprise.
Though tardily the British navy sailed
To mine the coast in Norway's neutral seas,
Enemy forces struck a bolder blow.
Whilst troopships crossed the narrow Skagerrak,
Luftwaffe Junkers carried paratroops,
Who fell upon Norwegian aerodromes -
The first descent of airborne troops in war -
To hold the landing strips for later flights.
In Oslo harbour brief resistance flared
From local sailors and the fortress guns,
When shore torpedoes sank the German ship
Transporting army staff and secret police.
Yet Oslo could not long withstand the shock
Of sudden landings by efficient troops.
The party led by Quisling took control,
Subservient to Germany's command -
Henceforth a name to live in infamy.

Disparity of power coerced the Danes
When Copenhagen fell to token force,
But Norway struggled on, in hope of aid,
As Germans landed on the western coast,

At Kristiansand and Bergen in the south,
At Trondheim and at Narvik's distant port.
King Haakon and his ministers proclaimed,
Amongst the valleys deeply scarred with snow
Where armoured cars pursued them to Hamar,
That all should fight for Norway's sovereignty;
And yet his army, slow to mobilise,
Could only muster ill-assorted groups,
Who clung to wooden road blocks till outflanked,
And suffered undefended from the air -
For German aircraft ruled the snow-filled skies.
So only on the coast could succour come
From new-found allies seemingly resolved
To land in force and drive the Germans out.

At sea, heroic action saved the pride
Of Britain's navy, which had failed to stop
Invasion by a much inferior fleet.
One destroyer - 'Glowworm' - left to fight
A lonely battle off the fjord coast,
Engaged the cruiser 'Hipper', though outclassed,
And through a smoke-screen rammed her in the side.
Then five destroyers sank ten Kriegsmarine
In Narvik harbour, and Warburton-Lee,
The captain of the 'Hardy', sent his crews,
As German reinforcements threatened them,
A last command - 'Continue to engage' -
Before he died from grievous injuries.

To retake Narvik was the foremost aim
Of Allied leaders, but they also sought
To land at Trondheim, sealing off the north.

Luftwaffe domination changed the plan:
Instead the French and British would descend
On Andalsnes and Namsos, to converge
From north and south on Trondheim's garrison.
The southern force was heavily attacked
By Germans better trained to fight in snow,
And progress south to Namsos was delayed
By shortage of supplies. Soon it was clear
The pincer movement was too hazardous.
Both forces were withdrawn through their ports.

Far north at Narvik, Austrian mountain troops,
With German sailors, dug in by the town.
Too long the Allies lingered at their base
At Harstad harbour fifty miles away,
Unsure of how to land in heavy snow
Beneath attack from bombs and coastal guns.
Though battleships could bombard German lines,
Scruples about civilians drew their fire.
Thus only tardily, with Norway lost,
Was Narvik town assaulted from the sea,
When reinforcements came of French and Poles
And brave Norwegian remnants undeterred.
Germans were driven out, but soon avenged.
It was too late; the Finns had come to terms,
And, on the western front, the surge of war
Was rising to o'erspill the futile wall
Built on the fear of widespread slaughter there.
The Allied soldiers ruefully embarked;
And Swedish ore was saved for Germany.
Now Norway's coast would harbour Nazi ships -
The mighty 'Tirpitz' and a U-boat fleet,

Whose sturdy crews would threaten to destroy
Whatever convoys sailed from Britain's shores.

The war machine that Hitler had compelled
To mount a project swift and perilous
Had won its laurels for professional skill,
At sea, by air, and on the hard terrain
Of central Norway, in a barren land
Where ice and snow impeded every move.
In expert fighting, leadership, supply,
The Wehrmacht had surpassed its enemies.
And yet the Kriegsmarine could ill afford
So many losses in the northern seas,
A weakness which reduced the future threat
Of armed invasion of the British Isles;
And, by his ruthlessness and disregard
Of Norway's people, Hitler had confirmed
That German soldiers fought with such prowess
For Nazi ends unworthy of their zeal.

Norway displayed the Allies' lack of will.
Unreadiness could no more be concealed.
Slow to respond, unsure and ill-equipped,
They proved their mettle only in defeat,
In rearguard actions or outgunned at sea.
Their populations feared a coming storm,
Like that which broke on Norway's neutral land.
When Finland was defeated, Reynaud won
The office that Daladier forsook.
So now, as Norway's freedom lay extinct,
The name of Neville Chamberlain gave rise
To questioning that augured his demise.

3 The Fall of France

Along the Rhine artillery proclaimed
The ancient feud of Teutons and the Franks,
As Hitlers' armies crossed the frontiers
Of Belgium, Holland and of Luxembourg.
The Allies' failure in the distant north
To rescue Norway from the Nazi grip
Cast doubts on Britain's appetite for war
And Chamberlain's capacity to fight.
Was he the man to lead the nation armed
Against the very powers he had appeased
With such assiduous, unwarlike speech;
Who had proclaimed his faith in Hitler's word
And peace with honour? Was not this the time
For unremitting war with every means

Against a foe implacable in hate?
The British Parliament, as oft before,
Awoke to meet a danger long ignored.
So now they summoned Chamberlain to go,
'In the name of God, go'[1], as Cromwell cried;
And, in his place, they called a mightier voice
To speak for Britain at this crucial hour.
Winston Churchill - scion of the line
Of John, first Duke of Marlborough, likewise called
To lead the British, allied in defence
Of those same small and violated States -
Informed the world of Britain's will to fight
For victory at all costs, and come what may.
Warlike adventure under many suns
Had long prepared him for this destiny;
For he had drunk the violent draught of war
At sea and in the air, and under fire
Commanding men on Flanders' battlefields.
For long he had perceived the Nazi threat,
And chastened the appeasers with harsh words.
Reluctant to be led in time of peace,
The British nation, now belligerent,
Acknowledged, in its peril, his renown.
As Churchill said himself, his were the words
The British lion, aroused from slumber, roared.

Once more the god of war cast forth his gaze
On lowly Belgium, formerly the scene
Of Marlborough's battles with the Sun King's arms
At Oudenarde, Namur and Ramilles;
Where recent war had stained with fresher blood
The fields of Passchendaele, Mons, Messines,

And shattered towns from Antwerp down to Ypres,
Where still the bugle rang at Menin Gate.
The German general, Manstein, had devised
A plan to circumvent the French defence
By driving through the hills of the Ardennes,
And thus outflank the fortress line of France
That stretched from Luxembourg along the Rhine.
Too late the cautious Belgians called for help,
No longer neutral as their country burned.
So British troops advanced towards the Dyle,
And French along the Meuse, but Liege fell
When airborne Germans swooped upon the fort
Of Eben Emael, believed impregnable,
And bridges on the frontier canal.
Through Tongres, Louvain, Wavres the Wehrmacht
    poured,
And entered Brussels' now deserted streets.

On Holland too the parachutists fell
To seize the bridges for the armoured force
That crossed the neutral border unforeseen.
Too late the sluice gates opened to the floods,
As Stukas, diving low at Rotterdam,
Compelled surrender by their terror bombs.
Queen Wilhemina fled to England's shores:
Five days of *blitzkrieg* broke that dynasty
Which years of fortitude had once empowered.

Now deep within the hills of the Ardennes,
The German columns steadily progressed,
Across the plateau heights of growing corn
To swift descents in thickly wooded vales

And arduous climbs beyond the bridging points,
With tanks and trucks ahead, and men behind,
Occasionally deployed against the French
At half-completed road-blocks. Few had thought
That armour could advance on such terrain,
Or soldiers move *en masse* through wooded hills.
Just as the Duke of Marlborough had deceived
The King of France, by crossing Wurttemberg,
Emerging from the forest near to Ulm
To win the glorious day of Blenheim field,
So now the Wehrmacht, swiftly on the Meuse,
Startled the French, who thinly lined the bank,
With sudden fears of imminent defeat.
The German troopers, trained to seize each chance,
Paddled their dinghies on the choppy stream,
Regardless of the light, sporadic fire.
Bridgeheads were made at Dinant, Montherme
And at Sedan - so ominous for France -
Then armour followed, crossing on pontoons.
Each German soldier felt expectant pride
Of militancy pregnant in his breast,
Of vengeance for his father's agony
On that black day when Ludendorff declared
An end of hope and tendering for peace.

No German planes had stemmed the Allied move
To reach the Belgians on the river line
Of Dyle and Meuse, behind the frontier.
For Manstein's plan depended on the hinge
Of German armies swinging to the south,
Whilst French and British mobile forces stood
Engaged in Belgium, helpless to support

The ruptured line along the French Ardennes.
Soon Wehrmacht *Panzers* raced towards the west,
Past Charleroi and Rocroi, Montcornet,
To Guise and Crecy, Cambrai and Peronne.
Only at Laon could the French attempt
To break the impetus of German arms.
Beneath that ancient rock where early kings
Had raised aloft the sacred crown of France,
A tank brigade, led bravely by de Gaulle,
Struck the advancing *Panzers'* southern flank.
Without support the sally was too weak.
De Gaulle was bitter when he saw how France
Let fall the sword of honour from her grip,
When French *poilus*, abandoning their guns,
Admitted Germans to the hallowed land
For which a million countrymen had died.
He promised then to make no armistice
Until the Hun invaders were expelled.

Yet now the Germans could not be withstood;
Their tanks sped on, with marching troops behind
In steady ranks with flags of red and gold,
Singing with sturdy voice and sullen zeal -
Hard warriors of iron, not long enrolled
From queues of unemployed in city streets.
When Churchill flew to France to meet Gamelin,
And asked him where the French reserves were held,
The old Commander shook his head and shrugged;
'*Aucune*' was his reply. Such was the state
Of that great army which had conquered once
The massive forces of the Kaiserreich.
Now archives burned in Paris offices,

As plans were made to leave the capital.
Not as before were people there resolved
To hurl defiance at the German guns
And fortify the queen of city's walls.

A new Commander, Weygand - older still -
Proposed to cut the German corridor
That now extended almost to the sea.
From north and south concerted thrusts would fall
Upon each flank of Rundstedt's salient.
Communications were not adequate
To carry out a plan thus improvised,
Nor fighting spirit strong enough, nor means,
In Allied armies shattered by the speed
Of *blitzkrieg* war, unparalleled before.
Some British armour, like de Gaulle's brigade,
Made a sharp lunge at Arras from the north,
But could not long delay the German drive
To reach the coast at Abbeville on the Somme.
Divided, outmanoeuvred and confused,
The Allied armies could do little more
Than stand steadfast from Verdun to the sea,
And stubbornly retreat through Flemish towns.

In this dread moment when the Allied line
Was breached beyond the hope of all repair,
Lord Gort, commander of the British force,
Alone decided that the time had come
To save his army from assured fate
Of swift encirclement, and seek a port
Whence to embark for England's safer shores.
Through Lens and Bethune, Hazebrouck, Cassel, Bergues,

From Lille through Ypres and Nieuport to the sea,
His weary army marched without dismay,
In fighting order, quick to turn about
And form a front of unrelenting fire
That slowed the onset of the German tide;
Just as at Mons the British rifle fire
Had thinned the ranks of Moltke's grenadiers
And heralded a victory on the Marne.
Past fields where still the poppies grew as red,
Across the ditches, through the standing crops,
The soldiers marched between their tanks and guns,
Which clattered suddenly on cobbled streets
In villages whose gloom foretold the loss
Of native freedom. Garlands now were few,
So recently bestowed on British troops
When to the Dyle canal they had advanced
As pledged defenders of the Belgian soil.
Now shutters closed on allies in retreat,
Except where children, unaware of fear,
And those too old to disavow the past
Could answer still the foreign soldier's smile.

Once more an English army was enclosed
Within encroaching jaws of alien arms,
Like Harry on the field of Agincourt;
But now no arrows' flight, nor English swords,
Nor daggers of the Welsh, nor royal command
Could stem the flow of overwhelming might.
From Abbeville on the coast the Panzers drove
To Gravelines and St Omer, where they stopped
On orders from the German High Command.
For even Mars, fierce patron of success,

Reserved a touch of mercy for the brave,
And let most live to call a second time
Upon the gods who favoured righteous war.

For crucial hours the Germans were delayed,
As Calais fortress, once again controlled
By English soldiers, mingled now with French,
On Churchill's orders made a final stand,
Denied all hope of rescue from the sea.
Yet, on the northern flank, a massive breach
Was opened in the line, when Leopold,
The king of Belgium, ordered a ceasefire,
And Belgian troops capitulated there.
But still in Hitler's mind a doubt remained,
For if the Wehrmacht's armour were engaged
Against a resolute and skilled defence
Within the flooded Belgian hinterland,
What would remain to turn upon the French
Who, numerous still in arms, might close their ranks
To save the capital, and with it France?

The boastful Goering, eager to extol
His powerful airforce, hitherto supreme,
Assured his master that the British troops
Could be destroyed entirely from the air,
Trapped as they were on twenty miles of coast
Behind Dunkirk from Gravelines to Nieuport.
In vain the Wehrmacht generals pressed their case
To order their victorious armour on,
To crush the British army with one blow
Against the steely anvil of the sea.
Hitler refused, and in that brief respite

The British reinforced their outer lines,
Formed a perimeter around Dunkirk,
And called upon the navy for relief.

One more decisive battle then was fought
Behind the beaches, in the Summer sky,
More brilliant blue for war's intensity,
Where German Stukas targeted the shore
Or were repelled by British fighter planes,
Striving to cordon off the precious sands
That stretched behind them, filled with waiting men.
In slow succession ships approached the pier,
And steadily embarked long queues of men,
Who waited patiently beneath the fire
Of solitary planes that raced above,
Or, screaming down, delivered sticks of bombs.

To carry men from off the open beach
Small ships were needed. Every kind of craft
In ports or bays, or on the rivers, sailed
From English harbours, manned by varied hands
Of weekend sailors, ferrymen, sea scouts,
Or crews of fishing boats, of barges, yachts,
Of pleasure boats at comfortable resorts.
Men long retired now hastened to enlist,
Called now to help their fellow countrymen
Beleagured on a narrow foreign beach,
Like the Achaeans when the Trojan host
Swarmed down upon their stranded ships of war.
Though boats were sunk, some grossly overfull
With weary soldiers lying on the decks,
Some hit by bombs, some by the strafing raids

Of German fighters, some by cannon fire
From distant guns beyond the Allied lines,
Yet most survived these hazards of the sea
And reached the tranquil ports of England's coast.
Too late the Führer realised his mistake.
No longer could the Wehrmacht leave its prey
Encaged by hostile sea; so tanks closed in
And German columns marched to their support.
The British soldiers held a tightening ring,
As valiant rearguards yielded step by step,
In flash of shells, the darkening land of France,
Beneath the pall of smoke from burning oil.
A German pincer movement caught, at Lille,
Five French divisions, who fought stubbornly
To save their comrades waiting at Dunkirk,
Exchanging life or freedom for their friends
And for what honour France still countenanced.
Three hundred thousand Allies thence escaped,
Snatched from unfriendly shores to disembark
In peaceful England, where the fields of Kent
And ripening orchards, late with blossom hung,
Lay quiet beneath the blue, unbounded sky.
Down weary gangplanks marched the battered troops,
Their main equipment left behind in France –
All tanks and vehicles and heavy guns –
But not defeated, though the fight was lost,
And strong in their resolve for liberty,
Which they had seen destroyed in foreign lands.

Churchill gave warning that if France succumbed
The Germans would invade the British Isles.
So now at last the issue was made clear.

From long complacency the British woke
To see the threat to all they held most dear –
Their 'earth of majesty', all it contained
Of gentle life, of justice, law and peace,
Of monarchy and Parliament, free speech,
Of native song and wit, of honesty,
Of wisdom hid in ancient practices,
Of greening fields and woodlands, gardens rich
With flowers of Summer, rivers swift or slow,
And briny air on cliffs and shallow sands -
Remembering in time of pestilence
A unity which few in peacetime knew.

The armies of the Reich wheeled southerly
To drive the French beyond their capital.
In vain the bravest soldiers died for France,
At village road-blocks, or in fields unripe,
Or, in the air, outnumbered helplessly,
Their deaths the shame of Frenchmen who had quit.
A final time the British leaders flew
To meet the Reynaud government, now at Tours.
Some still expressed the will of France to fight,
But French morale was low. How could their State,
Whose glorious armies had amazed the world
At Austerlitz and Jena and the Marne,
And at the Great War's final victory,
Have been destroyed in six short weeks of war?
As in an evil dream, the French observed
A German army at the Channel ports.
How had they crossed the Meuse? How so outflanked
The line of Maginot, whose guns and steel
No stratagem of war could ever breach?

Doubt paralysed the High Command of France.
Why had their soldiers rarely stood and died,
As they had done in thousands on the Marne,
Or at Verdun, or at Chemins-des-Dames?
Were Communists to blame, or Leon Blum,
Fifth columnists, or perhaps the Croix de Feu?
From Belgium refugees blocked every road,
Swelled by a growing flood of desperate French,
Who still recalled the barren years of war
In German hands. On carts or ancient cars,
By bicycle, on foot, whatever they
Could salvage at their side, they shambled on,
Shot at by German fighters, dispossessed,
And cursed by troops whose passage was delayed.
Across the Somme, across the Oise and Marne,
The Wehrmacht soon advanced. Would Paris fall?
To Reynaud's cabinet other figures came -
The aged Petain, Baudouin, Laval -
Who now began to plan what course to take
When Frenchmen laid down arms and sued for peace.

At this sad time for France, the vain Duce,
Who'd once proclaimed eight million bayonets
Would fight to reinstate the splendid days
Of Rome's *imperium*, now tardily
Invaded southern France to gain some spoils
Before the impending truce was duly signed.
The French defenders halted his attack,
But German troops then took the capital
And hastened southwards far in central France.
Reynaud himself, supported by a few -
Jeanneney, Herriot, Mandel, Georges, de Gaulle -

Insisted that the battle was not lost,
But Petain's words could no more be ignored.
The hero of Verdun, who'd once allayed
The desperate cries of army mutineers,
Proposed an armistice to end the war.
Hitler's reply was prompt; he came himself
To meet the senile Marshall at Rethondes.
In that same carriage where the truce was signed
Which stained the German army with defeat,
The Fuhrer now demanded his revenge:
France partitioned, ruled within the south
By Petain's spurious government at Vichy,
Collaborating with the German Reich
And claiming for the French a new ideal
Of Fascist order, and servility.
Wehrmacht troops would occupy the north,
And mark each day the Third Republic's shame
With goose-steps past the Arc de Triomphe's grave
Of one French hero from the other war,
And down the Champs Elysee to that place
Where once the old nobility had died.

But Charles de Gaulle, whom Churchill recognised
As one like him, a man of destiny,
Would not admit that France had lost the war.
He chose to fly to England from Bordeaux
And broadcast to the world his solemn word
To take upon himself the fate of France.
In that ungainly figure, tall, aloof,
The heart of France was carried overseas,
In exile whilst her people lay entombed
In vaults of Hitler's Nazi tyranny.

A battle had been lost, but not the war;
The flame of French resistance would be lit.
By his avowal phoenix France would rise
From ashes of despair and bitterness,
As oftentimes before in her distress.

4 The Battle of Britain

Churchill now saw the fundamental need
To save the fleet of France from Hitler's hands,
For reinforced with this the German power
To conquer Britain would be much enhanced.
A British naval force was sent forthwith
To Mers-el-Kebir on th' Algerian coast,
Where several battle cruisers lay at rest -
The 'Bretagne', 'Dunkerque', 'Strasbourg' and 'Provence'.
On Churchill's orders, Admiral Somerville
Demanded that the French should make a choice:
To sail for England, or for Martinique,
Or sink their ships at anchor where they lay.

If none of these were done, then, Churchill warned,
The British fleet would open hostile fire.
Commanded by Petain, the French replied
That they would not respond to such demands.
And so the British turned their guns on France,
Their erstwhile ally, and with ruthless fire
Of heavy salvoes and torpedo planes
They crippled that great fleet whose tricolor
No more betokened sovereignty of France.
The 'Bretagne' sank in flames, 'Provence' was beached,
The 'Dunkerque' ran aground; only 'Strasbourg'
Escaped to sea, and safety at Toulon.
At Mers-el-Kebir many sailors died,
And national outrage gave Petain support,
But wiser Frenchmen knew this sacrifice
Was offered in the cause of liberty.

Now all the world took note of British will
To fight without reserve, at any cost,
To win, as ever, mastery at sea
And strike, wherever circumstance arose,
For signal victory, with no quarter asked.
Hitler still hoped that Britain was content
To hold her Empire, whilst the Germans kept
All land secured by conquest in the war.
In this belief he offered Britain terms.
Fearing their country's weakness, some took heed,
But most agreed with Churchill, fearing more
The loss of native freedom, and disgrace.
Churchill himself was settled in his aim
To free the continent from Nazi rule.
His broadcast words, poetic in their force,

Dispelled all doubts of national unity,
And summoned up the will to fight alone.
Thus German plans were laid to cross the sea
And bring the *blitzkrieg* to those islanders
Who had too long frustrated all designs
To dominate the European lands.
How could the British army, ill-equipped,
Artillery and armour left in France,
Do battle with the Wehrmacht's brazen troops,
The terror of the vanquished Poles and French,
Whose '*Sieg Heil*' shook the heavens as they marched?

One question faced the German Kriegsmarine:
How would they ferry half a million men
Across the English Channel? What of tides,
Of wind and waves, that often had deterred
Such would-be conquerors? This was no stream,
Like Rhine or Elbe, for army engineers!
As Mers-el-Kebir had so lately shown,
The British navy would not hesitate
To sink a thousand barges full of men -
'Food for fishes', Winston Churchill claimed.
At threatened coasts the British were at work
On beach defences: wire, and pill-box guns,
With blazing oil and even mustard gas
To kill and maim whoever would invade
Their long-defended and inviolate shores.
One condition could reverse the odds:
Command of sky above the narrow sea,
Giving the fleet protection from the air
Between French harbours and the English coast
From Ramsgate to Lyme Bay.

Goering assured the Führer that with ease
His Luftwaffe could smash the RAF,
And even bring the British to their knees
By massive bombing of their ports and towns.
His force of bombers, fifteen hundred strong,
Though suited more to tactical support,
Was guarded by a thousand Messerschmitts,
Against nine hundred British fighter planes –
The Hurricanes which fought the war in France,
And all the Spitfires Dowding had withheld
When Reynaud wanted every British plane
To fly beside the French in northern France.
To bomb the British ports and thus induce
The RAF to fight in their defence
Was Hermann Goering's chosen strategy.

But heavy losses soon compelled a change
To bombing of the fighter aerodromes.
The Stukas had been driven from the skies -
In swift revenge for what they did in France.
Now Junkers came and Dorniers, pencil slim,
And snub-nosed Heinkels, pregnant with their load,
Emblazoned with the cross and swastika,
Littering sticks of bombs with heavy crumps
On glistening runways, hangars, office blocks,
And aircraft still inert upon the ground.
When fire bells rang at Hornchurch and North Weald,
At Manston, Tangmere, Eastchurch, Biggin Hill,
The waiting pilots scrambled hastily
To climb on high above the bomber host.
But often British radar could detect

Approaching aircraft far away at sea;
Then fighter squadrons rapidly converged
And dropped like hawks upon the teeming swarm,
With bursts of rapid fire that thinned their ranks,
As petrol tanks ignited, engines flamed,
And aircraft spiralled, bleeding black with smoke.

Yet soon the German bombers flew within
A screen of fighters - Me 109s -
As fast as Spitfires, faster in the climb,
Though slower on the turn in narrow arcs.
Thus in those Summer days a battle royal,
Miles high above the peaceful fields of Kent,
Above the ancient Weald, above the sea,
Was fought between those skilled protagonists,
Watched from the ground by anxious Englanders,
Who could not say whose burning aircraft fell,
Or whether of this breed of rival champions,
A German or an Englishman had died.

Each pilot seized the fleeting chance to hold
A slender profile in his gun-sight cross,
And pump the cannon-shells, or 303s,
With slow precision at the weaving tail;
Whilst on the flank his wing-man searched the sky
For sudden glints of enemy attack.
Crackling voices filled the itercoms
With cryptic messages. No time for hate
Nor sympathy; only the instant now,
When gloves of leather touched the magic fire
That burned an aircraft's paper-seeming shell,
And lacerated human flesh with flames.

As parachutes descended, floating free,
Like puffs of dandelion, the stricken planes
Burst into clouds of yellow-sprouting smoke.
Then suddenly the sky was clear again,
For fighters, short of fuel, had wheeled away
To far-flung aerodromes, and bombers fled,
Their shadows cast no more on England's fields
Of virgin crops and chequered symmetry.

Yet every day the ponderous raiders came,
In tight formation, escorts close beside.
At Uxbridge, where the fighters were controlled,
Each new attack was plotted on a map
By WAAF officials, swift as croupiers
To track a plane, or wipe away the dead.
Like old commanders on the field of war,
Or doughty admirals scanning leagues of sea,
So here, in that bland suburb, underground,
Air-Marshall Dowding followed every move,
Each second precious to command a flight
To scramble and engage the enemy,
For seconds counted in the deadly race
To gain more height before the Germans came.

For weeks the battle raged, each day a score
Of aircraft lost, of pilots maimed or killed,
British and Germans drowned at sea or burnt.
Some were famous –others no-one knew -
Lock and Lacey, McKellar, Carbury, Doe,
The Polish ace, Witold Urbanowitz,
The Czech Frantisek, South African Malan
And Nicolson, who won the lone VC,

And Douglas Bader, of the famed 'big wing',
Who boldly flew with artificial legs.
Some Germans had acquired their art in Spain,
Fighting for the Condor legion there,
Which first destroyed the town Guernica –
Like Werner Molders, Wilhelm Balthasar –
Others, like Wick and Oesau, Galland, Joppien,
Were veterans of *blitzkrieg* war in France.

None flinched, though one mistake of height or speed,
Or unseen 'bandits' hiding in the sun,
Might send an aircraft screaming to the earth,
Ablaze with petrol, scalding face and limb.
British reserves were short, so pilots flew
Until fatigue compelled their abstinence.
Those shot down unwounded faced again,
Within a few short hours, the same hard test
Of fighter's cannons or the bomber's gun.
Yet, though outnumbered, British planes drove back
The steady waves of enemy attack,
Destroying two for one, till Goering thought
Another strategy was then required
To force a victory from the stubborn foe.

A few chance German bombs had missed their mark.
They fell on London, and gave Churchill cause
To order a retaliatory raid
Against the German capital, Berlin,
Which Hitler had proclaimed would never hear
The sound of British bombers overhead.
Enraged by this attack, the Führer let
The baffled Goering change his plans once more:

The British people now would feel the weight
Of German bombs, of torment from the sky;
And when they saw their wives and children dead,
Their homes in flames, they would capitulate.

So London suffered; every night they came,
To light the eastern sky as dockland burned.
Crashing of bombs and sweeping searchlight arms,
Droning of aircraft, thud of ack-ack guns
And wailing sirens were the bitter dream
That Londoners recalled with every dawn.
And yet their pain was respite for the few,
The gallant pilots whose reserves were spent.
With aerodromes now free from constant raids,
Strength was rebuilt to fight again renewed.

Though still, as Autumn nights drew long with mists,
Great fleets of German bombers flew afar
To Coventry and Glasgow, Birmingham,
To Liverpool, to Bristol, Plymouth, Leeds,
To Manchester and Sheffield, each a place
Where goods, like aero-engines, were produced,
Or where the merchant fleet with constant toil
Delivered food and those necessities
Required to run a war economy.
Five hundred bombers shattered Coventry,
Unchecked by fighters, ill-equipped to find
The fleeting shadows on a moonless night.
Nor, whilst those other thronging cities burned,
Could British fighters see beyond the flames
To shoot the savage night intruders down.
Factories, docks, railways, plants and stores,

And many houses likewise were destroyed -
Mainly the local workers' terraced homes.
In every city bombed some hundreds died
From dire explosions, or incendiaries,
Or struck by masonry, or falling bricks,
Their bodies crushed by debris, choked by dust:
Women, children, men on factory lines,
People on buses, wardens at their posts,
Firemen, policemen, all alike arraigned
Before the cruel judiciary of war.
No clamorous voices cried, 'Enough of this!';
Most valued more than life their self-respect
And ancient freedom not to be compelled.
Most differences of status, wealth and speech
That bitterly divided them before
Were now forgotten in the common plight.
In unity their fear was cast away,
And Churchill spoke for all when he declared
That Britain would defend her island home
On beaches, landing grounds, or in the streets,
In fields and hills, on oceans, in the air,
And would not cease to fight, though all were lost
And distant lands became the battleground.

Just as the skill and courage of 'the Few' -
The fighter pilots of the RAF -
Had foiled the plans of Hitler to prepare
For German armies to traverse the sea,
So now the high nobility of folk,
Confronting war within their peaceful homes,
Made clear to Hitler that he could not bend
The British people to an alien will.

Nor could he now invade, as Winter came,
Enclosing Britain in the darkling gloom.

As if to underline this firm resolve,
An act of bravery occurred at sea.
In mid Atlantic, near the Iceland coast,
The German pocket battleship, the 'Scheer',
Attacked a British convoy, which had sailed
Without a naval escort. Forty ships
Were easy targets for her heavy shells,
But one armed merchant-cruiser, 'Jervis Bay',
Turned on the 'Scheer' alone, and with her guns –
Of minor calibre and feeble range –
Held her attention whilst the convoy fled.
For just an hour the struggle was prolonged,
As 'Scheer' kept out of range and flung her shells
Across ten miles of grey and acrid waves,
Until the 'Jervis Bay', aglow with fire,
Sank with her captain and heroic crew.
Too late the 'Scheer' pursued the convoy ships,
Now scattered on the dark and covetous sea;
Though five were lost, the rest escaped scot-free.

5 The Greek Disaster

Too easily were victory laurels won
By Mussolini when the French collapsed.
Despite his pride, he had not well prepared
His soldiers for a European war.
Only in Abyssinia did their might
Appear as strong as did the Duce's boast.
Whilst Hitler planned to cross the English sea,
His Axis partner threatened to advance
From Libya to the Nile, where British troops
Defended Egypt and the great canal
Which linked the Empire's vital waterways.
The Duce's army ponderously attacked,
As Wavell planned a British counterstroke.
Through Sidi Barrani, Bardia, Tobruk,
O'Connor drove the stunned Italians back

And occupied the El Agheila pass.
One step to seize the port of Tripoli
And all Italian soldiers would be flung
From that vast empire which the tyrant claimed
Along the shores of northern Africa.

Not yet, however, did the bells intone
The end of Mussolini's fragile rule,
Where once the Caesars held imperial sway.
For fresh appeal was made for British help,
Which national honour could not cast aside.
The ancient land of Greece, the home of art
And citadel of philosophic life,
Was once more harrowed by Italian arms,
Whose uncouth leader never would proclaim,
As once in Corinth Flamininus did,
The liberty of Greeks. Churchill resolved -
His generals would not willingly agree -
To send support from Africa forthwith;
For Greece, like Poland, held a British pledge
Against aggression by the Fascist powers.

At sea the British navy struck a blow
Against the Italian force about to seize
The isle of Corfu. Then Taranto port,
Though ringed by AA guns and searching lights,
Could not protect the proud dictator's fleet
When Swordfish bombers flew from carrier decks,
Armed with torpedo bombs beneath each wing,
And, in bright moonlight, sank the major ships -
One the Duce's new 'Littorio'.

Meanwhile, in western Greece, invading troops
Met fierce resistance from the angry Greeks,
Who thrust them back beyond the starting line.
What aid would Mussolini's ally give,
Who'd promised German help as due return
For acquiescence in the Anschluss pact?
Would British intervention thus provoke
The Wehrmacht forces on the Balkan front?
What would the Serbs decide? Would Turkey move
Against its ally of the former war?
All stood uncertain, as the Winter rain
Fell silently on Ares' dancing floor.
Hitler could not advance against the Greeks
Without free passage from the Jugoslavs.
Bulgaria was friendly; not the Serbs,
But German pressure made their government yield,
Until a coup by army patriots
Dismissed the king and challenged Germany.
Ill-used to such resistance, Hitler sent
His airforce to annihilate Belgrade.
Within two weeks the Jugoslavs were crushed.
Doubtless the Führer's secret strategy
To concentrate his forces in the east
And launch a violent, unexpected blow
Against the Russians was a further cause
Of such impetuous haste to finish soon
The Duce's untoward imbroglio.

The Greeks, more valiant for Serb defeat,
Now reinforced the Aliakhmon line,
Including troops from Australasia,
To hold the German drive from Monastir.

But Wehrmacht pressure, under air support,
Along the whole extended Allied front,
Stove in its western flank. Along the route
Of ancient battlefields, where earlier Greeks
Had faced a tide of massed barbarians,
The chastened force withdrew; through Tempe's pass,
In which, for days, New Zealand troops held firm,
Until the weary columns had defiled;
Then through Thermopylae of Spartan fame,
Across the plain of Thebes, and Attic hills.
Pursuit was swift; the Germans reached Patras
And Corinth bridge. The Allies in retreat
Could cross no more to safety in the south.
Invaders took the proud Acropolis,
As Persians, Bulgars, Turks had done before.
That place where great Athena Nike stood,
A beacon for the freedom loving Greeks,
Now flew the swastika; and down below,
Amidst the ruins of the Agora,
Where once the gadfly Socrates conversed
On virtue, love and immortality,
And nobly drank the hemlock unconcerned,
Jackbooted soldiers sauntered here and there.

The Greek defeat entrapped all British troops
A second time on hostile foreign shores;
But Britain's navy was no more prepared
Than at Dunkirk to let them languish there.
To Kalamata and to southern bays
And to the narrow tip that points to Crete
Flotillas came. Thousands were plucked away,
Though Nauplion saw tragic gallantry,

When boats that stayed too long at anchorage
To save more soldiers suffered hits and sank.
By Churchill's brave decision, those who died,
British and Greek, in mutual sacrifice,
Had nurtured freedom in those ancient groves,
Which still inspired the culture of a world
Whose liberty was now so perilous.

The isle of Crete remained in British hands,
So Churchill reinforced it, for he knew
That planes from Cretan aerodromes could fly
To far Ploesti, whence the Germans drew
Supplies of oil so vital for the war;
Whilst from the naval base at Suda Bay
The sea lanes were swept clear to Africa.
Yet Hitler would not quit the Balkan stage
Until the British were expelled from Crete.
The German General Student had command
Of one elite division, trained to drop
On any target to prepare the way.
Thus had they seized the fort, Eben Emael,
And river crossings for the vanguard tanks
Which broke the armies of the Netherlands.
Now paratroops would drop on aerodromes,
And hold them for the Junker transport planes
To ferry in the mass of infantry.
Churchill and General Wavell, seeing this,
Commanded Freyberg to defend the strips,
Especially Maleme, with his best troops -
Avenging Greeks and tough New Zealanders,
Still fresh from mainland war.

First, German aircraft bombed the Allied lines
To silence the defending batteries;
And Heinkels, Dorniers, Junker 88s
Then droned across the island end to end,
Releasing sticks of bombs on town and farm
With dire explosions, raising clouds of dust,
Until a shroud of black hung on the air,
Like engine smoke at London terminals.
Then Stukas followed, falling into line,
With dive brakes open, nacelle sirens on,
Chasing their strings of bombs, and peeling off
Three hundred feet above the shaken earth,
Where randomly dismembered bodies lay
In craters gouged from dry, calcareous rock.
The square-tailed bombers fled towards the north,
But then, in groups of three, came Messerschmitts,
Now sweeping faster, metres from the ground,
And strafing with machine-guns things that moved -
Soldiers, trucks, or Cretan shepherd boys.

Above the Sea of Crete troop carriers
Met no resistance from the R.A.F. -
Few British fighter aircraft were in Crete -
But at the German paratroops' descent
The sky was filled with deadly small-arms fire,
Like swarms of angry bees, disturbed by smoke;
Whilst far below the glint of bayonets marked
Where Allied soldiers quit the trenches' shade
And ran to butcher desperate German youths,
Who grappled with redundant parachutes.
At Maleme, beyond the aerodrome,
And near the tarmac strip of Retimo

A thousand fell in sun-drenched sacrifice.
Many who flew in gliders sooner died
From hideous crashes on the hard-baked earth,
Or hit before they reached a sheltering rock
Or grove of olive trees. Yet still they came,
Across the turquoise sea from Greece and Rhodes,
To fall like Icarus on burning Crete.

Retimo and Heraklion were held;
But Germans took the strip of Maleme,
When British troops withdrew, outnumbered there.
A night attack regained the airfield edge,
But daylight brought the Stukas overhead
And drove once more the dour defenders back.
Now German valour won its due reward;
For transport Junkers flew in relay flights,
Disgorging hundreds more of German troops,
Who only faced the scattered bursts of shells
From British batteries in distant groves.
Slowly the Allied forces were withdrawn,
Until the vital airstrips were foregone.
Allied commando forces put ashore
At Suda Bay withstood the Germans there
For long enough to let their comrades climb
Across the mountains to the southern coast.

At sea the violent outcome was reversed:
With crass ineptitude the Germans sent
A fleet of caiques across the Cretan Sea,
Without an escort, packed with infantry.
When British cruisers and destroyers fired
Repeated salvoes at this easy prey,

The Wehrmacht soldiers drowned in multitudes.
Not one invader reached the isle by sea.
Yet British shipping was itself attacked
By Luftwaffe planes, unchallenged in the air.
In swift revenge 'Juno' and 'Gloucester' sank,
Then 'Fiji', 'Greyhound', 'Kelly' and 'Kashmir'.
Across the high, impending spine of Crete
The weary remnants hastened in retreat,
Befriended by the Cretan villagers,
Especially those who had themselves made war,
With knives and hunting-guns in self-defence.
Down goat-paths to the sea slid British troops,
New Zealanders and Poles, Australians
And proud, embittered Greeks. From there by night,
Or harried in the dangerous light of day
By German bombers searching near the coast,
The navy took them off the narrow beach.

Yet still they had not slipped the grasp of war.
Whilst the unequal match off northern Crete
Between embittered gods of sea and air
Had carried off invading soldiers' lives,
This time the rain of bombs on heaving decks
That spat their feeble tracer fire in vain
Struck many down among defeated men,
Who'd recently survived the hard ordeal
Of landlocked battle. Now they died in ships,
In company of sailors ventured forth
To rescue them. Yet many soldiers lived
To reach the port of Alexandria,
In whose broad harbour couched a silent fleet.

Cretan victory cost the Germans dear.
Although they threw the British further back,
Stranded upon the shores of Africa,
The brave and youthful spearhead of their arms
Lay now in fragments - ardent paratroops,
Most buried on the field of Maleme.
Crete was a Pyrrhic victory, for its toll
Had gained an island but delayed the war.
The Führer's plans to turn the Wehrmacht's might
Against the Soviet Union were set back
By two more Summer weeks. He could survey
The Balkans with contempt, and dig the
Nazi heel in Grecian soil, but those who still
Remembered Turkish rule knew how to hate
This new barbarian. Hereafter would
The Greeks and Serbs resist, spurred on by those
Who'd stayed behind on Crete when all seemed lost
And British agents brought by submarine.
Nor would the Wehrmacht ever try again
To use as paratroops the crack elite
Of German youth. The many 'neath the dust
Of Crete's dry hills had proved their manhood well,
But by their deaths they also had convinced
Their erstwhile Fuhrer no more to attempt
Such rash invasion by an airborne force.

In Cabinet war-rooms underneath Whitehall,
The British leader followed every step
Of Freyberg's loyal defence and hard defeat;
But, far beyond the Cretan battlefield,
Another crisis challenged his resolve
With hourly news of sudden war at sea.

For in the grey Atlantic's vast expanse
The strongest ship afloat throughout the world,
The German 'Bismarck', threatened to elude
The British vessels tracking her escape
From Norway's fjords through the Denmark Strait,
To where she could assault with unmatched fire
All passing convoys - one, beyond the Clyde,
With twenty thousand soldiers for the East.
With 'Prinz Eugen' beside her, 'Bismarck' steamed
Through icy waters off the Greenland coast,
Until confronted by the flagship 'Hood'
And 'Prince of Wales', who chased her further south.
In one brief duel of gunfire 'Hood' was lost:
Her magazine exploded by a shell,
She sank in minutes, drowning all but three.
Yet 'Bismarck' had been hit and, leaking oil,
Continued on her mission of offence.
An air attack by nine torpedo planes,
Braving her fire, caused damage near the bridge.
Then, all at once, the conflict was reversed:
Pursuing cruisers zigzagged to avoid
A group of U-boats, and, as night advanced,
'Bismarck' was lost, concealed in wastes of sea.
Where would she turn - towards another prey,
Or to the haven of a friendly port?

From round the compass British warships raced
To find the unseen enemy, whose guns
Could still destroy each one of them in turn,
Or sink the convoy ships that crept unarmed
Towards the southern Cape. Then, from the air,
A sight was made again - 'Bismarck' alone,

And steaming fast for Brest. From 'Ark Royal''s decks
The Swordfish bombers rose aloft once more,
Torpedoes slung beneath each nether wing,
And soon had wrecked the 'Bismarck''s steering gear.
By night she floundered, held within a ring
Of five destroyers, waiting for the kill.

When daylight came, the British battleships,
'King George V' and 'Rodney', reached the scene,
And fought with salvos an unequal duel,
Until the 'Bismarck' listed far to port,
And 'Rodney' closed to just four thousand yards.
Her shells then silenced every German gun,
And shot away the mast. In flames and smoke
The mighty 'Bismarck' still refused to sink;
Nor would her valiant captain strike the flag
And offer to the British such a prize.
So 'Dorsetshire''s torpedoes smashed the hull,
And, undefeated, 'Bismarck' slid below,
To greedy ocean's cold and neutral depths.
No more would England need its battleships
To guard the Kattegat and other routes
For fear of one great ship. The navy was
Relieved for other work, in distant seas
And soon against new foes.

The colonies that Mussolini won
In eastern Africa by brutal force
Had now to be defended on all sides,
For British troops advanced – enough though few –
From Kenya, Aden and the Upper Nile.
First to succumb was Mogadishu port;

And then across the plains of tubbas grass,
And through the thorny desert to the hills,
Italian soldiers once again withdrew.

A second time Addis Ababa fell,
As British columns marched with shouldered arms
In welcome shade of eucalyptus trees.
More resolute were Carnimeo's men,
Where Keren, ringed by mountains, was the key
Which closed the route to Eritrea's coast.
At Dologorodoc their fortress held
Against successive waves of strong assault.
Wearied by climbing, British Empire troops
Were blasted back by automatic fire
And showers of small grenades, flung from the trench
That ringed the fortress wall of towering rock;
Until, at last, their heavy armoured tanks
With air support, broke through the sturdy line
Of Bersaglieri and Alpini guards,
Whose fierce resistance gave the lie to tales
Of how the Italian army could not fight.
Three thousand dead on Keren's lofty peaks
Recalled the days of Roman fortitude;
Yet, ill-equipped and often poorly led,
Italian soldiers rarely could defeat
Determined troops, like British or the Greeks.

The dream of Mussolini was dissolved:
Though shameful Adowa had been revenged,
The cloud capped towers of empire in the east
And hopes that Britain's rule would be defunct
From Alexandria to southern Cape

Were proven baseless. South African troops,
And native ones elsewhere, had fought beside
The English for one cause. Indians, too, had
Shown on Keren's heights their martial worth.
However proud, the British Empire stood
For rule of law against all tyranny.
Though Greece was lost and Europe now enslaved,
Whilst only in the air had Britain won
Decisive victory over German arms,
Success in Africa contained the seed
Of that resurgence which, in course of time,
United all the English-speaking world,
And struck the tyrants down, who sought to end
The precious freedom they could not pretend.

6 Barbarossa

For long the German Führer's febrile mind
Had looked beyond the borders of the Reich
For 'lebensraum', where Germany would seize
What land it wanted, scorning others' rights.
In Hitler's book, 'Mein Kampf', he had proclaimed
That Russian steppeland was the destined place
For Germans to invade and colonise.
They, as the master-race, would own the land
And force the Slavs to labour for the Reich.
His pact with Stalin was expedient,
Freeing the eastern front from any threat,
Whilst he could deal with France; but as he stood
And saw the cliffs of Dover through the haze,
The isles of Britain barbed against assault,
He cancelled any plans to cross the sea.
Instead he now indulged his early dream

To conquer Russia, and release a flood
Of German emigration to the east.
How then could England long resist his will?
All Europe would be his, from Finisterre
To where the Ural mountains barred the way
To Asian savagery. Now was the time
When Russia still was weak, her generals purged
By Josef Stalin's self-inflicted wound -
The trial of Tukhachevski and the rest.
Could Bolsheviks, corrupted by the Jews,
Withstand an onslaught by Teutonic arms,
Whose power destroyed the mighty hosts of France?
Again the blitzkrieg would unleash its storm
On men uncertain of their nation's cause
And forced to fight by leaders unprepared.

So whilst the British stubbornly endured
The Winter months of raids on crowded towns,
At one in their resolve to fight alone,
And fought to keep their perilous life-lines free,
Defiant still at sea and in the air,
All one in their resolve to fight alone,
The Nazi leader forged another plan:
To launch a massive drive against the Slavs
By that same army which now stood alert
To land upon the southern English shores.
Had Stalin not betrayed the recent pact
By sending troops to Riga and Tallinn?
Was he not threatening Germany itself
By seizing Bukovina as a base
To take the oil-fields, vital to the Reich,
Of Antonescu, Hitler's Fascist friend?

Pre-emptive action must destroy the power
Of Bolshevism and its hateful Tsar.
So troop-filled lorries crossed the autobahns,
And laden wagons rolled towards the east
To silent rail-yards, stocked with war supplies.
Victory of the British R.A.F. -
A new Trafalgar of the region air -
Had set the German tyrant on his way
To vast and dangerous continental war.
He too would cross the Beresina's swamps
And see his soldiers frozen on the steppes;
And, while his armies marched, he would contend
With British on the Axis' boundaries,
Above the German homeland in the air,
And on their natural element, the sea,
Until there came to Hitler and his arms
The dreaded war that burned on many fronts.
Then he would find that Russian arms outlived
The loss of millions and the stricken land;
And he would face a dozen Kutuzovs,
Allied with nations whose surpassing power
Would dwarf the coalitions hammered out
By William Pitt and Viscount Castlereagh.

The Greek adventure, forced on Germany
By Mussolini's ill-considered pride,
Delayed the Führer's plans for several weeks.
Only by June did Nazi flags unfurl
On Poland's border with the Soviets.
By then three armies were amassed to start:
Von Leeb, in eastern Prussia, faced the north
And Leningrad beyond the Baltic States;

Von Bock, east of Warsaw, would take the line
Of Moscow's highway through the central plains;
Von Runstedt, in the south, would drive his force
Upon Kiev, and enter the Ukraine.
A Panzer group accompanied each branch
Of this combined assault; whilst soldiers, too,
Of Hitler's Balkan allies joined the line
Of Runstedt's army, crouched along the Prut.

At height of Summer, whilst the Berlin crowds
Strolled at their ease along the *linden* way,
Beyond Warsaw the eastern sky was lit
By sixty hundred guns. Towards the sun
The scores of bombers climbed. Three million troops,
With armour, horses, trucks, crossed into Russia
Like a lava tide. The invasion's name
Recalled the splendour of the early Reich,
The realm of Barbarossa, Swabian king,
Whose 'Drang nach Osten' pacified the Wends
And sent Teutonic knights to distant lands.
But now no Christian king rode nobly forth
To civilise the Slavs; instead a pagan
Eager to destroy, and seize the land
For German settlement, while Russians learned
The 'untermenschen's' fate as manual slaves.

The Soviet defence was ill-prepared:
Though great in number, men were poorly armed,
With tanks no match for Hitler's Panzer groups,
And aircraft caught on forward aerodromes
By German strafing, even while they lay,
Uncamouflaged, exposed to swift attack,

Which left their ashen frames to mock the air.
Deep into Russia drove the armoured lines,
Followed, just as in France, by marching troops,
Sensing victory as each day advanced
Their steady progress through the shattered land.
No mercy here delayed the ruthless surge
Of soldiers told to breach the rules of war
By him to whom they'd sworn obedience.
Each captured village burned with beacon flames,
As straw and wood of desolated homes
Were wrapped in rasping fire and carbon smoke.
And yet the Führer did not plan to move
Too far within the vast interior,
But rather to defeat the Russian mass
Before it could retreat and fight again.
At Bialystok, then in front of Minsk,
The German pincers closed inexorably.
Soviet armies bled as thousands died
Or shuffled into cruel captivity.

Behind the Wehrmacht came the '*Einsatzgruppe*',
Trained to seek out Communists and Jews,
And quickly kill them with a gun or rope.
At first the German army looked aghast
At blatant murder. Officers resigned;
But most were satisfied that war prescribed
A soldier's duty in his country's cause
By whatsoever means. It cost them dear
To prostitute the law and give support
To spurious aims of Nazi racialists.
To infamous depths had war descended now:
Both sides abused their prisoners - lack of food

And constant marching, epidemics, cold,
Condemned the great majority to death.
Civilians were shot down, their houses burned;
And Russians in retreat laid waste the land.
Behind the German lines, the partisans
Wrecked vengeance when they struck with sudden raids,
Killing stragglers, wounding with sniper fire,
Derailing trains, and ambushing by night.
Those caught were hung or shot, with no regard
For age or sex, for uniform or rank.
A few were commissars, prepared to fight
For Stalin and the proletarian cause;
But most were Russian peasants, moved by hate
For Nazi cruelty and the German race,
Driven once more to save their native land,
As long ago their forefathers had done
When Bonaparte had crossed the Nieman stream.

Along the Baltic coast, past silent lakes
And ruined castles, high on distant crags,
Through forests dense with pine and silver fir,
The northern armies drove to Leningrad.
At Pskov, and on the Luga, they were held,
But only briefly, till the Russians broke.
As they approached the ancient capital,
They called upon the Finns to give support,
But Mannerheim was loath to move beyond
The boundaries so hardly reacquired.
Von Leeb, now weakened further by the need
To reinforce the Wehrmacht's central front,
No longer had the force for an assault.
Thus Hitler ordered that a siege begin.

How could a city run by Bolshevists
For long survive, invested on all sides?
He did not know what fortitude lay stored
Within the heart of old St Petersburg.
Meanwhile the centre armies reached Smolensk,
Where bitter fighting long delayed its fall.
Yet now the Wehrmacht saw within its reach
The glittering prize of Moscow. If that fell
Might not all Russia hail the conqueror?
But into this vast play of human strife
The force of Nature entertained a part.
Within the Pripet marshes' huge morass
Of watery scrub and pathless wastes of clay,
The invasion was delayed by partisans.
So Hitler ordered a diversion south
Of Panzer forces, otherwise deployed
To form the spearhead of the main advance
Along the Moscow highway past Smolensk.
Guderian's armour would not strike the blow
That emulated what he'd done in France.
Instead his tank commanders watched the dust
From endless miles of tracks on sun-scorched earth;
Till Autumn rain converted dust to mud,
And struggling horses sank knee-deep in mire
In heaving guns across the sodden land.
What had been roads became deep-rutted sloughs,
Impassable for trucks. The mighty Wehrmacht
Faltered in the mud, still harassed by the
Valiant partisans. In front of Kiev
Russian Cossacks fought, inflicting sabre wounds
On German troops, surprised within their tents.
Yet Kiev could not stand, and captive Slavs

Were crammed, like docile beasts, in railway trucks,
Which clattered off to loathsome prison camps.

Von Runstedt's drive across the Ukraine steppes
Brought hopes of seizing Russian oil supplies.
Beyond the Dnieper's stream, the way seemed clear
To Caspian shores and Baku's fields of oil.
But which of Hitler's aims would be achieved?
Would Leningrad be grasped, or Moscow first?
Would southern Russia, with its wheat and oil,
Become a prize more valuable than these?
Could all be seized before the Winter came?
These crucial questions were not yet resolved
By Hitler or the German High Command.
Some, like Guderian, saw Moscow's fall
As vital for a Soviet collapse.
Hitler himself feared Stalin's strength to fight
Within the depths of Russia's hinterland,
And therefore claimed his armies must ensure
The capture of the enemy's resource
In southern Russia, even on the Don.
On all three fronts advance was moderate,
Delayed by indecision, and the rain,
Until the Russian Winter took the stage
And made of Barbarossa one fell scene
Of German anguish.

Unrecognised by Stalin's godless rule,
A hand divine yet blessed his people now
With early snow and bitter, freezing wind.
The Wehrmacht was not clothed for Winter war.
Frostbite was rife; skin froze on things of steel;

Engine oil turned solid; withered horses fell;
And Germans felt within themselves the dread
Of dying in this pestilential land
Of scathing ice and endless plains of snow,
Far from their homes in sunlit Germany.
Von Bock, though weak from illness, drove them on
Towards the gleaming mirage of success,
When Moscow would submit to German arms.
At Briansk and Vyasma Russian troops
Were twice encircled with enormous loss.
With each advance, however, time expired,
Towards the zero point of German hopes.
Exhausted, numb with cold, the spearhead stopped,
Though eastwards from the Volga they discerned
The Kremlin turrets glinting in the sun.

For several weeks defences had been built
On Stalin's orders - dragons' teeth of pines,
Pill-boxes, ditches, endless miles of wire,
Constructed by the desperate citizens -
Women, children, men too old to fight
Who still remembered how the Germans came
Before the shades of revolution fell.
No longer could the Soviet army use
The endless space of Russia as its shield,
And by retreat attenuate the power
Of Hitler's armies as they spread abroad,
Far from their source of food and all supplies.
The enemy now stood before the wall
Whose breach would drown the capital in blood
And threaten to engulf the Soviet State.
Would commissars die here like those in Rome,

Who sat in currule chairs, till Gallic chiefs
Drew longswords from their sheaths and cut them down?
Would homes burn here in fire promiscuous,
While Hitler sat, like Bonaparte, enthroned?

Yet Stalin, now recovered from his shock
At Barbarossa's massive treachery,
Had realised that the Germans lacked reserves
To summon strength for a decisive blow.
The time had come for Russia's counterstroke:
He told Zhukov to order an attack -
A veteran of the Leningrad campaign,
Experienced in operating tanks,
T 34s, the German Tiger's match.
In Tokyo a Russian spy revealed
That Japanese aggression would not turn
Upon the Soviets, but to the south.
Thus fresh Siberian troops, immured to cold,
Were now deployed to hurl themselves against
The battle-worn invaders from the west.

As blizzards froze the Germans' flimsy camps,
The Russians moved through forests thick with snow,
Along the line from Klin to Zakharov.
Past ruined homes they drove the Wehrmacht back.
The Panzer forces on each German wing
Lost contact with the rest. Von Bock's response
Was orderly retreat, but in this plight
Would even German discipline withstand
Such loss of hope and image of defeat?
The Fuhrer would not risk catastrophe;
Nor would he contemplate the loss of land

So costly seized from Soviet control.
Each German soldier must endure the worst
And fight to hold the place at which he stood.
Guderian and Hoepner were dismissed
For ordering withdrawal on their fronts.
And so the Wehrmacht told its stricken men
To form *'Igelstellungen'*, hedgehog forts,
Defended to the final grenadier.
In freezing cold, frostbitten, short of food,
With few communications or commands,
Each German soldier faced the utter depths
Of physical distress, but did not yield.
Surrender meant a slower form of death
In Russian prison camps; there was no choice.
How many then recalled the brilliant days
Of pre-war Nazi rallies, when they'd marched
In shining jackboots, Nordic banners raised,
Eyes turned towards the Fuhrer, and the songs,
Of *'Deutschland uber Alles'*, *'Horst Wessel'*,
A million arms upraised, the beat of drums,
Women smiling, garlanded in flowers;
And then success in violent, swift campaigns,
In Poland, Norway, Netherlands and France,
Triumphant entrances in cobbled squares
Of Warsaw, Cracow, Oslo, Amsterdam,
And Paris, in July, when Hitler came
To praise his army, strident with success –
Deutschen Soldaten, born in times of gold,
When all seemed blessed, and victory justified
By destiny and purity of race?
Yet some, at least, in dire extremity
Awoke in conscience to the German crimes

Of making Hitler master of the Reich,
And listening to unreason's siren voice
Proclaiming national glory, undeterred
By moral shame and inhumanity.

Zhukov's offensive drove between the forts,
Unable to besiege them one by one;
Nor were the Russian forces yet equipped
To force encirclement. But Moscow stood,
And, as the Winter waxed, this cruellest war
Achieved a balance, till the Springtime thaw.

7 The Japanese Onslaught

Almost on the day when Zhukov struck,
Another force, more unexpected still,
Closed fast upon its prey far to the east.
South of the Kuriles Islands, deep in fog,
The navy of Imperial Japan
Sailed with the utmost stealth, denied all means
Of radio control, alert for ships
That might disclose its mission to the world.
Turning, past Midway, on a dog-leg route,
It laboured on through swelling ocean seas,
Refuelled by tankers, till it reached a point
Within the range of aerial attack
Upon America's Pacific fleet.
Before full light the planes had taken off:
Zero fighters, bombers primed to strike,

An air armada fit to make Japan
The sovereign of the eastern hemisphere.
Anchored in Pearl Harbour's sunny bay,
The boats of Admiral Kimmel were not warned
What tempest would descend on their repose.
Though radar had discerned approaching planes,
It was assumed they were B-17s
In transit from the Californian coast.
Eight battleships lay moored beside their berths;
Only U.S. carriers were at sea.

Over the verdant hills of Oahu,
The red-marked bombers skimmed in tight array,
And, when the leader saw the fleet below,
The coded words, 'Tora, Tora, Tora',
Conveyed the vital rapture of surprise.
Dive bombers struck at first on Wheeler Field,
Enveloping in fire the close-parked planes.
Above the harbour, with a low approach,
Torpedo bombers launched their deadly load
Into the broadside hulls. Further raiders
Bombed from altitude; others dived fast
Against the backdrop of the blue-green hills.
From burning ships, like cones no more extinct,
Great flames ascended, dark with petrol smoke.
A huge explosion killed a thousand men
As 'Arizona''s magazine was hit;
While 'West Virginia' sank on even keel
From gaping holes torn in her hull and deck.
The 'Oklahoma' rolled upon her back,
Propellers to the sky. Burning fiercely,
'California', too, sank on her keel.

'Nevada' left her moorings, bravely manned,
To reach the open sea, but, hit by bombs
From planes intent to block the harbour's mouth,
She beached herself upon the further shore.

Beneath the morning sun, obscured by smoke,
The tangled wrecks of untried warships lay,
Capsized or sunk, now lapped by gentle sea.
Sailors had died entombed in holds of fire,
Scarcely aware how death had struck them down.
As later waves of bombers dived in turn,
A few survivors grasped the working guns,
At risk from Zeros racing tree-top high;
Whilst rows of aircraft, parked on Hickham Field,
Were set ablaze in avenues of fire.

American naval power had failed to stem
The fierce effusion of the Rising Sun.
And yet the mastermind of this success,
The Admiral Yamamoto, could but say,
With premonition of his country's fate,
That they had woken but a sleeping giant.
No longer could Americans profess
Indifference to the old world's enmities.
Their dream of isolation was dissolved
By this one waking 'day of infamy'.

Why had Japan committed such an act
Of rash aggression, sowing thus the wind?
By threats and murders power had been acquired
From those, like Konoe, who wanted peace.
The sword of State was seized by violent men,

By Matsuoka, Hata and Tojo,
And army war lords in the northern wastes
Of mainland China, where they cruelly fought
With massed bombardment and the bayonet.
Nanking streets had run with mingled blood
Of children, men and women, killed alike
By Japanese unworthy to bear arms.
What was bushido then - the warrior's way -
Devoid of virtue, yet a potent force
In claims to empire, and in slavish will
To serve a State unbounded by the law?
Allied with Hitler, and with treaty made
To keep the Soviet Union at bay,
The masters of Japan had seized the chance
To march on Indo-China, when Petain
Had signed the armistice at Compiegne.
By this one move the Japanese became
A dangerous threat to other western powers:
To Holland's Asian empire, Britain's rule
In Burma and Malaya, and, not least,
The U.S. outpost in the Philippines.

For Roosevelt this was the final step;
He'd placed embargoes on strategic goods
For export to Japan, especially oil.
The war lords knew, deprived of these supplies,
Japan could not fight long. They must decide:
Withdraw from Indo-China, or march on
To death or victory in a total war.
Whilst Britain was involved with Germany,
And Russian armies desperately engaged,
Only the U.S. ships at Oahu

Could challenge an attempt to win control
Of eastern Asia and the western seas
For Hirohita's sacred dynasty.
Thus Admiral Yamamoto, who in youth
Had seen the power of U.S. industry,
Against his better judgment gambled all
For Japanese supremacy at sea.

This viper's bite of warfare undeclared
Had struck a fearful blow for tyranny.
Yet Winston Churchill saw the dread event
As not unwelcome in the greater cause
Of fighting to preserve the rule of law.
No longer would the British stand besieged
In lone defence of ancient liberties;
For now, at last, America would arm,
United in a new belligerence
Against the perpetrators of this deed,
The war lords of Japan. Well might they sing
In distant Tokyo their song of war:
'Across the sea, the corpses floating by;
Across the mountain, corpses on the field;
Only for the Emperor shall I die;
And not look back.'[2] But Churchill saw,
Beyond the cruel ordeal of lengthy war,
A hope of victory, allied with that power
Which shared the English tongue and common law,
And whose vast land and democratic life
Concealed the fires of unremitting might.

Yet even while the Zeros droned above
Pearl Harbour's stricken fleet, invasion fell

Upon the Orient. On scattered shores
The armies of Japan were not opposed.
Hong Kong, surrounded, fought for eighteen days.
Nor did Malayan jungle much delay
The skilful Yamashita's ardent troops.
Down through the neck of Kra his soldiers came
To seize Penang, whilst on the eastern shore
Another force drove south on jungle paths,
Outflanking road blocks, stealing river boats,
To leapfrog down the undefended coast.

Churchill, meanwhile, had ordered to the east
The finest of his navy's battleships,
'The Prince of Wales', escorted by 'Repulse'.
From Singapore courageously they sailed,
Devoid of air support from sea or land,
To intercept the invasion of Malay.
Off Kuantan a Japanese attack
From waves of bombers sank each ship in turn.
Above the 'Prince of Wales'' submerging decks,
Admiral and captain, standing at salute,
Redeemed the error of their fortitude.
No more would war at sea depend upon
Dead weight of steel and calibre of guns.
Now every mile of eastern Asia's coast
Lay open to the Rising Sun's advance,
Its navy paramount in all the seas
From Oahu to Straits of Malacca.

Towards Johore the British columns filed
And crossed the causeway into Singapore,
The teeming jewel of Britain's eastern crown,

Once key to her imperial domain,
Now without ships and vulnerable by land.
Yamashita's army was not slow
To cross the straits. The city was besieged;
Its heavy guns traversing empty sea.
Within its walls the people were convulsed
By swelling numbers and the growing toll
Of dead and wounded from the long campaign.
Incessant shelling and the rain of bombs
Brought mounds of bodies to the city streets.
Shortage of food and threat of cholera,
Then lack of water – for the Japanese
Had overrun the island's reservoirs –
Outweighed the waning pride of British arms.
Should thousands die to save a general's name?
So through the gates marched British officers
Behind the flags of empire and defeat.
It was the worst disaster, Churchill said,
In British history. Now white man's rule,
The vanity of empire in the east,
Had run its course. No law would temper now
The crude supremacy of martial power
In every land subjected to Japan.
Dishonoured in the harsh *bushido* code,
The British captives would for long endure
Abuse of victors, labouring as slaves
Beneath cruel masters on the Burma Road.

Meanwhile the swarming armies of Japan
Had landed on the island of Luzon,
And driven back MacArthur's ill-matched force
Of Philippinos and U.S. Marines.

Manila soon was lost, but on Bataan
A slow retreat cost heavy casualties
To Hommas's troops. Corregidor alone,
An island rock, remained to symbolise
The armed defiance of America,
Its fortress crammed with wounded and the flood
Of local people fleeing bombs and shells.
Within the hollowed rock of last resort,
The US soldiers, racked by dysentery,
Now short of food and sickened by the stench,
Found courage still to blast the Nippon boats.
Glowing, like Hades, deep in dreadful fire,
The Malinta Tunnel shook with falling shells,
Its occupants bemused beyond despair,
Contented by the company of death,
Eating their mule meat, whilst a lone Marine
Played wistful tunes upon a violin.

MacArthur had proclaimed he could defend
The Philippines against Japan's attack,
But sea-borne reinforcements were proscribed
By Yamamoto's devastating blow.
The ill-trained Philippinos, and Marines,
Could not protect those diverse islands long
Against the vigour of the Japanese,
Well-practised in the arts of jungle war
And brought by sea to any vacant coast
From Vigan in the north to Legaspi.
Yet though unsound, MacArthur's brave defence,
Fought by elite Marines who knew at heart
The oft-told stories of their fathers' wars -
At Little Bighorn River, Alamo,

At Chancellorsville and Chickamauga Creek,
In Cuba, and St Mihiel in France -
Now made Corregidor the latest tale
Of New World fortitude. Yet Homma's arms
O'erwhelmed the final line; and stricken men,
Already weak from wounds and dysentery,
Who fell into the hands of Japanese,
Were treated with contempt. Bataan's 'Death March'
Abandoned prisoners beaten, stabbed or maimed.
As for the rest, the years in hungry camps
With brutal guards meant few would long survive
The war they briefly fought upon Bataan.
But though above the fort Corregidor
The Rising Sun now flew triumphantly,
MacArthur would return, as he avowed.

In distant Burma, British troops withdrew
To Moulmein, as the Japanese advanced.
Only a day ahead, they could not stop
To offer help to desperate villagers.
Sometimes a wounded man was left behind,
Propped up against a tree, left to himself,
With food and water, one grenade and gun.
Outflanked by sea, they crossed the broad Salween,
But at the Sittang many men were trapped.
Too soon the only bridge was blown up;
None but the strongest swam the rapid flood.
Rangoon could not be held, though Churchill sent
A vaunted soldier to its doomed defence:
General Alexander, who had quit
The Dunkirk beaches with the last rearguard.
Nor could the courage of a tiny force

Of Allied planes, outnumbered in the air,
Preserve Rangoon from Japanese assault.
As British forces drove towards the north,
Through Prome, and then Myingyan towards Imphal,
The Japanese pressed on to Mandalay,
And, deep within the mountains of Shan States,
They cut the Burma Road at Lashio.
Only Stilwell's army now remained
Of those from China loyal to Chiang Kai-shek
And ardent to avenge their country's rape.
Across the Chindwin, in the Naga Hills,
The train of British, mixed with refugees,
Wove slowly up on paths of reeking mud
Towards Imphal and safety. Monsoon rain
Soaked into clothes and packs. Little welcome
Met the exhausted throng, who gathered there
On slopes above the town. Who could foresee
That these defeated men, diseased, half-starved,
Lying on sodden blankets in the night,
Would drive the Japanese from Burma's hills,
As surely as they'd come to plague the land?
Across the Irrawaddy's fertile plain
The springs of courage would run freely back.

One major goal remained in this first phase
Of Japanese expansion in the East:
The vast reserves of oil for waging war
Possessed by Holland in East India.
From Indo-China and the Philippines
Fresh troops set sail for Java, Sarawak,
Sumatra, Celebes and Borneo.
The Allied navies fought against the odds,

But in the Java Sea they were destroyed,
When Admiral Doorman, bravest of the Dutch,
Drowned with his ship. Darwin was struck by bombs,
Which raised Australian fears of swift attack
Across the Timor Sea. The Japanese,
However, now at large upon the Indian
Ocean's vast expanse, preferred to challenge
Britain in Ceylon, which, taken by Japan,
Would threaten British convoys round the Cape
And thereby Churchill's settled strategy
Of strengthening his African campaign.
Nagumo's fleet could heavily outgun
The task-force under Somerville's command.
Dive bombers struck Colombo, sinking ships,
And gallant British aircraft could not stop
Another raid upon Trincomalee.
Yet brute aggression, undiminished yet
In four short months of violent, ruthless war,
Was reaching out, in greed, beyond its grasp.

As fires abated at the burning wells
Across the Indies, and as smoke dispersed
Above the ships in Trincomalee's port,
The world took stock of what Japan had done.
The western powers had lost all they possessed
In eastern Asia. Japanese might fall
Upon Australia's unpeopled lands,
And cross Assam to where the British ruled
The restless millions of the Hindustan.
Would they advance, or seal their new-found realm
With chains of steel between the myriad isles
From Sakhalin to north Sumatra's tip?

As Tokio war-lords pondered on that choice,
War now was unconfined throughout the globe
On elements of land and sea and air,
And English-speaking people now in arms
Confronted it on every continent.
For Hitler - though he scorned them - said the Reich
Had common cause beside the Japanese.
Would Axis might prevail, before their foes,
Possessed of vast American supplies,
Could mobilise in liberty's defence
Against the claims of racial arrogance?

8 Axis Occupation

Aggression had repaid its devotees,
The Fascist powers, who'd seized their early chance
To strike against the western States and Russia.
Surprised by war, those ill-prepared to fight
Had suffered losses; till, defiantly,
The British first, and then the Soviets,
Had stemmed the fury of the first assaults.
On every front great armies paused for breath.
The thaw of Spring portended on the steppes
A new offensive by the German force;
In Africa the British also watched,
As Rommel planned to sweep them to the Nile;
Whilst on the Pacific rim the rival fleets
Disposed themselves for some decisive blow.

By now, in France, the fruit of Petain's rule
Was turning sere. Not since the time they'd shot
A Frenchman dead for brawling in the street
With German troops could Hitler's army pose
As friends of France. Their Gallic pride outraged,
The French began to chafe the Germans' power.
No more would they converse with German troops;
In city streets they misdirected them;
Books and pamphlets, printed underground,
Argued for freedom from the Nazi plague.
And bolder spirits took up secret arms:
Shooting soldiers, sabotaging trains,
Bombing factories, and threatening those
Who favoured German victory, like Laval.
Once Russia was attacked, the Communists,
Released from doubts about the pre-war pact,
Joined with ruthless zeal the violent course
Of armed resistance. When Hitler ordered
Ten French deaths for every German killed,
De Gaulle restrained his followers in France,
Till they could fight on later battlefields.
No scruples likewise moved the Communists.
Their acts of vengeance, planned in midnight rooms,
Did not abate. Innocent Frenchmen, shot
By firing squad, or hung from village lamps,
Paid heavily for such intransigence.
British agents, dropped on moonless nights,
Worked like leaven on the growing throng
Of French impelled by conscience to resist;
But all alike were prone to be betrayed,
To face Gestapo torture, like Odette,
Who did not name her fellow spies or friends,

Enduring total darkness for three months
Within the women's camp at Ravensbruck.
Czech parachutists, dropped by British planes,
Blew up the car of Himmler's deputy,
The dreaded Heydrich, in Bohemia -
The SS leader charged to rid the Reich,
And all its new dependencies, of Jews.
The two assassins died within the church
Of Borromaeus, shot by SS guards.
More blood of Slavs was sought for Heydrich's death;
A village - Lidice - not far from Prague
Was chosen for revenge. All males were shot,
Their families taken, every building burned
And ruins razed, leaving no trace behind.

By this time, also, systematic death
Was organised for European Jews,
By blood alone condemned as enemies,
As vile corrupters, traitors to the Reich.
The star of David, etched in yellow cloth,
Now stigmatised their children and the aged,
The sick, disabled, rabbis, unemployed,
Businessmen, students, rich and poor alike.
Germans and Poles, Austrians, even French,
Cast but a furtive glance at those frail ghosts,
Who, crushed in ghettos and bereft of means
To earn a living or maintain respect,
Languished in shadows, dark behind the wall
Of city quarters, separate from life.
They suffered now, like Him they had denied,
For in the streets of every German town,
And then in France, the Netherlands, the east,

Jews of all sex and age were rounded up
By agents quick to serve the master race -
To win promotion by an infant's death,
Or satisfy a bureaucrat's demand
For one old woman of a *mischling* birth
To make up numbers on a Jewish train.
Gendarmes in Vichy France preserved the lie
Of national sovereignty by their arrest
Of Jewish families sent to Drancy camp.
On Paris boulevards the yellow star
Marked out the race of David from the rest,
While Jewish shops stood empty, till the time
When gentile landlords deemed them fit to use.
Uncounted times when Wehrmacht troops entrained
For service on the many fronts of war,
And whilst the bombs of Allied aircraft fell
Upon their careworn families in the Reich,
Train-loads of Jews in filthy cattle trucks
Rolled slowly eastwards during night and day
To darkened sidings at a distant camp -
At Auschwitz, Chelmno, Belzec, Sobibor,
Or Maly Trostenets for Russian Jews.

Cardinal Galen preached in Munster's church
Against the murder of compatriots -
The senile, handicapped and those insane -
Till even Goebbels feared that such a crime
Might sap the will to work of those who heard,
And with reluctance ordered it to stop.
A few brave soldiers on the eastern front
Spoke out against the crimes committed there,
Like Michael Kitzelmann, whose Iron Cross

Availed him nothing when he showed disgust
For those who ordered such atrocities.
At Orel he was shot by firing squad.

Survivors from Bataan and Singapore
Now suffered cruelly at the hands of guards
Imbued with hate for those whom they despised
For willingly surrendering their arms.
Whips drove them on towards malarial camps,
To work as slaves beneath the tropic sun,
On railway lines upon the Burma Road.
Some chanced a levelled rifle to escape
And reach the jungle's fleeting sanctuary.
What did these victims make of memories now
Of peaceful gardens labelled Japanese,
Of ceremonial gates, of ritual tea,
Of Zen philosophy, of geisha girls,
Of lovely drawings limned in subtle shades?

Thus was foreshadowed what would long transpire
If Axis power were to predominate.
In every land the unchecked stain would spread
Of brutal men unmindful of the law,
Uncaring for the weak, obsessed by power,
Intolerant of those of other race,
Contemptuous of literature and art
Except what served their dismal purposes.
Meanwhile where love of freedom still waxed strong,
Men armed themselves to fight against the wrong.

9 The War at Sea

As soon as war began a U-boat force
Had taken station in the western seas.
Beneath the steely nets of Scapa Flow
Lieutenant Prien took his U-boat through
And sank the battleship, the 'Royal Oak' -
Proud vengeance for the Kaiser's Kriegmarine
That lay beneath the same expanse of sea.

Hitler knew that Britain could not fight,
Nor even long survive, without those goods

Conveyed from world-wide Empire and elsewhere,
And notably across Atlantic deeps -
Supplies of food, of metal, timber, oil,
Of arms and ammunition, ships and planes,
At first by Lend-lease from the USA,
Then from the same, now willingly allied.
German surface ships imposed a threat:
'Graf Spee' and 'Deutschland', 'Gneisenau', Scharnhorst',
The 'Admiral Scheer' and 'Hipper', 'Prince Eugen',
And, chief of these, the mighty-armed 'Bismarck'.
The British navy sought these battleships
Across the seas of every continent,
Tracking their routes to far-off neutral ports,
Or ocean rendez-vous for resupply,
Compelling them to turn their armaments
On better armed opponents than those boats
Chock-full of merchandise or unfused arms.
'Graf Spee' was scuttled, trapped by British ships
In Montevideo harbour; others sank,
Like 'Bismarck', battle-scarred, or lurked in ports,
Not keen to venture forth.

A harbour on the western coast of France -
St Nazaire at the broad mouth of the Loire -
Contained a dry dock large enough to hold
The one great ship, the 'Tirpitz', still a threat
To Allied convoys in the northern seas.
Thence, in the night, a strange armada sailed:
One battle-worn destroyer, 'Campbeltown',
Packed with five tons of high explosive charge
And followed by a swarm of motor boats.
Six hundred men, their faces blacked with cork,

Well-armed with knives and automatic guns,
Had heard Mountbatten tell them to ensure
That St Nazaire would never more be fit
To house the 'Tirpitz', if she were in need.
With this intent, Commander Beatty led
His motley convoy into St Nazaire,
While air force planes diverted coastal guns.

But suddenly the sweep of searchlight beams
Highlighted 'Campbeltown' as she approached.
From harbour batteries a criss-cross fire
Engulfed her decks and hull. Yet she plunged on,
Her crew prostrate, but still returning fire,
With Bren guns through the narrow gunwale ports,
Until her bows sliced through the massive gates
And, half within the dock, she came to rest.
Men poured ashore from all the convoy decks,
Shooting at Germans, running to destroy
The installations on the flagstone wharves,
And pulling wounded off the blazing boats.
But German reinforcements overcame
The small perimeter of British troops;
So death or capture was the lot of most,
Though five escaped, eventually to Spain.

When, some days later, German soldiers came
With women from the town of St Nazaire,
And strolled at leisure on the 'Campbeltown',
A huge explosion pulverised the ship
And wrecked the installations of the dock.
And yet, in spite of this, the British dead
Were buried there with military pomp;

And local people strewed their graves with flowers.
But still the 'Tirpitz', in its Trondheim fjord,
Preoccupied those warships forced to guard
The hunter's exit from a haven lair.

Now Doenitz, in command of submarines,
Convinced the Führer that his U-boat fleet
Could win the war by maritime blockade.
So scores of U-boats prowled the ocean depths,
Preparing to converge on convoy routes –
The Germans had deciphered British codes.
Through periscopes they watched the pale night sky
For silhouettes of Allied merchant ships,
Before they surfaced, closed to shorter range
To fire torpedoes, then crashed-dived away.
And submarines in wolf-packs could confuse
The navy escorts ringing convoys round.
The stricken ships capsized, or slid like whales
With gaping jaws aloft to silent deeps,
Dispensing men like insects on the waves,
Who grasped at rafts, or drowned in oily sea;
And through the dome of grey Atlantic cloud,
German aircraft –Junkers, Focker-Wolfes –
With nose machine guns and cascades of bombs,
Like blackened eggs from harpies in the sky,
Attacked in lines, till decks burst into flame.

No less the U-boat sailors felt the grip
Of near disaster in their coffin shells,
As, once submerged, inhaling leaden air,
They waited for the depth-charge pressure waves
To strike the hull and freeze the heart with fear,

And listened for the sound of creaking plates,
And watched the water from the loosened valves
That trickled down towards the duckboard floor.
Yet if they surfaced near the enemy,
They could not leave their boat till it was primed
To sink beside them, lest the British found
All kinds of secrets from the captured craft.

As yet there was an insufficiency
Of escorts, radar-sets and long-range planes
To stop the menace of the submarine.
Along the US coast the U-boats claimed
Their victims by the score from merchant fleets.
Offshore beside Miami's golden beach,
Lit by a million bulbs, their captains spied
The passing tankers etched against the light;
And further south the Caribbean coast
Saw wreck on wreck pollute the azure sea
With many tons of Venezuelan oil,
Bound for the war machines of western powers.

Off Freetown, Casablanca and Brazil,
The U-boats hunted further for their prey;
Whilst through the north Atlantic's fearsome swell
The furrows of the convoys tracked their way
From western Britain to Newfoundland's coast
And south to New York city; there to load
And turn again to face the bitter sea
And unseen predators. Though aircraft searched,
Like gliding sea-gulls hungering for fish,
The weary crews of snub-nosed Sunderlands
And Catalinas slung from upper wings,

Could not extend the quest quite far enough.
Within the broad Atlantic's surging leagues,
There lay a stretch of several hundred miles
Unreachable by air. Within that zone,
The silent U-boats lay in wolfhound packs,
Threatening each passing convoy with the shock
Of fierce explosions, sound of rending steel
And open wounds that sucked the sea within.
How many times on Admiralty charts
Had careworn plotters marked another loss
In that sea-filled abyss between the arcs,
Beyond the range the Catalinas flew?
How many times did Doenitz celebrate
Another victim sunk there by his crews,
Before he saw them home at Baltic ports
With guards of honour bearing Nazi flags?
Thus the Atlantic war continued long,
Each side employing brave and hardy crews,
'To watch the night in storms, the day in cold'[3],
Replacing those who died with new recruits,
Who also learned to fear the mute green sea.

Against the Wehrmacht's mighty war machine,
The desperate Russians needed every kind
Of new equipment that the West could bring -
Shermans, Spitfires, ammunition, guns,
Boots and clothing, medical supplies.
So Russian convoys faced the biting cold,
And braved the Barents and Norwegian seas
From Iceland to Archangel or Murmansk.
Yet Arctic weather was the lesser threat.
Occupied Norway sheltered on her coast,

Beneath the fjords' steep and barren slopes,
The 'Tirpitz', 'Scheer' and 'Hipper', armed enough
To wreck a convoy with their heavy guns;
Whilst hiding still beneath the iron-grey waves
Were greedy U-boats, now a hundred strong,
And on the Finnmark Plateau's distant field
A fleet of Kondors, loaded full with bombs.
About mid Summer, when the northern sun
Ne'er set upon the deepest fjord's gloom,
But overshone the wide, tempestuous sea,
Another convoy, PQ 17,
Left Iceland's coast and sailed north-easterly,
By Spitzbergen and Bear Island, on the route
Past Nova Zembla to Archangel port.
The German surface fleet quit Alta fjord
To intercept this convoy, but soon heard
That Allied battleships and carriers
Were near Bear Island and prepared to strike.
With memories of the 'Bismarck''s nearby fate,
The German admiral ordered the return
Of 'Tirpitz' and her escorts to their base;
But Britain's own commander, unaware,
And thinking of an imminent attack,
Gave to the ships of PQ 17
The order 'scatter', to avoid the shells
Of concentrated fire from 'Tirpitz'' guns.
Yet, to the scene, like foxhounds scenting blood
When all the mounted hunters have retired,
Came U-boats and the long-range Kondor planes,
To hunt down one by one the lonely ships,
Now unprotected from the sea or air.
Two-thirds were lost, with crews and precious loads,

On killing fields of never ending day,
Where men were buried deep in icy brine.
A few survivors reached the Soviet port,
While comrade Stalin raged at such a loss,
And Churchill dreamed of massive northern fleets
To sweep the Arctic ocean clear of Huns.

In seas far warmer Malta stood besieged,
That citadel of medieval knights
Whose lonely dedication had once held
Rapacious Islam, savage to destroy
The reign of Christ in European lands.
Now garrisoned by Britain, Malta lay
Between Gibraltar and the Suez route
To India and Empire's distant shores.
But, furthermore, the vital southern voyage
From Sicily to Cyrenaica,
By which the Axis succoured Rommel's troops,
Passed by the isles of Malta and Gozo.
Three biplane aircraft were the isle's defence,
'Faith', 'Hope' and 'Charity', of lasting fame,
Till Spitfire squadrons flew from carrier decks
To break the cordon of the Italian fleet.
As British submarines and aircraft sank
An ever-growing weight of Axis ships
With crucial cargoes for the desert force,
The Luftwaffe general, Kesselring, began
A fierce offensive on the island's ports
And on the aerodrome of Takali.

Each day the bombers came with swelling drone,
In close formation underneath a swarm

Of fighter escorts hidden in the sun,
To rouse the island, sunk in tremulous heat.
Above the aerodrome and harbour walls
Small puffs of black from anti-aircraft guns
Floated in futile gestures in between
The square-tipped wings of Junker 88s.
Above Valetta planes began to dive,
Like taloned eagles falling on their prey,
Smiting the decks of ships with wreaths of fire,
Or churning water high in white cascades.
Braces of Spitfires, racing to ascend,
Scattered the German fighters in alarm,
And undefended bombers, soon aflame,
Swept down in burning arcs to sudden death.

Rabat and Sliema, and the ancient walls
Of old Medina, silent on its hill,
Where once they'd watched the sea for crescent flags,
All suffered from the devastating raids;
But that Great Harbour, which had sheltered long
The major ships of every warlike race,
Sustained the worst attacks, and saw its stones
Upheaved by bombs, and splintered, bullet-scarred.
Maltese died in hundreds, like those times
When Turkish cannons smote the city walls.
Royal Navy ships were crippled at their berths,
And struggling convoys, seeking to relieve
The grave depletion of the island stores,
Lost many boats for want of air defence.
Hitler transferred four hundred combat planes
From central Russia, where their need was great,
And stationed them on parched Sicilian fields,

To dominate that area of sea
On which the fate of Egypt would depend,
The 'narrows' west of Malta, now become
The crossroads of opposing strategy.
Invasion plans were made - and cast aside -
For landings on the isle, and paratroops -
For Hitler still recalled the cost in Crete,
When brave resistance took so many lives
And thousands drowned in unescorted ships.

Thus Malta stood, the eye in storms of war
That waged on sea and air unceasingly,
As Britain sent relieving convoys there
From western straits and Alexandria,
Which fought the Italian fleet and German planes
At heavy odds. For this the Maltese gained
A high award, the name of George Cross isle;
Whilst British sailors and the airforce crews
Who died for Malta won their own renown,
At rest beneath the sea, whose wine-dark hue
Now lapped the walls of Ilium anew.

10 Midway

Quickened by wrath, America soon chose
To counter what the Japanese had done.
James Doolittle was chosen for the task,
With sixteen army bombers of long range,
To sail upon the carrier 'Hornet''s decks.
In that great western ocean, now possessed
By Hirohito's bold, triumphant fleet,
A picket line of warships intervened
To stop the US carrier's approach,
Forcing their planes to fly six hundred miles.
From decks too short for safety, they arose,
Near stalling with their heavy load of bombs,
Each climbing slowly, like a greedy bird
Reluctant to let fall too heavy a catch.

No Zero fighters came within their view
As they approached the mainland of Japan

And glimpsed the blue of Yokohama Bay.
Defenceless warships tempted them to bomb,
But they sped on; at treetop height they saw
The crowded wharves alive with busy men,
And then the houses, thousands row on row,
At last, their targets, factories of war.
They climbed apace to fifteen hundred feet,
And, through the warning puffs of ack-ack fire,
Dropped four bombs each at steady intervals,
Before they pulled away, and crossed the sea
To land in China on a friendly field -
Though one crew, baling out, were caught and shot,
Arraigned for killing unarmed citizens,
And one, who landed in Siberia,
Were soon interned by Soviet command.

Japan could not believe in such a raid,
That Tokio could burn with foreign fire.
Their war-lords had assured them none could reach
The sacred homeland, with a king divine
And cherry blossom ripe to burst in bloom
Beneath the snow of Fujiyama's cone.

For this dishonour only quick revenge
Would satisfy the Nippon High Command.
Defence of empire was unworthy now.
To fan the flames of hot, aggressive war,
And spread dominion of the Rising Sun
Across the wide Pacific to those lands
Where European races held at bay
The progress of the Asian destiny
Was now their theme: to seize the isle of Midway,

Then Hawaii; to occupy New Guinea,
The Solomon Isles; to threaten then
Australia herself, by cutting off
Her lifeline to the east; and in the north,
Where Arctic fog enshrouded all in gloom,
To make a landing on the Aleutian Isles,
And seek that route which once the Inuits trod
Towards Alaska and the brave New World.

Taking Port Moresby on the southern coast
Of east New Guinea was the first bold step
By which to threaten north Australia;
But US naval experts had for long
Deciphered what the Nippon navy sent
By radio transmission. Thus forewarned,
A carrier fleet approached the Coral Sea
To intercept the troopships moving south.
A similar force of Japanese appeared
To challenge the American attempt
To save Port Moresby. Rival fleets were found
By searching aircraft; both despatched their planes.
In ten brief minutes 'Shoho' was capsized;
But 'Shokaku', defying several hits,
Would fight again beneath the Imperial flag.
Torpedoed from the air and hit by bombs,
The crew of 'Lexington' abandoned her.
The Coral Sea, however, was no prize
To risk outright defeat; each side withdrew,
A few score aircraft lost, and other ships
Of lesser consequence. No longer would
Port Moresby live in fear of sea invasion
By the Japanese. One lesson, too, was learned:

That major naval battles could be fought
Without shots fired from any battleship.
Just as the British flagship, 'Prince of Wales',
Was sunk by air torpedoes when she'd sailed
In hostile seas devoid of covering planes,
So now two carrier fleets had long engaged
By means alone of aircraft flying far
To bomb the opposing fleet, and then return
To roost in triumph on their carrier perch.

A greater battle than the Coral Sea
Would prove this true. The carrier 'Yorktown',
Damaged in the fight, returned to dry dock
At Pearl Harbour base. Three months were needed
To make full repairs, but Admiral Nimitz,
Now the C-in-C, ordered her ready
In so many days, and furious workmen,
Skilled in many arts - riveting, welding,
Wiring, armour, guns, mechanics, steering,
Stores and painting - soon transformed the hull,
Like termites on a new Leviathan.
Thus 'Yorktown' sailed to join Nimitz' fleet.

Intelligence foretold a fresh attack:
A Japanese assault on Midway Isle,
A coral atoll less than two miles square,
With double specks of land, yet stepping-stone
To that great port where Yamamoto struck.
But more than this was sought for by Japan:
The Tokio generals knew Nimitz must fight
With all his fleet to safeguard Midway Isle.
Thus would the threat entice him to engage

Against the might of Yamamoto's force -
Eight carriers, two hundred other boats,
And battleships, including 'Yamato'
Whose armament was guns of eighteen inch.
The US fleet contained no battleships;
All were assigned to western coast patrols.
The 'Enterprise', the 'Hornet' and 'Yorktown'
Carried, however, air torpedo planes
And Dauntless bombers, recently supplied,
Though pilots were ill-practised in their use.

A Nippon force of carriers was sent
To seize the Aleutian Isles, thus luring ships
From Midway Isle whilst Yamamoto struck.
Meanwhile he sent Nagumo's powerful fleet
Ahead to Midway, ready to attack
The island's airstrip, furnishing the way
For transports full of soldiers to invade.
His own position, with the battleships,
Lay to the westward, waiting to engulf
The US fleet in devastating fire:
A worthy plan to use superior force,
But for one factor, unbeknown to all,
Except Commander Nimitz and his staff -
The Nippon naval code was being read,
Even as Yamamoto left Japan.

Just as Nagumo closed upon Midway,
The US carrier fleet and escort ships
Hove to beyond the line of sea and sky,
Their pilots eager for a bold assault
Upon the alien race whose treacherous blow

Had killed their countrymen at Oahu.
Nagumo's bombers were the first to strike,
Damaging Midway, but with small effect.
US land-based aircraft flew in turn
And likewise failed to make decisive hits.
Although Nagumo feared an air attack,
With rash contempt he filled his carrier decks
With bombers armed to strike a second time.
But even so, when US aircraft came
To drop torpedoes at the heaving decks
Of 'Kaga' and 'Akagi' and 'Soryu',
The prowling Zeros shot them down in flames.
Nagumo and his captains were convinced
The day was theirs, the battle all but won.

Then, suddenly, as quickly as the wind
Whips up the ocean from serenely blue
To raging, mountainous waves, all was reversed.
For whilst the Zeros hunted down their foes,
A cloud of new attackers overhead,
The snub-nosed Dauntlesses, whose untried crews
Peered through their canopies from four miles up,
Now steeply dived, and fell like silver rain
Towards the deck of 'Kaga' and the rest.
Decks, control towers, gun posts burst in flame
From half-ton bombs, like flakes of bursting shale,
And in an instant new explosions flared,
As loaded bombers caught the spreading fire.
Those Zeros in the air lacked height to catch
The Dauntless bombers skimming out to sea,
Their pilots jubilant at such success
And unaware of how their comrades died.

For those torpedo planes that first drew fire
Had left the Zeros unprepared to fight
A second battle in the distant sky.
Like stingless wasps, they lay on littered decks,
Or cruised too low in futile zig-zag flight.
The dead had also reaped their victory.

All was confusion in the Nippon fleet,
Command posts gone, and orders unobserved,
As men were trapped on burning lower decks
And oil fires flamed with black, consuming smoke.
Exploding magazines and cavernous gaps
Consumed machines and men with equal lust.
Admiral Nagumo left his sinking ship
To keep command from elsewhere in the fleet.
Not so the proud commander of 'Soryu',
Yanagimoto, who, with sword in hand,
Stood to attention on the ruined bridge
And sang, until the waves enveloped him,
The national anthem of the Rising Sun.
One carrier, the 'Hiryu', was not hit;
She sent her planes, with furious revenge,
Against the 'Yorktown', starting several fires,
Until the US bombers dived again,
And wrapped the 'Hiryu' in devouring flames.
Yet 'Yorktown' also sank, her final blow
Delivered by a Nippon submarine.

Could Yamamoto still complete his task
By waiting till the US fleet advanced
Into his overwhelming cannonades
From 'Yamato' and other battleships?

Amid the heat of victory, Spruance saw
This final danger, and with wise restraint
Recalled his carrier fleet beyond the reach
Of Yamamoto's guns. Unnerved by loss,
The victor of Pearl Harbour now withdrew.
Far northwards, where the pale Aleutians lay,
A meagre prize was won, two empty isles;
So small an acquisition could not match
The Midway victory in the scales of war.

What now prevailed round half the world's vast seas
Was rough equality. The US fleet
Was short of capital ships, and yet Japan
Defended now a great perimeter,
Patrolled by naval forces overstretched
To keep supplied the islands in her sway.
Her hasty claims to empire cost her dear,
Demanding war on many fronts at once:
In mid Pacific, on Australia's fringe,
In Burma, and where still the embers burned
Of Chinese hatred in their brutal plight.
Even on the Amur's marshy banks
The Nippon soldier languished at his post,
On guard in case the Russians broke their pact.
Was not Japan an ally of that power
Which threatened to destroy the Soviet land?
At any moment Stalin might command
A Russian force to cross the Amur's bounds
And draw a circle round the Japanese,
As they had done at Nomonhan before.
And yet Japan retained her greatest strength -
The willingness of all her hardened troops

To die for her Sun-king, in hope of life
In that Valhalla where their heroes dwelt.

America, initially so weak,
Adapted her great industries for war.
Detroit, Chicago, Pittsburgh, Baltimore,
Texas and the Californian ports
All now produced an ever-growing stream
Of aircraft, ships and tanks, whilst men were trained
To fight in every element and clime.
Henceforth Japan would face a crescent foe,
Relentless to avenge her injuries.
The warlords of Japan mistook the might
Of those whom they impulsively had struck.
The giant, awake, would never rest again,
Till those who had awoken him were slain.

11 The Dieppe Raid

In southern fields of England lay encamped
Those British soldiers charged with home defence.
Once Churchill knew invasion threats had passed,
He grew impatient at their lack of use.
Was not Stalin desperate for relief,
And calling for a western second front
To claw the enemy back from where they stood
In millions on the Russian motherland?
Roosevelt, also, urged a quick assault
Across the Channel to re-enter France,
And strike directly at the conquered lands.
His generals were impatient when they heard
The caution of the British Chiefs of Staff.
Alanbrooke, like Churchill, could recall
The slaughter of the Somme and Paschendaele,
But only General Marshall could attest

How many Yankee youths had died in France
To win a mile or two of foreign land;
And even he rejected British plans
For devious war on far peripheries,
As Chatham fought to cull the powers of France,
Or Wellington on torrid fields of Spain,
Or Anzacs at the bloody Dardanelles.
Churchill acknowledged, too, that war must come
Once more to France to drive the Germans out,
And offer, to the Allied armies, routes
That pointed to the heartland of the Reich.
In Britain only could sufficient force
Be mustered to invade the coast of France.
So Churchill gave Mountbatten the command
To plan a great exploratory raid,
Before full-scale invasion might ensue,
That Britain, now a bastion of defence
Might soon become the springboard of attack.

In waning Summer, when the tides were high
And only stars gave dim, concealing light,
A large flotilla left the Sussex coast
And crossed the Channel to the chalky cliffs
Along the Pays de Caux, where lay Dieppe.
Canadian troops outnumbered all the rest.
A German sea-patrol was soon destroyed,
Though, cramped in landing-craft, each soldier feared
A warning to the coastal batteries.
No Allied aircraft bombed the German guns;
No naval salvoes broke apart the wire,
Or other obstacles along the beach,
For fear of killing French inhabitants.

Even before the crash on hostile stones
Of cold, metallic ramps, the guns had fired.
Beneath a smoke screen infantry debouched,
With bayonets fixed and safety catches off,
Straining their eyes to spot what they'd been told
By expert staff in sunlit training rooms.
Machine-gun bullets hit them; many fell.
Some tripped on bodies bleeding in the dark;
Some reached the esplanade and crouched below.
On either wing, commando units climbed
Through narrow gullies, hazardous with wire,
To reach the pending cliff-top batteries
And kill with razor knives the startled crews.
Now Hurricane fighters turned above the beach
To strafe the German troops, whilst mortars flared
To cover an advance upon the town.
Churchill tanks descended from the boats,
And, lumbering across the pebble beach,
Were hit by shells, and lay as burning wrecks,
Like pyres of steel for ancient warriors.

Pinned down by cross-fire, few men quit the beach;
Most hid behind the wall or stranded tanks,
Or lay prostrate within a bed of stones.
Only the sterile sky, now bright with dawn,
Did not emit the rattling sounds of death,
Except where, high above, there wheeled and dived
The British aircraft, now once more engaged
In saving comrades on a beach in France,
And settling scores for many casualties
Lost on their fighter sweeps of northern France.

Not from the Luftwaffe was help at hand
For German soldiers fighting in the town,
But on the road from Abbeville, whence fresh troops
Were driven unimpeded to the fray.
As enemy action grew yet more intense,
And no more ground was won above the beach,
The Allied soldiers realised they were trapped
Within a margin bound by cliffs and sea,
A mere appendix to the soil of France,
Of salty pebbles, tainted now with blood.
Sea-borne evacuation under fire
Was all their bold initiative had won;
Nor even that for some, like Captain Foote,
Who carried wounded men across the beach
And, at the call for all to re-embark,
Stayed with those left behind, to tend their wounds.
Over a thousand died upon the beach.
Many remained as captives. Few returned
To breathe, unwounded, scents of Summer air.

'Reconnaissance in depth', the raid was called.
Lessons, indeed, were learnt: that major ports
Could not be lightly taken by assault;
That therefore open beaches were the place
For new invasion plans; that floating harbours
Might provide for ships; that long bombardments
From the sea and air must precede infantry;
That arduous training and new kinds of arms
Were prime requirements for amphibious troops.
The Germans drew one lesson in reverse:
To fortify the western ports of France.
And all along the Nazi littoral

From Belgium to the Bay of Biscay shores,
New gangs of workers laboured to construct
The long Atlantic Wall of concrete forts
And seaward facing guns in pill-boxes,
Where ageing troops surveyed the hazy sea.
And plans were made to hold a mobile force
Behind the beaches, ready in reserve,
In case, one day, when tides had cleansed the stones
Which soldiers dead had stained with maple hue,
An expedition sailed to France once more,
Not doomed like them to founder on the shore.

12 Bomber Command

In Leningrad starvation did the work
Of German arms, and while the northern wing
Of Hitler's forces tarried in the siege,
The rest began a campaign on the Don
Towards the oilfields of the Caucasus.
Once more the Russian armies faced the tide
Of Wehrmacht ruthlessness and expertise,
As tens of thousands died, or lingered on
In prison pens unfit for humankind.

What then could Britain do to show the worth
Of her participation in the war?
In Africa she fought to stem the flood
Of Rommel and the Axis partnership;
At sea the navy struggled to perform

Escorting duties on the convoy routes;
Whilst, in the air, the R.A.F. patrols,
Designed to draw the Luftwaffe away
From aerodromes along the Russian front,
Could not provoke the enemy to fight.
For all his zest to turn the war around
And prove the British urgent to attack,
Churchill yet knew no 'second front' could come
Till it was long prepared in strategy,
And Britain filled with vehicles of war.
Would Russia keep her armies in the field
And see her land laid waste, her cities burnt,
Both youth and age heroically destroyed
In scenes of carnage rarely paralleled,
Whilst, to her mind, the western allies moped
And waited off-stage till the play was done?
One way alone remained to satisfy
This need to wage a new aggressive war:
To strike the enemy heartland from the air,
As had been done at Warsaw and Belgrade,
At Rotterdam and Britain's ports and towns.

So far the R.A.F. had tried to bomb
Strategic targets - factories, railways, ports -
And sought to minimise civilian deaths.
Expert economists gave much advice
On what effect such bombing would achieve,
But air reconnaissance showed small success:
Most targets were not hit, and damage done
Was soon repaired by German industry.
So, with misgivings, Churchill gave assent
To those, like Harris, who approved the change

To massive air attacks on German towns.
The bomber force would now be re-equipped
With long-range aircraft, flying four miles high,
Well armoured in defence, and carrying guns
To shoot the fighters down that dare attack.
Incendiaries and high explosive bombs
Would bring to German homes what was endured
When British cities burned so savagely.

At first the targets were the western towns
Close to the Rhine; then, on the Baltic coast,
Lubeck and Rostock, ancient Hansa ports,
Which, Harris noticed, offered no defence
And, built of timber, were combustible.
In clear night skies, to bombers flying low,
The silver Baltic gave Lubeck away.
The inner city blazed from end to end,
As laths and plaster crumbled in the heat.
For four successive nights the flames were fuelled
In Rostock's wooden core. Low level planes
Attacked the Heinkel factory near the town.
When Hitler heard, retaliation came
With sudden raids on medieval towns -
On Canterbury, Bath and Exeter -
Until both sides renounced 'Baedeker' raids.

Thus far the British had not tried their power
Against a major city of the Reich,
So Harris next resolved to demonstrate
How bombs alone could terminate the war,
By planning for a thousand bomber strike
Against the Rhineland city of Cologne.

From diverse airfields every type of plane -
Halifax, Stirling, Hampden, Wellington,
And new four-engined Lancaster - all flew
To vast assembly points in southern skies.
Across the North Sea droned the pregnant horde,
Its crews alert for 'enemy coast ahead'.
From perspex cabins gunners scanned the sky
To spot the Messchersmitts or Junkers rise
Against the faint horizon's eastward glow.
Soon they had crossed the dread Kammhuber line -
A chain of radar stations, interspersed
With 'boxes' where assembled fighters flew,
Until the ground control directed them
To home upon a target bomber group.
This time a thousand bombers swamped the screens
And few were lost to enemy attack.
Below the ground was dark, all lights blacked out
In village, town or highway, everywhere.
Only paths of water, shining grey,
Denoted still the unoffensive earth.

But then a sudden cannon flash revealed
That Messerschmitts had infiltrated them
And roamed at large within the bomber swarm.
Exploding aircraft fell in streams of flame.
The rest pressed on regardless. Each man knew
The god of numbers reaped a tithe of deaths,
And gave himself to his appointed task
Of holding firm the steering column's throb,
Or watching dials beside the pilot's hand,
Or calculating, in a cone of light,
The triangles of distance, wind and drift,

Or checking Browning guns and feeder chains
Of shining bullets soon to be discharged,
Searching with weary eyes the dangerous night
For that one mote that meant a German plane.
Eastwards the distant dawn glowed paltry red,
But down below the city shone with fires
That flickered through the streams of rising air,
Like bleeding wounds on bodies cauterised.
Through bursting flak the beams of searchlights veered,
Whilst lighter guns deterred a low attack.
Yet, steady on their course, most planes flew in
Through avenues of smoke to drop their bombs,
Then climb the midnight sky with empty wombs.
Once more they ran the gauntlet of the 'line';
Until the sea drew forth from weary crews
A muttered chorus of profound relief,
Like cries heard long ago by Euxine shores.
Of those shot down, a few escaped unharmed,
Rescued from angry mobs by German police,
But most were trapped inside their stricken craft,
Or drowned in northern seas. One pilot - Manser -
Controlled his damaged plane just long enough
To let the crew bale out before he crashed.
And many died, their deeds unrecognised.

Few British airmen thought what havoc reigned
Below them in the city of Cologne.
They did their duty, constant in the hope
Of taking part in Germany's defeat.
Were they obliged to think how houses fell
And buried families under smoking stone,
How children burned alive in upstairs rooms,

How water mains had burst and flooded homes,
How bombed out people waited patiently
For transport to prefabricated camps,
How some looked up, enraged, and swore revenge,
And others wept for pity, now awake
To what war really was, and did not blame
The hapless English flying overhead?
Would the airmen even have believed
That some Cologners sang in their despair,
'Fly on, dear Tommy, farther to Berlin,
They are the ones who always shouted '*ja*'!'[4]

The British public welcomed this display
Of how their air force, with a thousand planes,
Could repay what the Luftwaffe had done
At Coventry and all those other towns
Where shattered buildings marked the absent dead.
Harris himself was adamant to break
The will of Germans to sustain the war.
He did not know how much they could endure,
Nor how the grip of Nazi secret police
Constrained their protest. Others rationalised:
Non-combattants' were incidental deaths,
The cost of bombing war facilities –
Factories, plant, communications, mines –
If aircraft proved they did not have the means
To hit a target smaller than a town.
Churchill, in this dilemma, chose the path
Which, in his judgment, made one outcome sure:
That Stalin would not make a separate peace,
If he observed how Britain did not flinch
From any way to strike the Nazis down.

The Russian leader saw the news-reel film
Of cities razed and German suffering,
And knew his country did not fight alone.

Not all could rest content at how the war
Forgot the ancient code of chivalry –
That only men in arms should be attacked.
Bishop Bell and some M.P.s condemned
The area bombing and civilian deaths
As contrary to international law.
Government and people were less scrupulous.
Just as Kurukshetra's ancient plain had seen
The bronze age warriors cheating in the fight;
Or as proud Achilles, on Hector's death,
Around the walls of Troy demeaned his corpse;
Or as the cultured men of Attica
Put all the Doric Melians to death;
Or as the ardent faithful in the wars
Fought in Catholic or Reforming cause
Had pitilessly killed their Christian foes;
So now the character of war itself,
Its unrestrained ferocity and hate,
In killing face to face, by distant fire,
By drowning, starving in blockade or siege,
By cruelties scarcely dreamt in time of peace,
Hardened the hearts of once pacific men
And deafened them to cries of moral law.

As for the airmen, bombing German towns
In face of flak and fighter cannon shells,
When every mission had its toll of planes,
Familiar faces absent in the mess,

When crews were maimed, or blinded, burnt with oil
Or carried dead to air force mortuaries,
This was for them as much a battlefield
As any fought with bayonet or gun.

America, too, had few such moral qualms,
Though when her bomber forces first began
With daylight raids by Flying Fortresses,
They claimed precision bombing would succeed.
From targets of low range in northern France,
Like marshalling yards at Rouen, they returned
With few aircraft destroyed; but when they flew
Much further to the Reich, and met in daylight
German Messerschmitts, their rate of loss
Became intolerable. Mustang fighters
Later would escort the US bombers
Far to target zones; till then their airforce,
Like the British, mainly bombed by night.
The RAF attacked selected sites,
Such as the Schneider works in Burgundy,
But area bombing could not be renounced.
To Essen and the cities of the Ruhr,
To Bremen, Kiel, and Frankfurt on the Rhine,
To Hanover and Mannheim, Osnabruck,
Great fleets of bombers found their target zone
By radio pulses from an English base;
For science, too, assumed a hangman's mask,
As executor of a lawful task.

13 El Alamein

From where the vast Atlantic beat on France
To Russian steppes and Norway's Arctic Cape
The tide of Europe's war had reached its height.
Where Hitler's name now ruled in place of law,
The continent became a fortress armed
To keep itself enslaved against the world.
No straight assault could yet bring victory,
And British Chiefs of Staff were now convinced
That first north Africa should be secured.

A war of movement crossed the desert sands,
Its prize the Nile and Egypt, where converged

The sea-borne route to India and the East
And that land bridge which linked two continents.
In southern Russia German troops now held
A line that almost touched the Caspian.
Were Rommel to advance beyond the Nile,
The way lay open through the Middle East
To enter Russia from the southern flank
And close the ring of Wehrmacht sovereignty.
The fate of Russia would be thereby sealed,
The place of neutral Turkey jeopardised,
And oil assured to meet all German needs.
How then could Britain fight, her force destroyed,
Like Bonaparte's, amidst Egyptian sands,
With ships deprived of Alexandria
And Suez as a passage to the East?
The European war would be resolved
In Hitler's favour, and the British lion
Encaged within the once imperial isle.

For this conclusion Erwin Rommel strove.
His brief campaign in France had won him fame.
An opportunist on the battlefield,
Inspiring loyalty in all ranks of men,
He soon reversed the pendulum of war.
Across the dunes of Cyrenaica,
Through Libyan wastes and fast along the coast,
By swift advances inland in the night
With captured stocks of oil and food supplies,
The German *Panzers* drove the British back.
Though Auchinleck fought hard in fierce campaigns,
And, at Tobruk, Australians did not yield
But threatened to disrupt the tenuous line

Of thin-skinned trucks that left Benghazi port,
The Axis army crossed the frontier
And stood in Egypt, eager to advance.
Tobruk surrendered, and at Bir Hacheim,
Where, in their desert fort, French legionnaires
Had reaffirmed their country's pride of arms
By holding off for days a *Panzer* force
Contriving to outflank the British line,
The order was 'withdraw'. A bold attempt
By Rommel to attack, and with one blow
To scatter from the Nile the British troops
Who formed the 'tail' of Auchinleck's command,
Was only stopped by valiant defence
Amidst the shifting sands of Alamein.

At these reverses Churchill was dismayed:
Where were the reinforcements he had sent
At heavy cost across the dangerous sea?
Why could the British army not respond
To Rommel's smaller force? And Auchinleck –
What had he planned? A counterstroke must come!
Churchill was not deterred by dire reports
Of British armoured cars devoid of guns,
Of German tanks' superiority,
Of how, so often, British armour failed
In desert gullies held by infantry
With deadly fire from anti-aircraft guns
Converted to a low trajectory.
So, pressed by Stalin, and by Parliament,
For some aggressive action, Churchill went
To study for himself the desert scene.
Though Alanbrooke declined to take command,

In order to remain by Churchill's side,
Yet Auchinleck was ruthlessly dismissed
And General Gott appointed to succeed -
A man experienced in desert war,
But tired from months of fighting and retreat.
A quirk of Providence now intervened,
For Gott was killed - his aeroplane shot down -
And in his place a man of destiny
Was chosen to confront the 'Desert Fox',
As Rommel now was called for his exploits.

Montgomery had no doubts; it would be him,
Not Rommel, who would dominate henceforth
This theatre of the war, and choose the time
To strike one final, devastating blow.
All orders to evacuate were burned;
'Eighth Army will stay here in Alamein
And on Ruweisat ridge. If not alive,
Then let us stay here dead. Let Rommel come;
If he attacks again, we'll not delay
Our own campaign to finish him for good,
And rid all Africa of German arms.'[5]
Laconic, brusque and free of sentiment,
The new commander woke within his troops
A spirit of relentless energy,
A will to victory rarely found before.
Training began in earnest, no small task
Neglected as unworthy to be done,
Each man prepared to sacrifice his life,
While he held arms and stood unwounded there.

Across Ruweisat ridge the Germans too
Made ready for a final enterprise:
To reach the Nile by sweeping past the flank,
Between the minefields and the southern sands
Where Quattara depression barred the way
To heavy armour and artillery.
Montgomery guessed that Rommel, once again,
Would send his *Panzers* in a swift attack
To draw opposing armour out of line
And into gullies, where the hidden guns
Could strike pursuing tanks as they advanced.
Though Auchinleck had built a sound defence,
New tactics were required to meet this threat.

Montgomery placed his armour on the ridge
Of Alam Halfa, skirting to the north
The *Panzers'* route. His orders were to wait,
And when the Axis tanks were in their sights,
The British would then fire, without pursuit,
From hull-down placements on the upper slopes.
And when the Tigers came, some new-equipped
With longer barrels, firing-power enhanced,
Expecting as before a running fight
Of quick deployment, feigning of retreat,
And sudden ambush in the rolling dunes,
No answer came. So German *Panzers* wheeled
To face the louring Alam Halfa ridge,
And drove in range of British guns and tanks;
But none advanced from where they were deployed,
As they had done at heavy cost before
At battles for Gazala and Tobruk.
Each time the *Panzers* struck, they met the fire

Of tanks entrenched above them on the ridge.
Their losses grew, their petrol stock was short;
Then bombers from the east assailed them too,
And, with reluctance, Rommel drew them back.

Was this the time to win the desert war?
Montgomery ordered Freyberg to advance;
New Zealand troops might cut the Germans' line
And leave their armour trapped without supply.
But still the British lacked the expertise
To innovate attack and seize the chance
To catch the Desert Fox beyond his lair.
Fearing riposte, Montgomery held his hand.
The *Panzers* turned and reached Himeimat ridge.
There they would stay until the breaking storm
Of one last battle fought for Egypt's prize.

Already British plans were underway
To launch their own climactic counterstroke.
From Alamein, beside the coastal road
And south across the ridge of Ruweisat,
Almost to where Quattara blocked the way,
Deeper minefields fringed the British lines.
Enlivened by success, Montgomery chose
A bolder means than anyone before
To challenge Rommel in a final test.
He would not turn the southern flank with tanks,
And then swing northwards to pre-empt the ground
Behind the Germans, cutting off retreat.
Instead he would assault the Axis line,
With infantry at first to clear the way
And then with tanks to draw the Panzers on,

Whilst his main force would fight a 'killing match',
A battle of opposing infantry
In which superior numbers would prevail.
Thus would the German armour be compelled
To intervene on ground the British chose,
And lose in detail precious Tiger tanks
To close defensive fire and air support.

Elaborate plans were made to misinform
The German air force and their ground patrols
Of where the main attacking thrust would fall.
A dummy pipeline slowly grew each day
Towards the southern sector of the front.
False stocks of ammunition and supplies,
And wooden tanks and guns and cut-out trucks
Disguised the desert with imagined arms,
Whilst real-life soldiers hastened to and fro
To multiply the estimate of men.
North of Ruweisat ridge were camouflaged
Authentic arms assembled for the task
Of breaking into Rommel's strong defence.
Here lay the heavy guns and armoured cars,
Crusader tanks and Shermans just arrived
From freighters docked at Alexandria.
In new-dug trenches infantry prepared
Their gleaming weapons – rifles, bayonets, knives –
Their hand-grenades, and digging tools, and food,
Bottles of water, razors, morphine pills.
Montgomery had resisted all demands
To hasten his attack before the time
When men were trained and everything complete.

Nor would he move before the next full moon
Gave light to sappers clearing out the mines.

Already desert war had struck a blow
Against the Axis armies leaguered there:
For Rommel lay unwell in Germany.
But in their trenches dug in barren stones,
From glistening sea to thirty miles inland,
His faithful soldiers crouched on constant watch.
One-sixty-fourth Division by the sea,
Below the hill of Tel el Eisa rock;
Then Trento, Bologna, Ramke Parachute
(No longer airborne since the Cretan fight);
Brescia and Folgore in the south;
Behind them armour, ready to deploy:
The Fifteenth *Panzer* and Littorio;
And on the southern flank, where it was thought
The main attack would come, the Twenty-first,
Flanked by the Ariete on their right -
Old comrades of the German desert Korps -
With Pavia Division in reserve.
Westwards along the coast, the Ninetieth Light,
With them Trieste, waited to engage
Wherever they were needed in the line.

Confronting this array of Axis power
Were many nations bound in one command:
Ninth Australian held the northern flank -
With some who'd fought so bravely at Tobruk -
Fifty-first Highland waited on their left;
New Zealanders, survivors out of Crete,
South Africans, and on Ruweisat ridge,

Manning its northern slope, Fourth Indian.
These were the men of Leese's Thirtieth Corps.
The Greek Brigade, Fiftieth, Forty-fourth,
Then Seventh Armoured - famed as 'Desert Rats' -
And last, upon the left wing of the force,
The French Brigade who'd fought at Bir Hacheim,
Now camped beneath the rocky pyramid
Of Quaret el Himeimat in the south:
These were the men of Horrocks' Thirteenth Corps.
Behind them, in the north at Alamein,
First and Tenth Armoured were the main reserve,
Whose role would be to reinforce the drive
To smash the Axis line, and then break free
In open desert west of Rahman track.
In trenches and beside their tanks and guns
Two hundred thousand men now quietly slept,
As sentries stood alert and listened hard
To casual sounds of odd grenades or guns
That burst and rattled in the chill of dusk.

Then, all at once, a thousand flashes lit
The moon-grey desert sand and wastes of rock,
And flickering shadows fell across the dunes,
As thunderous gunfire rolled along the line.
Just as at Passchendaele and the Somme
Artillery was prologue to the fight,
So once again the British gunners shelled
The mortal path their infantry must tread,
To burst the buried mines and barbed defence
And scar with flame the waiting enemy,
And countermand, with seething fire, his guns
Which burned, when they were hit, with ruddy glows

Beyond the ridge against the western sky.
Already now the sappers had advanced
In covert groups to clear the narrow ways,
Peering by moonlight at the pitted sand,
And even, when detectors were at fault,
Prodding with bayonet point to feel the mines -
And not for them the glory of the fight,
But only the uncertainty of death
Beside the rotting shells of desert snails.
Now, at last, the starting-line was crossed,
As infantry advanced through drifting smoke,
Guided by rays of light from tracer shells
And searchlight beams that arched towards the night.

The Axis High Command could not discern
The focus of attack. Rommel, though ill,
Flew back, at Hitler's wish, from Germany.
He feared the bell had tolled for his decline:
Supplies were short; the British navy and
The Maltese airfields threatened every ship
That brought his precious cargoes to Tobruk.
How could the *Panzers* move deprived of oil?
But Rommel's doubts did not disarm his mind.
Were not the Germans' deep defensive lines
Well laced with eighty-eights and other guns
To enfilade a wadi, or entrap
Unwary armour reckless in pursuit?
Though Rommel did not know, for all his guile
Learnt in a hundred desert escapades,
That his opponent's tactics were reversed.
Nor did he know Montgomery would eschew

A turning action on the southern flank
And concentrate on Miteiriya ridge.

But there, in fact, the plan had gone awry:
For well-concealed machine guns and small arms
Brought constant fire upon the British troops.
They could not clear sufficient paths for tanks,
So armour must advance and cross the mines,
Though eighty-eights awaited their approach
With eager gun-crews crouching over sights.
How could they reach the Miteiriya crest,
As tanks exploded, wrecked by mine or shell,
As German snipers shot the bravest dead,
Who ventured out, regardless of their lives,
High on their turrets, searching through the dust
For passages through camel-scrub and mine?
All was in doubt, until Montgomery told
His tank commanders no-one would withdraw.
With grim obedience the armour reached
Beyond the top of Miteiriya ridge,
And formed a ring to shield the infantry.

The fury of the battle rose afresh,
When British troops advanced in cautious lines,
Crossing the stony waste with wary steps,
Until the crump of shells and pattering fire
Had raised within the warrior blood of old,
And wild abandon raged on every side,
Till bodies lay ungainly, dead and maimed,
And wounded staggered rearward, led by friends.
Yet Axis strength remained, as veterans,
In grimy gun-pits, mustered their reserves

Of camaraderie, professional pride
And bitterness towards the English foe.
They had not come so far across the sands
To contemplate defeat for want of spleen
Within a slit trench or a sand-bagged post.
Would not invincible *Panzers* sweep the field,
As at the 'Cauldron' and Gazala line?

Montgomery's runners brought him dismal news
Of infantry exhausted, and of tanks
Contained once more by firm defensive fire.
Unmoved by such reports, he looked elsewhere.
Towards the north, the Ninth Australian
Had made good progress, which he could exploit.
A breakthrough there would bring them to the coast
And threaten to roll up the Axis line
By flank attack. So while the centre held,
He ordered General Morshead to advance
With British armoured units in support.
Around Hill 28 and Kidney ridge
The battle flared on ground profuse with blood.
Elite formations fought to hold each yard
Of worthless desert. Bersaglieri took,
By desperate charge, the westward-facing slopes,
But soon withdrew. Dive bombers struck the massed
Australians, till fighter planes and
Anti-aircraft fire shot from the burning sky
The stukas and the slow piaggios.
Surrounded by his comrades' wrecked machines,
One British sergeant, 'midst Italian tanks,
Set fire to six with well-aimed cannon shells.

To this new crucible, where many died
In personal combat, caught in streams of fire,
Or bombed and strafed by sudden air attack,
Rommel committed most of his reserve.
And though his outposts fell, the Axis line
Withstood each thrust of British infantry.
Outnumbered, ill-supplied, and subject now,
As air support was lost, to constant raids,
The German troops still fought tenaciously.

The crisis was at hand. Montgomery saw
That in the north no further ground would yield -
His second strong assault had passed its height -
But, through the dust of battle, he discerned
A new disparity in strength of arms.
For Axis forces lay upon the rack,
With armour now engaged, and tiring men
Reliant on their own resource of pride,
But sensing a defeat. Now was the time
To draw the bowstring taut, and with one shot
Pierce through the screen of improvised defence,
Drive in the broken line and, once beyond,
Exploit with armour in the desert range.
So from the British lines were ordered back
Freyberg's New Zealanders, the Highlanders,
And one brigade of tanks. The battle flagged;
As Axis troops, relieved from fresh assaults,
In hope renewed, refortified their lines.

Far from the stage of war grave doubts were felt
About Montgomery's real intent to win.
Had Rommel once again shown more resolve?
Must Churchill bow to Marshall Stalin's taunts

That British soldiers lacked the will to fight?
Even the patient Alanbrooke now feared
That victory had eluded British arms.
Only Montgomery showed no signs of doubt,
But quietly reinforced his new reserve,
Gave orders for intensive bomber raids,
And kept the Australians active in the north.

Then 'Supercharge' was launched near Kidney ridge.
At dead of night the infantry began
To cross the start-line, rifles at high port.
Two thousand yards of close sporadic fire
Illumined desert sand with dangerous light,
Where stumbling soldiers died or fell in pain,
Before the clumsy tanks were signalled through,
Each firing at the enemy ahead,
Revealed by silent flashes of their guns.
Now ponderous armour clashed like beasts extinct,
With shattered carapace of blackened steel
And vacant turret bleeding to the sky.
Night, dark with smoke of battle, hid the deeds
Of men embroiled in turning points of war;
No quarter for those bayonetted unseen,
Or trapped within a burning vehicle,
Or crushed alive beneath the treads of tanks.

A gap was forced within the Axis line,
Its hinges smashed by shells, the armour through.
At last the British tanks could move beyond
The dreaded mines and levelled eighty-eights.
The morning sun above the Nile confirmed
Their rapid progress on the Rahman track,

Now west of Kidney ridge and spreading fast
To intercept the Axis in retreat.
Aware that he had lost, the Desert Fox
Prepared to save the Wehrmacht's mobile troops,
But, in dismay, he read the Fuhrer's call
To fight for final victory or defeat.
For just a while the order was obeyed,
But seeing men destroyed to no avail -
His loyal companions since he'd first arrived
To fight the British in North Africa -
Erwin Rommel scorned his master's will
And ordered every mobile unit back.

Abandoned infantry and stranded tanks,
Made captive by the desert, could but wait
To be released by erstwhile enemies.
A few, like the Ariete, did not yield
Till every tank was out of fuel or burnt.
General von Thoma, chief of *Panzer* Korps,
Would not desert his Tel el Mampsra camp,
But stayed alone when all had been destroyed,
Standing erect beside a burning tank,
As British armour circled him with fire.
That night he dined within Montgomery's tent,
Discussing with his captor future plans,
And claiming still - the irony of war -
The Wehrmacht's true invincibility,
Before the prison cage enclosed him round.

Pursuit began towards the coastal road,
Armoured columns struggling to make haste
On stony tracks or sinking dunes of sand.

Then heavy rain turned desert into bog.
A few stray tanks were caught, the rearguard strafed,
But Rommel was as wily in retreat
As formerly in that full flood of war
When Axis armies raced towards the Nile.
With swift withdrawals far on moonless nights,
His remnant army reached Agheila bend,
And in Tunisia, the Mareth line.

Below Hill 28, past Kidney ridge,
Between the Rahman track and Miteiriya,
The littered desert lay in havoc's wake,
With charcoal wrecks of tanks and trucks and guns,
Peopled by rifles thrust in dirty sand,
Like barren saplings, marking where men fell.
Were trenches dug foreseeing then the need
For massive graves of slaughtered infantry,
Dismembered by the shells and casual bombs?
Here lay the grenadier, whose girlfriend's card -
A photograph at home - said on the back,
'*Vergissmeinnicht*'[6] in perfect gothic script,
And those for whom the English bells would ring,
Unheard beneath the sea of furrowed earth.
Who could condemn these dead of either side,
Hated no more for emblems once so proud,
Alike in death and buried in those dunes
Where they had fought Montgomery's killing match?
Who truly were the victors – those who'd won
The right to clear the rotting battlefield
And march again to enterprise of war,
Or those tomorrow's battles would not see,
Who'd conquered death with such temerity?

14 Stalingrad

Obedient to Hitler, German troops
Throughout the Russian Winter held their forts,
And cut off any Soviet advance.
Once more the Führer claimed he had foreseen
His army's prospects better than his Staff.
Now, in the Spring, could he assume command
And lead the Wehrmacht on to victory?
Though generals, like von Rundstedt, said withdraw
And shorten German lines, he hoped to seize
The rich Caucasian oil, the southern steppes,
And then the crucial gap at Stalingrad
Between the rivers, Volga and the Don.
The war could not be won, so Hitler thought,
Without regard to economic needs

For wheat and oil, nickel and manganese,
Which only southern Russia could provide.

Soviet forces, mindful of success
In front of Moscow late the previous year,
Were first to launch offensive Spring campaigns -
One south from Kerch to free Crimean ports,
One to retake Kharkov. Both were stopped,
When swift ripostes broke up the massed attacks.
Not yet were Russians ready to outfight
The German soldiers, freed from Winter's grip
And still possessed of arrogant belief
In *Herrenvolk* invincibility.

Between the Don and Donetz German tanks
Now rolled across the steppeland, pushing back
The Soviet armies weakened by defeat.
Russians deserted, or were quickly shot
By secret police or party commissars,
Sent to preserve the revolution's cause
In Stalin's name. Retreating units burned
Each village down, polluted water, spoilt
The stores of grain, and slaughtered every cow
On State-owned farms or workers' meagre plots.
Again the Wehrmacht revelled in success,
Anticipating how the sunlit plains
Would serve as *lebensraum* for German stock,
Where peasant Slavs would labour to supply
The master race of pure Teutonic blood.

Now Hitler's plans enlarged: List's army group
Would seize the Black Sea coast, and cross the woods

Of Caucasus' steep range to take Baku.
Weich's army would move eastwards from the Don
To capture Stalingrad, thus sealing off
The Russian armies on the southern steppes;
Then hasten north along the Volga's banks
To threaten Moscow. Only too aware
Of what logistic problems were involved,
Of Russia's vastness - how the enemy
Had traded it for time till Winter came -
And how the partisans claimed heavy tithes
Behind the German lines, the Chief of Staff
Was bold enough to question Hitler's scheme;
But all in vain, for Halder was dismissed,
Replaced by Zeitzler, who objected less.

As German *Panzers* drove the Soviets back,
So, like a spring compressed, resistance grew.
Within the foothills, tanks could not proceed,
Whilst, on the Kalmyk steppe, advance was slow
Across the arid Mongol pasture lands,
Where ancient mounds were auguries of death.
Yet Paulus' army closed on Stalingrad,
His northern flank stretched far along the Don
And held by troops not from the Fatherland -
Rumanian and Italian infantry.
Both armies strove to reinforce the front:
Hoth's *Panzers* hurried north; Richthofen's planes,
Which long ago had bombed Guernica,
Now burned the standing wheat and roofs of straw.

Then, north of Stalingrad, the Germans reached
The heights of Mother Volga's western bank,

Where far above the yellow river's flood
Their mortars fired on Rynok's vital bridge.
Was once again a Russian army trapped,
Without supplies, marooned on native land,
Awaiting, when the armoured jaws had closed,
The spurious haven of a prison cage,
Where cold and hunger emulated death?
What those in Warsaw heard, and Rotterdam,
And those at Belgrade, when the Germans came -
The drone of aircraft, slow with weight of bombs -
Now filled the sky above the western streets.
Yet as the fire bombs burned the suburbs down,
Turning the Volga redder than the dawn,
This time, within the gutted concrete shells,
Amidst the debris smoking now with pyres,
There lay an army tempered in the fire.
Fresh men and guns were sent; then Zhukov came,
The hero of the Muscovite defence.

But Adolf Hitler, unaware of this,
Believed that here the hinge of war would swing,
Revealing future vistas of success,
Of armies shattered, all defences gone,
Of land and people prostrate at his feet.
In Hitler's vision Stalingrad became
A symbol of his will and Russia's doom.
The Volga's banks would hear the death knell ring
For Bolshevism and the Jewish plot
To overturn the German destiny -
An error, long ago, that Croesus made,
When, at the Halys river, he attacked
The might of Persia, sure in his belief

That what the Delphic oracle foresaw -
Destruction of an empire - would ensue.

Although the Wehrmacht held the river banks
To north and south, it chose head-on assault,
Contemptuous of the Russian will to fight.
Panzers advanced through ruined city streets,
But in the rubble, hid by brick or stone,
Concealed in cellars, shell-holes, lofts or roofs,
Lay snipers, men with hand-grenades and mines,
And anti-tank gun crews, whose sudden fire
Burst plates of steel, or slaughtered infantry.
Tanks burned in narrow streets, or turned around
In slow confusion from the cross-fire hail.
This was no more the battlefield of old
On plains of France in early Summer sun,
Or in the standing wheat of Russian steppes.
Even the Tiger's high-explosive shells
Failed to destroy the inner city blocks,
Where marksmen, perched on rafters high above,
Could rifle tank commanders in the head,
Or shoot at will the leading officers.
New tactics were required, with heavy guns,
And air attack, before the soldiers came
To crawl in dust, beside unburied dead,
And toss grenades through vacant window frames,
And charge past broken doors with bursts of fire
At shadows seen in ruins dark with blood.
The time had come for conflict face to face,
For duels with sharpened blades or pistol shots,
With hands and nails, with bricks or concrete slabs,

When men lay wounded, blinded by grenades,
Entrapped by fallen beams, limbless or dead.

On Matreyev Kurgan hill the battle raged
For many days to take the central heights,
Where Chuikov had moved his field H.Q.;
While near the southern flank the Germans strove
To occupy the elevator towers,
Held by Russians desperate for supplies,
And now beset by flames from burning grain.
Beside the Volga, on the western side,
Three ruined factories were the last redoubt.

Russians on the river's further bank
Maintained by night the waning garrison.
Across the water, shining red with flames,
Towards the hollow structures near the shore,
The ferries slid with minimal reserves,
Barely enough to save the men besieged.
For Zhukov planned to turn to good account
The German zeal to make of Stalingrad
A signal victory for the *Herrenvolk*,
By building up a great offensive force
Along the eastern banks and on the Don.
Those men who held the city's ruined heart
Were forced to fight with only what he judged
Would hold the Germans there, and thus allow
Onset of Winter to attenuate
The mighty war machine of Hitler's Reich,
Till struggling groups of isolated men
Would tremble at the dark and biting snow.

Within the wrecked confines of inner streets
Only a heap of bricks or shattered wall
Marked off the front-line troops on either side.
Like animals at bay, with staring eyes,
They watched for movements from the hidden foe,
Or struggled forward, scarcely now aware
Of what the body feared - a bullet's blow
Or bayonet's sudden thrust. Amongst the Germans
Questions now arose, unspoken doubts
That fed on each event, on deaths and wounds,
On strong attacks repulsed, on stories told
Of prisoners shot or starved, and, worst of all,
Of Russian Winter, and of no return.
They had not heard what Chuikov had said –
That for the Russian army 'time is blood'.
For time his men would die, day after day,
To build reserves to mount a fresh attack;
Nor had the Russians heard, on Volga's banks,
Trapped in the factories by the water's edge.
No turning back for those of either side;
To turn meant death from zealous pistol shots
Of officers or party commissars.
Each day the ratchet rose for those who stayed.
Their grains of fleeting time, their chance of life,
Like blood of corpses littered on the streets,
Seeped through the earth with every passing hour.

Who were these soldiers, incubi of hell,
Come from the distant corners of each land,
From German forests, far Siberian plains,
From city streets in Moscow or Berlin,
To this small core of what was Stalingrad,

A stench of ruins, deep in dust and smoke?
What crimes had they performed in lives before,
Dwelling in sunlight, free in Summer air,
In former days before this swift descent?
How many were redeemed, alive or dead,
Absolved by acts of brave audacity,
By saving comrades, comforting the sick?
How many, in a moment, turned from rage
To see in enemies the face of God
And love itself in fury's very heart?

Rodintsev's Guards were ferried to support
The dwindling forces in the narrow strip
That stood between the Volga and the foe.
Their task was not to make a final stand,
For Chuikov had ordered otherwise:
To harass Germans, let them never rest,
With mortars, rocket guns, grenade and knife;
To wake their sleep with fear of every sound -
A falling brick, a rat, a taunting voice -
With fear of snipers trained to wait like cats
And with a single bullet stem a life.
No longer could the dead be buried there,
When they would die who sought to bury them.

Those German wives who read their letters home
No longer heard of triumph and return;
For words now spoke of men with hopes denied,
Condemned to fight an unremitting war,
Of comrades killed or wounded, and the fear
Of Winter's ineluctable advance.
What did such women think, by Autumn fires,

As, on the air, they heard the Führer speak
From Burgerbrau in Munich of his plans
For taking Stalingrad 'with small assaults',
Because he did not want Verdun again?
Within their dug-outs German soldiers heard,
And looked with unbelief, as though betrayed.
What was this sacrifice of German blood?
What was the cause for which they fought and died?
Who was this man to whom their oath was pledged?

Each day drew shorter and, where bodies lay,
The flakes of early snow brought wreaths of white.
Behind the icy Volga, Zhukov massed
A Russian army well prepared to fight,
In Winter great-coats, hats of beaver fur,
Supplied with newer tanks and air support.
Across the Don they broke the German line,
West of the city, where the allies stood -
Rumanians half-heartedly at war -
And reached the bridge at Kalach in the rear
Of Paulus' forces held in Stalingrad.
Too late the Wehrmacht saw its front exposed,
And tortoise-like could not withdraw its head,
The brave Sixth Army now surrounded there.
Though Weichs, and even Zeitzler – wiser now -
Thought Paulus should retreat, they were ignored,
For Hitler had assumed supreme command
When Jodl was dismissed for making clear
He disagreed with what the Führer planned.
The name of Stalingrad possessed his mind;
He saw the place as 'schwerpunkt' of the war,
Which, like Verdun, was fateful to each cause:

Here was the clash of master race and Slav,
Of Nazi might and Bolshevism's hate,
Where victory would release the German flood,
Northwards to Moscow, south-east to Baku,
And make the Russian hordes subservient,
Their burning farms the German promised land.

As Paulus' troops heard of encirclement,
A second seal of Winter chilled their hearts.
Beyond the suburbs, units driven back
Converged upon the city. Many fell,
Exhausted from their wounds, frost-bitten, starved,
And soon their bodies lay as snowy mounds,
Ignored by sunken eyes of passers-by,
Intent upon their own approaching fate.
No trenches could be dug on frozen ground,
Where shells threw up huge granite clods of earth.
Men huddled into pot-holes, heaps of bricks,
And, looking back on wastes of endless snow,
Fired futile shots at moving specks of black
That pressed them ever closer to their end.
Lice-ridden, dirty, wrapped in bloody swathes,
In tattered field-grey, some devoid of boots,
The remnant army gathered in those streets
Where German arms, exultant to succeed,
Had scorned the Soviets not long before;
Whilst now on Volga banks, the deathless foe
Defended still the twisted frames of iron
That once were factories. What help might come?
The Führer ordered Paulus to refrain
From all attempts to break the Russian ring,

Assuring him of Luftwaffe support
Until the Wehrmacht organised relief.

Von Manstein was appointed to command
A *Panzer* army hastening from the south.
In violent actions on the frozen wastes
The tanks advanced as far as Mishkova;
There the exhausted spearhead came to rest.
Only a break-out by von Paulus' men,
Inspired by desperation, would suffice,
But though von Manstein urged him to attack,
The beleagured general, hamstrung by command,
Preferred to stay, dependent on the planes
Which flew through blizzards to an ice-bound strip.
For Hitler knew Sixth Army's infantry
Absorbed the major part of Soviet force.
Whilst they remained encircled, other troops,
Endangered far beyond the lower Don,
Might be withdrawn. If Stalingrad were lost,
Zhukov could move south-west upon Rostov,
And cut off all retreat. So Hitler left
Sixth Army to its doom; Manstein withdrew.

No aircraft landed now at Gumrak strip.
Only a few brave pilots dropped their loads,
Like tokens of despair, from leaden skies.
On Christmas Day the horses were destroyed,
Eaten by starving men with brief good cheer.
A soldier spoke of home, of candles, trees,
Even of peace, even of Spring to come,
'That if we should return, to find warm hearts.'[7]
Another wrote of frost-bite in his hands,

Of fingers missing, pianos in the street,
Of groups of men escaping through the snow,
Of Russian troops at Gumrak, and the end.
When all were soon to perish, Paulus sought
Permission to surrender, but in vain.
At last, he disobeyed the Führer's will
And led his army to captivity.
An endless line of men dispirited,
Ragged, limping, starving, grimy men,
Once, in their pride, entitled '*Herrenvolk*',
Now marched away, through banks of frozen snow,
To die obscurely in far distant camps,
Like ghosts of those defeated Greeks who'd slaved
In Syracusan quarries far from home.

Deep in the Caucasus another force
Lay in grave danger from the Russian drive
To cut the slender Rostov bottleneck.
Von Kleist, however, led them swiftly back,
Past villages abandoned in the snow
And hazards from the local partisans.
Once more the Germans formed a Winter front,
And mighty armies stood exhausted there.

But news of Stalingrad brought sudden fear
To German homes within the Fatherland.
Was this a warning of impending doom?
Envenomed by their people's long ordeal,
Would godless armies now invade the Reich?
Midwinter darkness conjured in some minds
The final bullet, when all else were lost.
This was the total war that had to come,

Since that dread day when Hindenburg had said
That Adolf Hitler would be raised to power.
Anger, depression, fatalism, hate:
Such were engendered by the word 'defeat',
And by the news that thousands were bereaved,
That German manhood lay in graves of ice.

Others, at Munich, chose a braver path.
The White Rose movement said what none had dared:
That Hitler had destroyed the nation's youth,
All freedom, honour and morality,
That expiation must annihilate
The godless leaders of the present Reich,
That Germany would ever be despised,
Unless the Nazi government were expelled.
'The dead of Stalingrad adjure us now;
Rise up my people, signal fires ablaze!'[8]
It was not long before they were betrayed:
Huber and Probst, Hans and Sophie Scholl,
Soon tried in People's Courts and hung in shame,
Whose courage counted more than battles won,
Though they lay, too, in cold oblivion.

15 Guadalcanal

Defeat at Midway had not curbed the will
Of Japanese aggressors. Still they sought
To drive on southwards past the Asian isles
That laboured now beneath the Imperial flag.
A line of Nippon troops in jungle green
Marched out of Buna on New Guinea's coast
To cross the Owen Stanleys and attack
That Allied base, Port Moresby, earlier saved
By naval battle in the Coral Sea.
Through swathes of kunai grass and mangrove swamps,
Past gorges dense with trees, and towering peaks,
Along a narrow, humid jungle track,
Like patient ants, the weary column climbed.
Those who fell sick were left aside to die.

Australians opposed them on the trail,
With small effect, for many were half-trained.
So Japanese, though hungry and diseased,
Persisted to the summit, whence they saw
Port Moresby far below. Could it be saved?
Or was the gate now open to invade
The white man's land beyond the Coral Sea?

Far eastwards war had reached Guadalcanal,
Where, in a jungle clearing, engineers
Were building airstrips ready for the planes
That bore the symbol of the Rising Sun.
This scar of runway, cut in luscious green,
Marked out the empire's current boundary,
Where burgeoning growth might presently embrace
The archipelagos of half the globe.
But Nimetz and MacArthur made a plan
For bold offensive action in response.
Rabaul would be encircled by two moves:
A staged advance along the Solomon Isles,
And in New Guinea reinforced attack
To seize the northern coast and capture Lae.

It did not take them long to win the field
Where Japanese construction workers toiled,
But 'leathernecks' - Marines - were cast ashore
Devoid of air support, with little food,
To listen hard for Zeros, and to scan
With anxious eyes the blue Pacific sea.
Around them lay the jungle, thick with vines,
With creepers, ferns, gigantic twisted roots,
Great hardwoods, palms and mangroves, rushing streams.
Beset by insects, soaked by constant rain,

Soon many had contracted dysentery;
And yet they held the vital aerodrome,
To which they gave the name of 'Henderson' -
After a dead Marine at Midway Isle.

The Japanese Command was swift to act:
A naval force sailed fast along the Slot,
The narrow passage through the Solomons
By which reserves were shipped by transport craft -
Dubbed by Marines 'the Tokyo Express'.
'Long-lance' torpedoes and their heavy guns
Destroyed four cruisers of the U.S. fleet.
Made confident by earlier success
In short campaigns against colonial powers,
The Japanese invaded with a force
Too small to sieze the airfield; most were killed.
Now Wildcat fighters occupied the strip.
Perimeter defence gave lines of fire
Through spaces cleared of jungle, littered still
With bodies from the premature attack.
Meanwhile at sea the carrier fleets engaged
In violent battles costing many lives;
Invading transport ships were strafed or bombed,
And soldiers died who never reached the shore.
For Yamamoto and the High Command
Now chose Guadalcanal to be the crux
Of Japanese advance towards the south.
Likewise MacArthur saw he must not lose
This stepping-stone to Australasia.

A more elaborate plan and greater force
Were brought to bear by Kawaguchi's men.

Aircraft and ships bombarded the Marines;
Then waves of infantry attacked their lines,
Till they withdrew upon a narrow ridge
A thousand yards from where the airstrip lay.
For days and nights a vicious struggle raged
With bayonets, grenades and bursts of guns.
Twelve times one night the Japanese attacked
By crawling up the slope of kunai grass
And screaming as they crossed the stony rim
To face the leaden hail of rapid fire.
From high machine-gun nests grenades rolled down
To burst amongst the enemy below,
And others, lobbed in slow, descending arcs,
Scattered their lethal fragments in the grass.
Marines - some wounded - tightly clasped their guns,
Slamming their rifle bolts, or feeding chains
Of shining bullets past a belt-feed pawl,
Sometimes removing ruptured cartridges,
Manhandling heavy weapons, hot from fire,
To move them to a newly threatened post
Along the blind perimeter of night.
Now hand to hand they fought with bayonet thrust,
With boots, with fingers, grappling in the dark,
Oblivious of everything but life,
To keep or take it, self or enemy.
At last, the remnant Japanese withdrew.
The ridge was held. They left their dead behind,
Piled high on slopes made slippery with blood.

Yet, free from Wildcat sorties in the day,
The Imperial navy ruled the sea by night.
Destroyers brought in fresh reserves of men

And, once again, a great assault was planned.
Torrential rain disrupted the attack.
A desperate charge against the final ridge
Was met with sweeping fire and primed grenades,
Until, again, the mounds of bodies stood
As mausoleums of the Nippon dead,
Obedient ever to their emperor-god.
Above malarial swamp a stony crest,
Set on the ocean's brim, was charnel-house
For warlike peoples, proud of nationhood,
Of samurai, of western frontiersmen.
Such was the clash of fierce, unyielding wills,
Embittered by antipathies of race.

The pendulum had swung. Now the Marines,
Elated by their courage and success,
Prepared to break out on the western flank.
Equipped at last with tanks and heavy guns,
They forced the enemy back, until despair
Drove some to launch a suicide attack,
With cries of '*banzai*' shrill on dying lips.
Guadalcanal was won. The Rising Sun,
Whose tinted light traversed the western seas,
Had reached its height. Upon the furthest bounds
Of new-found empire shadows now were cast.
By order of the Emperor himself,
Guadalcanal survivors were withdrawn.
Only his word could overrule the wish
Of officers preferring in their pride
A futile death than life with honour dead.

Above Port Moresby, General Horii,
His troops exhausted from their fearsome trek,
Had been commanded to withhold attack,
Whilst his reserves were sent across the sea
To lend support to Kawaguchi's men.
By now the Allies, strongly reinforced,
Could sieze Milne Bay, and push Horii back
Along the Kokoda Trail whence he had come.
MacArthur set his pincer move in train,
To drive along the north New Guinea coast
And clear the Solomon Isles to Bougainville.
The ebb of empire left a rotting corpse
For every yard where battle had ensued.
Thousands more would die before the end;
But that low ridge above the jungle strip
Of Henderson upon Guadalcanal
Had been, indeed, a watershed of war.
Unlawful force had met its nemesis.
That Japanese defeat would long portend
The Asian war's apocalyptic end.

16 The Clearance of North Africa

No second front in France could be maintained
Until the Allies were of greater strength,
Or Axis power reduced. The theatre chosen
For a new campaign, north-western Africa,
Would threaten Rommel on a second flank
And, once the coast was cleared from end to end,
The passage of the sea would be relieved
To Malta, Suez and the southern fringe
Of Axis territory. This was the chance,
Which Churchill long had sought, for Britain
And America to fight with joint command
Upon a battlefield of their own choice.

Along the Clyde the crowded quays gave proof
An expedition was now imminent -
To Norway, Hitler thought - whilst from the west

A giant flotilla sailed three thousand miles
Directly to the ports of Africa,
To Casablanca and Oran, Algiers,
And furthermost to Bone. Bound by their oath
Of due obedience to the Head of State,
The Vichy French fired on the landing grounds.
German victory served the ends of France,
Laval declared; but Admiral Darlan,
Head of the Marine, then in Algiers
To see his crippled son, ordered cease-fire
When information came that German troops
Had contravened the terms of armistice
And occupied the southern half of France.
No more could Petain claim to occupy
The seat of sovereignty, for now he spoke
As one compelled by supervening power.
As at Mers-el-Kebir, Darlan's concern
To save his fleet from enemy control
Drove him to order Toulon to resist
The German claims to commandeer his ships:
All seventy were scuttled in the port.
Whom now would French Algerians obey -
The soldiers, Generals Giraud or de Gaulle,
Or Admiral Darlan, welcomed by all those
Who had for long obeyed the Marechal?

On Christmas Eve the question was resolved:
A young fanatic shot the Admiral dead.
As Churchill wrote, Darlan had kept his word -
Despite his hatred for the British cause -
To keep the fleet of France in Frenchmen's hands.
De Gaulle and Giraud were induced to meet,

And with reluctance shared the reins of power;
But deep divisions lingered still in France,
For who had served the fallen nation best -
Those loyal to what they called the 'legal' State,
Or those resisting on the soil of France,
Or one who'd left to carry on the war
With sympathy and help from Englishmen?

In Casablanca, where the US troops
Had shortly landed in the roaring surf,
The leaders of the western Allies met:
The ebullient Churchill, eager to engage
The Axis forces where and when he could,
And Roosevelt, who from a sick man's chair
Controlled the free world's residue of power.
Where to proceed when Africa was won?
Should every man and weapon be withdrawn
To summon up the strength for one great blow
Across the Channel into Picardy,
Or should they sally northwards from Tunis
To threaten Italy or southern France,
Or help revolt in Jugoslavia?
What then of Turkey, loth to intervene,
Yet fearful to incur the victors' scorn
By weak neutrality? And what of Spain?
Might Franco close the Straits, and starve a force
Deployed against his Fascist counterparts?
How should air power be used? Was Harris right
To claim his bombers could destroy morale
And bring the German people to their knees?
Or should more aircraft fly in close support
Of ground attacks, or rather escort ships

Imperilled once again by U-boat packs
That, from the Bay of Biscay, roved the sea
From Iceland to the coast of Africa?
It was agreed already that the war
To free all Europe from the Nazi grip
Was paramount. Yet in the Solomons,
In China, Burma and the ocean wastes
That stretched unbroken west of Midway Isle,
The Japanese remained, coercive, brute,
And frantic to defend what they had won.
What forces could be spared to chastise them -
To make Guadalcanal a turning point
For further action in the Carolines;
To rescue Burma, strengthen Chiang Kai-shek?

Such were the questions tabled for debate
In peaceful villas, circled by armed guards,
Amidst the palms of Casablanca's shore.
Agreement was soon reached, though Admiral King
Demanded for the war against Japan
The landing craft forthwith to be required
For moves against the long periphery
Of Nazi Europe. Decisions thus were made:
That first the U-boat danger must be met,
And Soviet forces nourished with supplies;
That Sicily should be invaded next
To threaten Italy and sway the Turks;
That bombing raids should be intensified
Against the sinews of the German power -
Their industries of war, their docks and mines,
Their railways, bridges, dams and services -
Amphibious forces should continue raids

164

On enemy coasts wherever chance arose;
In Britain Allied armies should be held
In constant readiness to land in France,
If ever a decisive moment came.
And pressure should be kept upon Japan,
Until a full offensive could be launched.
Re-entry into Burma was agreed,
And staged advances to the Carolines.
The air support for China was confirmed.

One final controversial choice was made:
The declaration of the Allies' will
To force surrender unconditionally.
This grave demand recalled the former war,
When Germany had claimed the armistice
Was based on Woodrow Wilson's fourteen points.
The Allies now would not prevaricate:
The justice of the victors would prevail.
As Churchill argued, better this than terms
Too harsh for any German to accept,
Like those that Marshall Stalin might demand -
Fifty thousand sentences of death,
And Germany's complete dismemberment.

Yet, even so, within some German hearts
The will to fight for Fatherland, and die,
Rather than stoop for mercy from a foe
Composed, they thought, of Bolsheviks and Jews,
Of haughty British, brash Americans,
And all those nations, occupied by force,
With living memories of how Hitler ruled,
Waxed stronger than before. Nazi leaders
Could not look for peace, short of a total

Victory or defeat; their names were hated
For their odious crimes, committed in
The Reich, against the Jews, and everywhere
Beneath the swastika. They would compel
The people to their cause, till all was lost,
Proclaiming, in their arrogance, the right
To lead the German nation to its fate,
The *Gotterdammerung* of Nordic myth.

Even the Kreisau circle of von Moltke,
Until that time anticipating help
From friends abroad to strike the Nazis down
And form a free and democratic State,
Were now dismayed by this severe demand.
Could not some cautious gesture of support
From Roosevelt or Churchill have been sent
To Goerdeler, Leber, Tresckow, Trott zu Solz,
Bonhoeffer, Olbricht, Yorck and many more,
Who, in despite of Himmler's secret police,
Continued plotting Hitler's overthrow?
The western leaders - generous, quick to praise
The courage of compatriots and friends -
Knew little of von Moltke and the rest.
Or did they fear how Stalin might perceive
The merest contact inside Germany?
Were he suspicious of a separate peace,
He might pre-empt it, leaving Hitler free
To turn the mighty Wehrmacht to the west,
And make invulnerable his Nazi realm
From Arctic Circle down to Sicily.
And so those Germans, men of honour still,
Continued, irrevocably alone.

French troops now served in Eisenhower's command
As Allied armies reached Tunisia.
Montgomery, also, chasing Rommel back
Along familiar roads through Libya,
Was reinforced by Frenchmen, joining those
Who'd fought so stubbornly at Bir Hacheim.
Leclerc's patrol had crossed Saharan sands
A thousand miles from Chad to Tripoli,
Eager to see the dust of battle rise.
He vowed he would not stop until he flew
The tricolor in Strasbourg's Place Klebert,
For which a million French *poilus* had died.

Against advice the Führer now decreed
That, at all costs, Tunisia be held.
Until it fell, the Allies could not mount
Sea-borne attacks upon the Axis coasts
Of France or Italy. Strong reinforcements
Made the Germans bold. At Kasserine Pass
Their seasoned troops drove back the raw recruits
Of Patton's U.S. force. With British help
The counterstroke was blocked. At Medenine,
Montgomery's veteran army was attacked
As they arrived, but he was swiftly told
Of every move the *Panzers* were to make,
For Churchill sent him Rommel's planned attack,
Decoded from 'Enigma' intercepts –
Before the war the Poles gained one machine,
And British experts based at Bletchley Park
Translated German coded messages.
This time the *Panzers* faced well-sited guns.
No memories now of proud ascendancy

Could long survive the sight of blazing wrecks
And swift retreat within the desert dunes.

One strong defensive line remained to guard
The south perimeter of this redoubt
Of Axis power in northern Africa:
The Mareth Line, built formerly by France
From Gulf of Gabes to the Matmata hills,
With ditches, concrete pill-boxes and wire,
And, by the sea, the Wadi Zigzaou.
A first assault was easily repulsed;
The second crossed the Wadi's steep incline,
But violent riposte forced its countermand.
Montgomery had prepared another plan:
New Zealander and British columns drove
Far westwards through the desert to a pass,
Whence, after heavy fighting, they debouched,
Supported from the air by Allied planes,
Whose sorties were precisely planned to match
Whatever moves the ground commanders made.
Rommel's soldiers, threatened on two fronts
And weary from their arduous retreat
Past mirages of former battles won,
Fought with accustomed valour, but in vain.
The jaws were closing on the Tunis cape
Which housed an army once so near the Nile.
Rommel was summoned home; von Arnim came,
To hold in Africa a shred of land.

A broad advance now pushed the Axis force
Towards the Gulf of Tunis, whilst at sea
The British navy sank Italian ships

That hazarded supplies past Malta's shores.
An air armada, crammed with fresh reserves,
Was met by Allied fighters off Cape Bon.
Spirals of smoke and wreckage on the sea
Dispelled the dream that Hitler had indulged
Of building a redoubt of Axis arms.
Nor could the balmy Spring for long avert
A final sequel to El Alamein
Beside the palms where ancient Carthage fell.
Naval patrols prevented all escape;
"Sink, burn, destroy", was sent throughout the fleet.
Scattered in pockets, short of fuel and food,
The German army lost the will to fight,
And steadily the prison cages filled.
Von Arnim brought resistance to an end,
Despite the Führer's orders. Much was lost
That Germany would need in Italy.
Conquest of Tunis promised even more
Than hauls of prisoners and the final end
Of Rommel's escapade to reach the Nile.

Confined to Europe, Hitler now must wait,
And, like a spider, mend the breaches made
Along his vast perimeter of steel;
Whilst on the Soviet front a mammoth war
Devoured his soldiers ineluctably.
How many more must garrison the west
Against invasion's hydra-headed threat?
How many, too, must guard against unrest:
Suppress the 'bandits' active now in France,
Fight Tito's rebels in the Balkan hills,
Administer the ghettos and the camps

Where millions lingered, starved of all but pain?
Initiative had passed from German hands,
Though even now the U-boats could destroy
The dual power of Anglo-Saxon arms,
Sustained by slender transatlantic ties
Of merchant vessels packed with war supplies.

17 The Warsaw Ghetto

Ancient dislike of gypsies, Slavs and Jews,
Insinuated long in German minds,
Was made by Hitler's vitriolic words
Into a systematic creed of hate.
From Jews especially many Germans shrank,
Taught to deny their human dignity,
And thinking them unclean, diseased and cruel,
Exploiters of their economic power
In law and banking, merchantry and trade.
Their gradual persecution in the Reich -
By local violence, laws of Nuremburg
And then by terror on the Kristallnacht,
When many died and Jewish shops were wrecked –
Forced hosts of Jews to leave, and those who stayed
Accepted deprivation as their lot.
Few could predict iniquities to come,
When war's dark night would cover heinous crime

And conscience, blindfold, see no infamy.
Poland, defeated first, was first to feel
The unrestrained brutality of hate.
Both Slavs and Jews were treated with contempt.
In Warsaw, Lodz and Krakow ghettos formed,
To which the Jews were moved without regard
For status or profession, age or health.
Forced to abandon what their homes contained
Of family heirlooms, furniture and art,
Concealing on their persons what they could
Of jewellery, coins, mementoes, sacred things,
In lorries or on foot they crossed Warsaw
To occupy the chosen quarters there,
Whence Polish Christians had been likewise moved.
The walls were sealed, extended ten feet high,
Infilled and topped with wire, house windows bricked,
And every gateway manned by German troops.
All who went through required a yellow pass,
With those of Jewish workers marked in blue,
Until the time when even Jews who made
Essential items for the Wehrmacht's needs
Were not employed. The population grew,
As Polish Jews were brought from Warthegau.
All wore the star of David on their arms.
No contact was allowed across the wall;
To seize a loaf of bread, or tendered hand,
Incurred a bullet from a watchful guard.

Conditions worsened in the narrow streets,
So crowded now that none could freely pass.
A dozen people lived in every room,
With little water, meagre scraps of food,

No heat to ease the bitter Winter's pall.
Dirt and starvation bred alike disease;
Typhus became endemic; ghostly forms,
With sunken eyes and sagging, yellow flesh,
Haunted the streets. And starving children begged,
Who now forgot the greenery of parks
With childrens' slides and swings and roundabouts
And singing birds beyond the ghetto's walls.
They only knew the crowded tenements
And felt the loneliness of filthy kerbs.

Coaches of 'Kraft durch Freude' often came,
Usually full of eager soldiery,
As though on sojourns at the local zoo.
Some struck with whips, as they drove slowly past,
Or, with their weapons, knocked the children down.
Some stopped for photos next to Jewish graves,
Of genre scenes of mourners with a corpse,
Of rabbis flanked by smiling SS men.
For them, such degradation was a proof
That Jews were Untermenschen, and should die
To purify the German Herrenvolk.

Beside the peaceful Wannsee near Berlin,
Amongst the Winter trees, brushed now with snow
That fell more thickly on the Polish plain,
The SS leader, Heydrich, had convened
A meeting to resolve the fate of Jews.
The words of Adolf Hitler were their guide –
The Jew, the enemy of all the world,
Since time began, will play his final role.
The Jew must pay for what he has begun,

A second war imperilling the Reich.
And so a mass migration to the east
Would be enforced; and further, Eichmann wrote,
Experience grows of great importance yet
For what will be the Jewish question's end.

Outside the Reich, in Poland's bitter land,
Death camps were built: at Kulmhof, Sobibor,
At Majdanek and Belzec, Birkenau.
For Warsaw's ghetto, eastwards of the Bug,
Treblinka was especially enlarged.
By Himmler's word the 'cleansing' then began.
Each day in Warsaw Jews were rounded up
For emigration to the eastern lands,
And thousands then embarked on cattle trains,
To stand for days, neglected, hungry, sick.
Within Treblinka's walls they were assessed:
A few to work, the greater part to die.

In silent columns, watched by brutal guards,
They shambled forwards to the 'bath house' block,
A star of David nailed above the door;
Then trudged along a darkened corridor,
Through curtains taken from a synagogue,
Passing beneath the Hebrew words inscribed,
'This is the gate through which the righteous come'[9].
There, standing naked, they were slowly gassed,
By diesel fumes, or, later, Zyklon-B.
The gold was taken from the corpses' teeth,
And women's hair was cut to make warm socks
For U-boat sailors. Fearful rumours spread;
In Warsaw's ghetto few assembled then

To take the daily train towards the east.
The Jewish Council, desperate to appease,
Offered their people meals of bread and jam
To tempt them to another promised land.
The trains continued, filled again with Jews,
Migrating, in their ignorance, to death.

One day, in Winter, German troops were met
With sudden firing in the ghetto streets:
A secret group of Jews had gathered arms,
And in the fighting fifty soldiers died.
Shipments were halted; Himmler was informed.
On Hitler's birthday, during Passover,
As Jews remembered how they'd once escaped
From thralldom to another tyranny,
The SS Führer launched an *Aktion*
To purge Warsaw of every trace of them.
Two thousand Germans, well equipped with arms –
Tanks, rapid-fire artillery and gas –
Now fought against guerilla bands of Jews,
Supplied with pistols, rifles, homemade bombs
And one machine-gun seized from German troops.
Led by Anielewicz, who long had claimed
That armed resistance was the only course,
The Jews fought on, sustained by hopelessness,
As bunkers fell to gas and petrol flames;
Until Anieliwicz himself was killed,
And other leaders took their own frail lives.
A few, like Itzhak Zuckerman, escaped,
Crawling through sewers to the 'Aryan' side.
Yet hundreds of the enemy had died,
And Jews rejoiced to see a German fall,

Or scream in pain, or turn and run away
From terror of a Jewish gun or knife.

A month of killing left the ghetto stained
With blood of thousands, bodies in the streets,
Whilst, in the ruins, broken families starved.
The *coup de grace* was made by General Stroop,
Whose troops blew up the ancient synagogue.
All those who lived were straightaway embarked,
Not for Treblinka, but for Majdanek,
Where all, near fifty thousand, died at once,
Machine-gunned in the ditches they had dug,
Behind the 'house' where other Jews were gassed.

Across a continent the hapless race
Were driven from their homes, deprived of rights,
Suffered and died by virtue of their birth.
Out of the depths the cry of Israel came,
But Allied will was baffled by their plight,
For, in Bermuda, where their cause was raised
At that same time the Warsaw ghetto fell,
No plan was made to save Jews from their fate
As victims of the Nazis' morbid hate.

18 Crisis in the Atlantic

No single battle fought upon the land,
Or in the air above, could end the war;
Not even Stalingrad, nor Alamein,
Ensured the Reich's defeat, nor would success
At Mount Cassino, Kursk, nor at Falaise
Do more than mark the long and arduous road
To final victory; but yet, at sea,
Were mastery achieved by U-boat war
A stranglehold on Britain would be won,
Forcing surrender. Could the nation stand
Against starvation and the loss of arms?
Churchill himself, no prey to anxious fear,
Yet dreaded what the weekly charts portrayed
Of U-boat sinkings in the western seas,
The cargoes lost of food and oil and guns,

Of tanks and aircraft, steel and high-grade ores,
Machine tools, timber, and the ships themselves,
With all their complements of hardy crews;
And sometimes even U.S. servicemen.

Much had been saved by escorts, now equipped
With 'hedgehog' mortars, fired to form a ring
Of contact fuses round a U-boat's hull.
Aircraft, also, threatened wolfhound packs,
Especially near their Bay of Biscay ports,
Where radar of a new short frequency
Detected U-boats in the fog or dark,
Which, caught in searchlight beams before they dived,
Met swift destruction from a bomb or charge.
Yet still the convoys faced a stern ordeal,
For though the Allied aircraft flew afar
From Scotland, Iceland, Newfoundland, Azores,
Eight hundred miles of sea lay in between
The furthest ranges of their air patrols.
In mid-Atlantic, during four long days,
The slow-hauled convoys crept, with fearful haste,
Aware of danger, blind to its approach,
Watching the sea for any distant sign
Of surfaced U-boats, or torpedoes' wake.

Two Allied convoys' fates, conjoined in one,
Assumed the crisis of Atlantic war.
They gathered in the Hudson, loaded up
With steel and iron ore, bauxite, copper, oil,
Sugar and cocoa, timber, grain and meat -
Some old, decrepit freighters, others new.
The slower convoy left three days ahead,

With both protected by an escort group:
Corvettes with depth-charge launchers on each deck,
Slim destroyers, manoeuvrable and fast,
Some old four-stackers from the US fleet,
And British frigates recently equipped
With forward-firing launchers to prevent
A diving U-boat hiding underneath.
Not yet, however, could the navies spare
A carrier for convoy escort work,
Nor were there any catapaulted planes,
Mounted on a merchantman's fore-deck,
To seek out submarines or Focker-Wolfes,
And take their chance on ditching in the sea.

German B-Dienst decrypters ascertained
When both these Allied convoys would depart.
Three wolf-packs were assembled on their route:
A forward screen, named 'Raubgraf', of fourteen,
Then, within the air-gap, two more lines -
'Sturmer' and 'Dranger' - counting twenty-eight.
Two 'milch cow' tankers resupplied their fuel.
A week of heavy gales obscured all sight
Of both the convoys; then a light was seen
By one patrolling U-boat, which informed
The German Admiralty of time and place.
From Admiral Donitz came a swift response:
The 'Raubgraf' pack were ordered to withdraw
To meet the rest advancing from the east.
Every Allied ship would be enclosed
Between the U-boats' fast approaching jaws,
And caught beyond the range of air support.

One convoy was a hundred miles ahead.
Just at torpedo range, the escorts clung
To lines of merchantmen, disposed to keep
The dangerous cargoes at the convoy's heart.
Already seven U-boats were in touch,
All cruising at the boundaries of sight,
Where they could dimly see the convoy masts,
And caught a glimpse, upon a rising wave,
Of funnels and of bridges etched on sky.
Above the commodore, a two flag sign
Sent out the fearful news of submarines.
As twilight fell, the nervous tension grew:
Which ones would be torpedoed in the night?
Could anyone survive in icy sea?

Between the escort screen, as darkness fell,
A single U-boat stole, and roamed about,
A killer shark in search of easy prey.
In quick succession four torpedoes ran;
One hit the 'Elin K', whose Nordic crew
Took to their lifeboats, while their vessel sank.
A second U-boat entered through the screen;
The frigate, 'Zaanland', settled where she lay,
Her boiler smashed, her decks alive with sparks
From running anchor chains. 'James Oglethorpe',
A US cargo ship, her steering jammed,
Was never seen again by friend or foe.
Attacked by one corvette, a U-boat dived,
But, in a moment, sonar contacts drew
A depth-charge cluster, damaging the hull:
She slid away to seek a Biscay port.
Torpedoes struck two other cargo ships;

One quickly sank - the 'Harry Luckenbach' -
Though crews escaped in boats, they were not saved,
But died upon the vast Atlantic wastes.

Whilst U-boats turned about to reload tubes,
The hunted convoy watched for their return;
Until, once more, the deadly missiles came.
Freighters and one large tanker soon were hit.
Though threatened by the flames, a ship gave help,
But panic on the 'Irenee du Pont'
Cost several lives, when lifeboats did not wait.
'Nariva''s crew were saved; she stayed afloat.
Despite the heavy swell and flooded decks,
The captain and two officers went back
And briefly were marooned when their corvette,
Spotting a U-boat, turned to track it down.
'Nariva''s engines could not be revived.
Watching a wisp of disappearing steam,
The three men stood, abandoned on the deck,
Till, failing in pursuit, their wayward boat
Returned to save the valiant castaways.
'Coracero' was next to be attacked.
The engine-room exploded, killing five.
The Dutch ship, 'Terkoelei', then was hit,
Capsizing on two lifeboats filled with men.
Meanwhile, the old four-stacker, 'Beverley',
With brave persistence, tracked a U-boat down.
By sonar contact, depth-charges were fired
And cracked the U-boat's hull, though far below.
Yet, driven up by batteries, she fled.

By night-time all was quiet. Depth-charge attack
Had driven off remaining submarines.
But still, next day, five more torpedoes struck.
Some army families, fleeing Singapore,
Who'd narrowy escaped imprisonment,
Now met their end on board 'Canadian Star';
Whilst 'Walter Gresham''s gunners, as she sank
Fired off their shells, contemptuous of life.

The second convoy faced a single threat:
Commander Kinzel's U-boat 338.
Machine guns fired on Kinzel as he turned,
But through the convoy ran the deadly wakes,
Until four ships were sunk: 'Alderamin',
'Fort Cedar Lake', 'King Gruffyd', 'Kingsbury'.
'Alderamin''s commander, Captain Os,
Refused all help until his men were saved.

Beneath the devastation they had caused,
The crew of 338 consumed a meal
In celebration of their grim success,
Whilst Admiral Donitz sent a signal back:
'Bravo! Stick to it. Do the same again.'[10]
Six more of *'Dranger'* wolf-pack were informed
Of where to intercept the Allied fleet.
Yet Captain Kinzel was not satisfied;
Four more torpedoes from U-338
Ranged through the convoy; one more ship was struck -
The freighter, 'Granville', quickly broke in two.
Twelve crewmen died before they could escape.
This time a bold attack by two escorts
Drove Kinzel down below six hundred feet.

But now another hunter intervened.
To U-boat 305 the silhouettes
Of convoy ships against the moonlit sky
Stood out like targets on a fairground range.
The 'Zouave' sank in minutes, dense with iron,
Her ancient rivets flying as she split;
'Port Auckland' stayed afloat, her engines dead,
Until a second missile rent her hull,
And ocean's flood embraced the bodies there
Of those who'd died within the engine room.

Through heavy seas the shocked survivors sailed,
Expecting any time the tearing crash
And rush of water from a sudden hit.
Imagination saw the heaving deck
With growing list and men entrapped below,
The slide beneath the waves and drowning breaths.
But grave necessity drove fear away,
And every sailor clung to duty's task
To hold the compass course, or man a gun,
To read a gauge, or stoke the boilers up,
To stand upon the bridge, as though in port,
And pass the time of day with due aplomb,
But still with eyes alert for tell-tale tracks
That signified a swift torpedo's trail.
Those most in peril were not navy men,
Whose choice had been to fight an ocean war,
But rather those whom peacetime had enrolled
To live in amity by foreign trade,
And meet but nature's storms and turpitudes.
Now merchant sailors were impressed for war
And faced bombardment on the open sea,

Where none could feel the touch of mother earth,
Or find the shelter of a trench or wall.
Nor was Poseidon partial, drowning men
With equal disregard for friend or foe.

And yet one day, within the leaden sky,
They saw a single Liberator plane,
A thousand miles beyond its Ulster base.
What elixir of life to weary crews!
What dove of Noah, returning from afar,
With 'olive leaf pluckt off' to mark the end!
Henceforth the ocean lost its boundlessness.

Then aircraft came from other distant fields –
Sunderlands and Flying Fortresses -
From Iceland, Belfast and the Hebrides.
At their approach the German U-boats fled,
No longer safe upon the level sea,
But harried from the air by swooping planes,
Machine-gunned, bombed, and depth-charged in the
    deep.
With freedom to attack, the escort ships
Pursued the U-boats, driving them below.
A Flying Fortress caught U-384
Upon the surface, hiding in a squall.
Depth charges sank her, leaving gouts of oil
Above the grave of fifty men, who'd sung
One time too many songs of Kriegsmarine.
The plane's report, deciphered by B-Dienst,
Confirmed the view that Donitz had received:
The battle tide had turned; the hour had come
To break off contact and withdraw his fleet.

Two convoy ships were sunk before the end:
The 'Carras' and the 'Matthew Luckenbach';
But then the order came - no more attacks,
Except on stragglers, or when opportune.

Which side had won this transatlantic duel?
Of merchantmen the loss was twenty-two;
Of escorts none; of U-boats two were lost,
And seven forced by damage to retreat.
Yet Admiral Horton, at his Mersey base,
Was hopeful that the trend had been reversed.
Losses to U-boats were at record heights;
And he foresaw the pendulum of war.
This battle was the great climacteric;
Henceforth the U-boat menace would be met
By growth of air-power from more land-based planes
And escort carriers, to hunt and kill
Where U-boats dared to surface on the sea.
The German naval code, unbroken now,
Would soon be cracked; and better radar used.
The ratio of losses would be turned,
And U-boats driven back to coastal seas,
Where they could lay submerged with schnorkel tubes.

Like Goering's Luftwaffe, the Kriegsmarine
Had failed to break the islanders' resolve.
Starvation was no more a present threat,
Nor lack of key supplies of goods and arms.
New World production flowed across the seas
And soon would come a million men in arms
To fight the second front against the Reich.
As ever in the past, Great Britain's power

Was made secure by victory on the sea.
Whilst Hitler's eyes were fixed upon the east,
Churchill looked west beyond the ocean's bourne,
At giant America, whose untold might
Would countervail and set the world to right.

19 The Dambusters' Raid

Whilst German soldiers fought on distant fields
In Africa and Russia, or stood guard
Where subject peoples writhed with discontent
In eastern Europe, Norway and in France,
Within their homeland ruined cities burned.
In steppeland camps or dug-outs in the sand,
The wretched troopers heard the baleful news
Of families killed, of wives or children maimed,
Of homelessness, of cherished places wrecked.
British by night, by day Americans,
Carried their tons of massed incendiaries.
Commander Harris, jealous of his planes,
Still argued that the war could be curtailed
By ceaseless bombing raids on German towns.
No other aim should prejudice this means,
Not even the demands of U-boat war,
Nor army cries for tactical support,
Nor the defence of empire in the East.
Destroy all German industry by rote,

Especially in the heartland of the Ruhr!
Though factories might survive, productive power
Could not outlast the loss of social life,
Of transport, homes and public services.

Such was the rationale of bombing raids,
And with it a persuasive claim was made
To circumvent the need to land a force
Upon the coast of France and fight campaigns,
Like those which saw the youth of Britain slain
In Flanders fields against the Kaiserreich.
Yet Harris' area bombing had not won
The Allied leaders' unreserved consent.
Churchill and his Chiefs of Staff had doubts;
So, too, had General Eaker, who advised
A joint attack on air production plants
To undermine the German fighter force.
The problem still remained: no planes approached
At heights where they could accurately bomb.
Enemy guns and fighters drove them off
From most precision targets in the Reich.

A pre-war plan, however, re-emerged:
To bomb the dams that held the waters back
Which served the needs of millions in the Ruhr.
A special squadron practised flying low.
Their leader, Gibson - only twenty-five -
Had flown a lot more sorties than his due,
Including one, alone, to Altafjord,
To bomb the 'Tirpitz' in its northern base.
To smash the dams a special bomb was made,
And, after many trials, pronounced as fit.

Dropped at high speed from sixty feet above -
Two aircraft lights converged to show the height -
It bounced across the water, then submerged
On contact with the surface of the dam.
The Springtime maximum of water's depth,
As well as brilliant moonlight, were required.

Towards the darkening east the bombers flew;
A crew of seven manned each Lancaster.
Silvery shores of England slid away;
Then hostile coast appeared, and sullen isles,
From which arose the lazy tracer shells
Of German guns. One plane was hit and crashed.
Across the surface of the Zuyder Zee
Another flew too low and lost its bombs;
Damaged by water, it returned to base.
They followed next the length of a canal,
Shining like glass between the earth-dark fields.
One hit a cable, dived and burst in flames.
In Germany the villages were quiet,
But now there came the leaping tracer lines,
In arcs of coloured light, that sought in vain
To draw the nerveless pilots from their course.
Along the Rhine they turned towards the hills.

The Mohne lake was silent, black and deep.
Gibson, the leader, dived towards the dam,
And with the moon behind him, flew at speed
Two miles across the water, spotlights on
To calculate the height at sixty feet.
As German gunners sighted on the beams,
The yellow tracer rose in casual lines,

But engines roared and water sped below.
A bomb was falling, bounced and hit the dam;
Like gushing oil, a cloud of water rose,
And then a thunderous crash that shook the plane.
Its Merlin engines laboured as it climbed.
A Very light burned red to mark success.

For several minutes planes were hid by hills.
Then one began a second slow attack,
But German tracer hit a petrol tank;
A wing blew off, before it crashed and burned.
Behind the power-house, just beyond the dam,
Its bomb exploded, with a ball of smoke.
Whilst Gibson circled, drawing German fire,
The other aircraft hit the dam with bombs,
Until the face split open at the last,
And rolled away to let the water through.
Now aircrews saw a torrent unrestrained,
A racing wave descending down the vale,
Seizing buildings, sweeping trees away,
Engulfing cars that fled too ponderously,
Whose headlights shone a fading sickly green.

Guy Gibson's group of Lancasters flew on
Towards the Eder, deep in wooded hills.
Beside an ancient Schloss, each dived in turn,
Dropping to sixty from a thousand feet,
And running down the lake to bomb and climb -
There were no gunners on the Eder wall -
With sudden swerving on a starboard tack
To circumvent the mountain straight ahead.
One plane bombed late and blew itself apart.

As dawn approached across the eastern hills,
A final bomb was dropped; the dam collapsed.
Down to Kassel surged the foaming mass,
Flooding houses, inundating farms,
Drowning people as they woke from bed,
And blacking out the early morning lights.

Night fighters chased them back to Hollands' coast,
Shooting one down beyond the Zuyder Zee.
Fifty-six aircrew perished in the task.
Only a single Lancaster had reached
The third Ruhr dam, the Sorpe, which in fact
Was built invulnerable to any bomb.
Without its loss the Ruhr's great industries
Were not unduly troubled by the floods.
The Eder breach affected mainly farms;
The Mohne's did not seriously harm
The war production vital for the Reich.

What then did Gibson and his crews achieve
By such a skilful and audacious raid?
Theirs was the finest operation yet
With that precision Allied forces lacked.
Henceforth a master bomber was the key,
The leader who would light the way with flares,
Whose fast, unarmed Mosquito could escape
A fighter screen and ring of eighty-eights.
Guy Gibson later flew such master planes.
One raid complete, he told the other crews,
'Now beat it home'; but he himself would die
In his Mosquito, shot from Flanders' sky.

20 The Battle of Kursk

Ever a gambler, Hitler now conceived
A daring plan to save the eastern front.
A second Spring in Russia had condemned
The German army to defend a line
From where they still surrounded Leningrad
A thousand miles to Rostov-on-the-Don.
A brilliant thrust by Manstein had reversed
The Russians' progress westwards from the Don
And seized once more the city of Kharkov.
'*Sichelschnitt*"s creator - that bold move
Which sent the *Panzers* through the Belgium hills -
Proposed to step back from the southern line
And let the Russians reach the Dnieper's banks,
In order to expose their northern flank
To armoured onslaught from the Kharkov front.
But ceding ground was never Hitler's choice;
He looked instead for some offensive stroke
To gain once more the war's initiative.

The salient at Kursk gave such a chance:
To pinch it out would throw the Russians back,
Disrupt their plans, weaken their other fronts.
The Germans knew they did not have the strength
To reproduce their earlier attacks,
Which brought the domes of Moscow in their sights,
And almost claimed the derricks of Baku.
Two armies would advance from north and south
Against the shoulders of the salient,
Meeting at Kursk and Tim to block retreat
By Soviet forces trapped towards the west.
Surprise was crucial; yet there was delay.
Wehrmacht generals were beset by doubts:
For Jodl said reserves must be maintained
To use in Italy or further west.
Kluge and Zeitzler favoured the attack.
Hitler could not decide, and made excuse
That all must wait until the Panthers came -
His newest tank, not battle-tested yet.

Meanwhile, the Russians saw the threat to Kursk
And, when at last the Führer's mind was set,
They soon observed how units were prepared
For what the Germans code-named 'Citadel'.
As time advanced, the salient became
Indeed a fortress. Was it a Verdun,
Where German armies bled themselves to death?
The Soviet Stavka built defensive lines,
Thick-sowed with minefields, twenty thousand guns,
Katyusha rocket throwers, tanks hull-down,
And hordes of soldiers, many trained to lie
In hidden trenches, whence they could emerge

And kill the crews of damaged German tanks.
'Pakfronts' of anti-tank guns lay in wait
With broadside fire on channels through the mines.
The Fifth Tank Army of T-34s
Formed in the rear a tactical reserve.
Russian aircraft, too, were well prepared
To dominate the battle zone at Kursk.

Yet German armoured tactics took account
Of that tenacity they'd often met
Since Russians had recovered their morale.
No longer were the *Panzers* just a sword
To cut a swathe through vulnerable defence.
For now the Tigers led an armoured wedge,
Followed by lighter tanks with infantry,
Then mortar units, mounted now on tracks.
Would not these men, these Teuton *Herrenvolk*
Of SS *Totenkopf*, SS *Das Reich*,
Gross Deutschland and *Leibstandarte* SS,
And all the rest, of chosen Wehrmacht troops,
Who'd conquered Europe in the blitzkrieg war,
Prove once again the might of German arms,
Exposing how the Communist deceit
Had forced the Russian peasantry to fight
For Stalin's hated ideology?

Both sides lay still in sultry Summer heat.
A Czech deserter to the Russian lines
Informed them of the date of 'Citadel';
And so assembled Wehrmacht troops were hit
By waves of shells from massed artillery.
Despite their losses, they advanced on time

And broke the outer screen of the defence.
From sunken lanes and dried-up river beds,
With hatches closed, the German tanks rolled out,
Across the billowing crops towards the mines.
Crippled by fire, some lay in burning fields,
Their crews soon killed by shells or infantry.
Protected by their thicker armour plate,
The Tigers led, but progress was delayed.
Swollen by Summer rain,the lateral streams
Had turned to swamp the nearby fields of corn.
Gross Deutschland troops advanced at heavy cost
Through villages with roofs of blazing straw.

Hoch's southern pincer broke through several lines,
As diving Stukas bombed the Russian tanks,
Or raked them with repeated cannon fire.
His infantry fought on by day and night,
Creeping in darkness through the littered fields
To meet in mortal combat hand to hand
The Russians sent to kill the crews of tanks.
But General Model's northern pincer force,
Lighter in armour, could progress no more.
Its Porsche tanks, devoid of infantry,
Though well-equipped to match T-34s,
Had no machine-guns, and were soon destroyed
By Russian soldiers leaping on their backs
And spraying air vents red with searing flame.

The Germans only chance was to exploit
A short advance made on their eastern flank,
For elsewhere they were stopped by Russian fire
From well-directed guns in hills or woods.

Hoch ordered all his tank reserves to group
And break out northwards in a race for Kursk.
But, to the east, near Prokhorovka town,
The Fifth Tank Army waited in the rear,
Nine hundred tanks, unused and freshly armed
With SU 85s, a Soviet gun
To match the dreaded German 88s.
The death ride of the *Panzers* had begun.

In stifling heat the armoured forces met,
To fight all day in clouds of blinding dust,
Which obfuscated targets from the air.
Behind the grinding tanks, small groups of men,
With bayonets fixed, or carbines raised to fire,
Ran on through showers of mud from bursting shells,
Or fell in pain, transfixed by flying steel.
Exploding tanks sent trails of oil aloft
In sky already black with burning thatch.
No warriors upon the plains of Troy,
Adorned to fight in glistening chariots,
Nor medieval knights in full array
Of oriflamme or eagle, keen to spur
Their splendid stallions on, with lances raised,
Had seen such ponderous clash of heavy steel,
Nor heard such crude cacophony of fire,
Nor seen the midday sun turn slowly grey
And dark descend on afternoons of war,
Nor smelt ubiquitous burning on the field,
Nor seen men crushed like insects in the mud
Beneath the weight of lumbering machines.
Nor was this like the time when German tanks
Played havoc with the Polish cavalry,

Or when Guderian, beyond the Meuse,
Had raced across the champaign fields of France.
As veterans now they fought with stern intent,
Against the odds, on Prokhorovka's plain.

Beneath the glare of shells and Very lights,
White tracer tracks and orange stabs of fire,
Both grenadier and *kolkhoz* peasants lay,
United by obscure and violent death.
But Fifth Tank Army mustered fresh reserves;
None were forthcoming for the *Panzer* corps.
A battle of attrition would be won
By Russian generals prodigal with men.
The Kursk attack had drawn the Russian fire,
And found it stronger for its bold defence.

Another conflict occupied the mind
Of Adolf Hitler and his General Staff,
For while the tank war raged, far to the west
An Allied force embarked for Sicily.
Conscious of Italian weakness there,
The Führer ruled that from the Kursk attack
An SS *Panzer* unit must withdraw
And be transported to the southern front,
A move confirming Kursk would not be won.
Though Manstein claimed that Russian tank reserves
Could be consumed in Prokhorovka's fire,
The Fuhrer ordered Hoch to turn about.
Kursk was, as Marshall Koniev later claimed,
'The swan-song of the German armoured force.'[11]
The Stavka had prepared a counter-stroke:
A flood of Russian forces reached the line

From where the Germans started 'Citadel'.
They crossed the Donetz, took Kharkov again,
And looked towards the Dnieper's western bank.
Northwards, too, the German lines were thinned;
The Orel salient quickly was regained.

As one defeated German general said,
'At Kursk we were positioned like a man
Who seized an angry wolf by both his ears
And realised then he dare not let him go.'[12]
Gambling had failed. At Kursk the Wehrmacht lost
Its tank reserve along the eastern front.
Henceforth the Russian army would advance
By hammer blows that echoed down the line,
Testing each sector till its strength was found,
Then moving to adjacent ones with ease,
Like pianists' hands upon a row of keys.

21 The Fall of Mussolini

North Africa was cleared of Axis arms.
Should war be carried next from there to Rome,
As in the ancient days of Hannibal?
The Allied High Command remained unsure
Of where to strike against the hostile coast
That ranged from Norway to the isles of Greece.
For British strategy, like Pericles' -
Which threatened every shore of Spartan Greece -
Relied traditionally on naval power.

Americans, however, believed in force
Brought massively to bear upon one front,
As Grant had done within the Wilderness,
And Foch in France. Although it was agreed
To make a landing on the Channel coast,
General Marshall, U.S. Chief of Staff,
Suspected that the British might defer
A grand assault in favour of their plan.
The British leaders, only too aware
From history and their own experience
How many lives the first Great War had cost,
Envisaged a peripheral campaign,
Probing Axis strength in every place
Where smouldering resistance could be fanned.
With German manpower stretched on many fronts,
Due time would come for one decisive blow.
Already British agents worked in France,
And helped guerrillas in the Balkan hills.
Were not Aegean islands vulnerable?
Could neutral Turkey also be aroused?
Even in Norway, Churchill thought the time
Was opportune for some aggressive move.
But Marshall could recall Gallipoli,
Whose bloody failure some attributed
To Churchill's love of injudicious schemes.
And who could say what might ensue again?

Alanbrooke, however, Chief of Staff,
Who wisely tempered what his master planned,
Offered a strategic compromise.
To him success in Tunis was a step
Towards invading European shores.

For Allied forces waited, coiled like springs,
To jump across the Straits of Sicily.
A swift attack on Italy would compel
The German High Command to reinforce -
Even from Russia - just as long before,
When Mussolini seized Albania.
Peripheral war, for Brooke, had dual aims:
To draw the Wehrmacht from the Russian plains
And, from the west, divert whatever arms
Stood in reserve to face the Allied threat;
Thus would the French invasion be secured.
Was that great Allied force, said Alanbrooke,
Which triumphed in the African campaign
From Egypt to the headland of Cape Bon,
To be disbanded, or to wait off-stage,
Until the scene was set to land in France?
The case was won; and Sicily preferred -
Not, as some thought, Sardinia -
For from that isle the Luftwaffe had struck
At Allied shipping passing through the straits.

A clever ruse concealed the Allied plans:
Upon a beach in Spain a corpse was found,
Dressed as a British officer of rank,
Amongst whose papers was a secret note
Referring to a plan to land in Greece
And, at the same time, in Sardinia.
The Führer was deceived, and ordered troops
To reinforce in Greece and southern France.
Meanwhile, the Allies gathered in their ports,
At Haifa, Suez, Alexandria,
Tunis, Bizerta, even on the Clyde,

The greatest war armada yet to sail;
To land, in all, near half a million men.

An angry wind whipped up the southern seas.
In landing-craft the waiting men were sick,
But, as the beaches came, they jumped ashore
And raced for cover by a dune or wall.
Defensive fire was light, for on the coast
Only a line of weak Italian troops,
Half ready to surrender, were deployed.
Axis reserves - Panzers and grenadiers -
Were leagured inland, hid in olive groves,
Or camouflaged in orchards, whence they saw
The flash of coastal guns, and in the sky
The scattered parachutes of Allied troops.
They did not see the many gliders lost,
Cast off too early by their cautious tugs,
And falling to the unforgiving sea.

Within a week the British had advanced
Along the eastern coast past Syracuse,
But, at the Primasole bridge, were stopped,
As Germans moved to guard the narrow pass
Between the towering Etna and the sea;
And further west the Panzers now emerged,
And struck at Gela on the southern coast.
Refusing to retreat, the U.S. troops,
Listened from fox-holes to the creaking tanks,
And waited to confront the grenadiers.
Near Gela beach a desperate duel was fought,
When guns were rushed, as soon as they were beached,
To face the tanks debouching from the plain.

Naval gunfire then was brought to bear,
And lightening salvos split the armoured hulls.
With half their number left as burning wrecks,
The Panzers turned and fled into the hills.
Held at Catania, Montgomery sent
A second column west of Etna's peak.
Americans advanced across the hills,
Through ripening vines and ancient olive groves
And apple orchards cool with dappled shade,
Where homely farms of terra cotta brick
Might hide the deadly fire of grenadiers.
They reached Palermo with a final thrust.
Italian troops, unwilling now to fight,
Soon flocked to compounds, fenced around with wire.

Mindful, perhaps, of Robert Lee's request
At Appomattox Court House, in defeat,
That men should be released to plough the earth
Before the frosts of Winter intervened,
General Patton sent home to their farms
Sicilian prisoners held in U.S. camps.
Meanwhile in barren fields across the land,
As hungry peasants watched the palls of smoke
That signalled burning houses and the dead,
Weary families kept their children home,
And brought their donkeys close within the walls.

To demonstrate the Allies' full intent
To drive Italians out of Hitler's fold,
A bombing raid was made on Rome itself.
And even while the Axis leaders met
Beside the peaceful Adriatic Sea,

The eternal city saw the fires of war,
As railway yards were hit by sticks of bombs.
When Mussolini's plane returned to Rome,
A huge, black cloud of smoke obscured his view
Of monuments to many emperors.
In palace rooms where once the Duce spoke
To cheering crowds below the battlements,
So near to where the first of Caesars died,
The Fascist Council was, at last, convened.
Adorned in black, they heard their leader speak
Of how the Italian people must react
To this attack upon their sacred land:
Just as Cavour had fought for liberty,
So now this war was Mussolini's cause,
And all must rally to the Duce's side;
But no more did they cheer with arms upraised.
When Carlo Grandi called upon the king
To take upon himself the powers of State,
Even the Duce's son-in-law approved.

When, next day, the Duce met the king,
Carabinieri guarded every room.
Victor Emmanuel, in Marshall's dress,
At last could speak with royal authority:
'Italian soldiers have no will to fight.
You are more hated here than any man;
I am your only friend; you will be safe,
But I shall choose Marshall Badaglio.'[13]
As Mussolini walked towards his car,
He was arrested there, and driven off,
And, on the isle of Ponza, soon interned.

Thus ended two decades of Fascist power,
When that proud land which once had ruled the world,
And since become its fount of art and style,
Submitted to an arrant demagogue.
Though motorways were built, and marshes drained
And Roman *fora* splendidly revived,
How many died in dirty prison cells,
Or were coerced by 'olive and the club'?
Though Mussolini knew the brutal means
By which the Führer governed Germany,
And did not like the murder of the Jews,
Yet he had chosen wilfully to side
With tyranny, and all its consequence.
For vain ambition led him to exploit
The Nazi victory won in northern France.
Henceforth he was the Führer's copy-cat,
Aggressive in the Balkans, quick to send
Italian soldiers to the eastern front.
Defeat undid him; first in Africa,
And now in Sicily, where native troops
Disliked their German allies more than those
Who'd brought the war to their misguided land.

Patton had seized Palermo; now he sped
Along the northern coast past Cefalu,
Where on the hillside stood the ancient church,
Whose apse depicts the Saviour of the World.
Each side of Etna, British troops advanced,
Impeded on the narrow coastal road
By demolitions of each cliff-top bridge.
Troina was bombed to force the Germans out,
Its screen of smoke concealing those who died,

Sicilians and grenadiers alike.
The race was on to reach Messina port.
Outflanking German rearguards from the sea
By rapid landings, Patton sought to trap,
Within the island, all the Wehrmacht troops.
But near the straits lay anti-aircraft guns
That filled the sky with clouds of bursting flak,
And nullified the hope of air support.
With shortened lines, the German force withdrew,
And crossed to Reggio with little loss,
To fight again in Italy's defence.
Though Sicily was won, the Duce gone,
The Germans stayed, to bring, like Hannibal,
The ugliness of war to vineyard slopes
And ancient hill-top towns of sweet renown,
To mountains parched beneath the Summer sun
And village streets where barefoot children ran.

22 Jean Moulin

De Gaulle in London struggled to attract
The boldest of the French, who would not bend
To German might or Petain's compromise.
'Collaboration' was a hated word
To those believing France must be renewed
By unrelenting war, however long.

A set-back at Dakar did not prevent
Much of the Empire turning to de Gaulle,
Though Indo-China yielded to Japan,
And Syria resisted Allied force.
The aged Petain could not long defend
The wealth of France from Germany's demands
For food, materials and, worst of all,
Deported youth for labour in the Reich,
Though Laval claimed the doubtful recompense
Of bringing back French prisoners of war.

Resistance grew, as individuals chose
To harass Germans, publish hostile tracts,
To gather information, or to kill.
Within the northern zone, clandestine groups
Made war upon the German army there.
The southern zone of Vichy offered more
To men prepared to live amongst the hills
In maquis groups, like those named 'Franc-Tireur',
Or Henri Frenay's movement, called 'Combat'.
Though all resistance kept alive the flames
Of French integrity and moral life,
The strong diversity of time and place,
Of aims and methods, weakened the effect.
How were numerous streams to flow as one
And overwhelm the occupying power?
As often, when invaded, France had found
A national hero prompt to offer life -
Bertrand du Guesclin, Joan of Arc, Villars,
Or one like Emile Driant at Verdun -
So now one man exemplified the will
Of all prepared for such a sacrifice.

Nearby the church of Chartres, whose windows then -
The proudest gift of medieval art -
Were blind to see the shame imposed on France,
The Prefect, Jean Moulin, had stood to meet
The German officers who took the town.
Efficiently he'd organised supplies,
Maintained the law, and cared for refugees;
But then he was required to testify,
Although he knew the charges were untrue,
That negro soldiers, brought from Senegal,
Had carried out atrocities of war.
When he refused, the Germans tortured him.
Imprisoned in a cell, he cut his throat,
But did not die, and later was released.

A perilous boat trip brought him to de Gaulle,
Who saw in him an image of himself -
Dispassionate and brave, of rational mind,
A servant of the State, whose love for France
No fear, nor other obstacle, could shake.
Moulin, also, recognised the man,
Embracing national honour in himself,
Whose lofty vision was the hope of France.
Though many Frenchmen criticised de Gaulle
For leaving France in time of greatest trial,
Or even as a traitor to Petain,
Moulin had faith in his integrity.
He'd seen collaboration growing fast
By Fascist groups and simple apathy;
How deep disunity beset the French.
He also knew the strength that still remained
In those who were resisting, and their need

To work together under one command.
De Gaulle would be their leader - as he was
Of colonies whose troops were now engaged,
Of all who'd rallied to his broadcast words
To fight beneath the banner of Lorraine.

Moulin was eager to return to France.
Commissioned by de Gaulle to act for him,
He dropped by parachute within the south
To meet Frenay and other chiefs of groups.
Some, like 'Combat', hesitated long
Before conforming to a national scheme
Of French resistance under Charles de Gaulle.
The Communists already had refused
To stop their killing Germans, though de Gaulle,
To save civilian lives, had ordered it.
And yet by dint of patience long applied,
Of secret meetings in resisters' homes,
Or in obscure locations unbeknown
To Germans and collaborating French,
Moulin obtained agreement to his plans.

At *Rue du Four*, in Paris in the Spring,
When lime trees flowered on vacant boulevards,
Behind closed shutters on the second floor,
A meeting of nineteen, at last, convened.
'Ceux de la Liberation', 'Front National',
'Ceux de la Resistance', and 'Combat',
'Liberation Nord et Sud', and 'Franc-Tireur',
'Organisation Civile et Militaire',
And all the parties of the Right and Left,
Trade Unions, and Jean Moulin himself,

Accepted there the need for unity.
Already Charles de Gaulle was in Algiers
To re-assert the nationhood of France,
Until, on their domain, the French might choose,
In place of Vichy, a new governance.
Yet other dangers threatened post-war France,
For Roosevelt's advisers were deceived
By Charles de Gaulle's facade of arrogance.
They warned the President against a man
Who scorned belief in French democracy,
And mocked its long debates and party strife.
Another soldier, Giraud, was their choice
To lead the French, until the war was won.
With mainland France now all in German hands,
And only to be freed by Allied power,
Would 'liberating' foreign soldiers come
To occupy the land of France again?
Hence, in Algiers, de Gaulle was loath to meet
The nominee of Franklin Roosevelt.
Only when Churchill threatened to withdraw
All British help to forces of de Gaulle
Would he relent. Disdainfully he shook
His rival's hand, and shared the leadership.
Moulin's success, however, had assured
The movement of de Gaulle its proper right
To represent the cause of liberty.
Except where Petain's image lingered still,
On desks of bureaucrats, in bourgeois homes,
Or in the minds of naïve patriots,
And where the stain of Fascism had spread
Indelibly across the land of France,
His symbol stirred the people to resist.

De Gaulle's authority could now withstand
The challenge of Giraud. The stage was set
For that commanding voice, which spoke alone
In bitter days when France was overrun,
To speak again, from liberated France.

Gestapo information, gleaned from those
Who sold their native land for greed or hate,
Was gaining ground on 'Rex', Jean Moulin's name
Within the network of resistance groups.
In Lyons' alleyways and Marseilles' lanes,
From house to house the fugitive escaped.
The groups that he convened still made their plans
To fly in agents, gather drops of arms,
Report to London where the Germans were,
Sabotage a factory, blow up trains,
And generally co-ordinate the war
Now fought by the Resistance 'arms in hand'.
Yet every meeting threatened to disclose
The whereabouts of 'Rex' to German eyes.
One traitor in their midst would soon reveal
Where Moulin could be found. And then, at night,
The French *Milice* would summon him from sleep.
Already General Delestraint was caught,
Whose 'Secret Army' was to be the force
To rise against the Germans on that day
When Allied troops would finally invade.

Moulin proposed a meeting in Lyons
To fill the vacant post of Delestraint.
He did not know how close pursuit had come.
Gestapo agents found where they would meet -

A doctor's office, high above the town.
Resistance leaders waited nervously,
For Jean Moulin was late. At last he came,
Up on the steep Caluire funicular,
Then on the tramway, number thirty-three,
Alighting at a square called *Castellane*.
A maid led Moulin to the waiting room.
Milice and Gestapo came at once,
Kicking in the door and firing shots.
Handcuffs secured the 'patients' one by one.
A Frenchman, perhaps a spy, escaped arrest.

The Gestapo chief in Lyons, Klaus Barbie,
Had no idea which one was Jean Moulin;
So all were beaten, till one gave away
Moulin's identity. The hard ordeal,
Predictable if ever he were caught,
Was undergone in prison at Montluc,
Where trains passed by en route to Summer Alps.
They tortured Moulin there; then ordered him
To Germany by train, but Moulin died.
Within the French resistance he knew more
Than any man alive, but gave away
No comrades' names. He had not spoken once.
All those he knew he saved, for love of France.

23   The Bombing of Hamburg

A means of jamming the Kammhuber Line
Had been discovered. Strips of metal foil,
Dropped from the air, obscured all radar screens.
Known as 'Windows', this had not been used,
In case the Germans would reciprocate.
But when the threat of bombing had declined,
With German planes deployed far to the east,
Then Churchill ordered its experiment.
So Hamburg was selected for its use,
A city of two million, densely built,
Still proud of its imperial renown,
Of medieval streets, and splendid homes

Constructed in the wealthy Kaiserreich.
Few people left when English aircraft came
And dropped their warning leaflets in the streets.

Lancaster bombers, seven hundred strong,
Approached the city from the Baltic Sea.
Pathfinders dropped three sets of coloured flares,
That marked the target, yellow, red and green.
The bomber stream flew in, almost unscathed.
No radar screens gave warning of attack,
For 'Windows' had obliterated them.
Frantic searchlights roved across the sky,
Whilst heavy guns shot blind, and eighty-eights
Could only sweep on dimly sighted planes.
Few German fighters reached the battle zone;
Their ground controllers, baffled by the foil,
Had no idea of where the target lay.
So Hamburg city felt the deadly rain
Of high-explosives and incendiaries,
Until the central area was ablaze.

For two more days the bombing did not cease,
As U.S. aircraft flew on daylight raids,
Before the mass of Lancasters returned,
Again by night, and almost unopposed.
Once again the smouldering wreckage flared,
Like energy compressed in furnaces.
Above the pavements rose a ball of flames,
A blazing fragment torn from hell itself,
Sucking upwards everything that burned -
Trees and bushes, roof beams, human flesh.
Tornado air-streams scoured the city streets,

Hurling bodies through the scalding heat
And spreading fire with incandescent sparks.
To darkened cellars stricken families ran,
Listening in terror when the flagstones shook,
Until the greedy tongues of flame reached down
To light the bunkers, stocked with coal and coke,
Combusting slowly, with yet crueller flames.
In air-raid shelters thousands died from fire,
Or breathed monoxide gas, and lay to burn
In vast incinerations of the dead.
Only those few who ran into the lake,
Or lay in streams, or braved the Elbe's flow,
Were safe from burning and the storms of air.
A million people fled. With them went word
Of this new terror of ordeal by fire.

In other cities murmurings were heard
Of cataclysmic raids destroying all,
And in the High Command, unspoken yet,
There lingered now the single word - 'defeat'.
Speer told Hitler that if six more times
A city was attacked to such effect,
Then German armaments could not be made;
Whilst even Goebbels feared for the morale
Of German citizens, tormented thus.
The Führer merely said to Albert Speer:
'You'll straighten all that out.'[14] And so it was.
Two months of Hamburg's output could be found
Within the Reich's complete economy.
The R.A.F. was not, indeed, so strong
That it could interdict the war machine
Of Nazi Germany. Hamburg was near,

And 'Windows' had prevented its defence;
The Ruhr was further, Berlin was remote.
Though the Kammhuber Line was now defunct,
Luftwaffe fighters quickly improvised
New 'wild boar' tactics, hunting eagerly
Where flares and searchlights and the fires below
Revealed the stream of bombers in the night.
Yet daytime fighters took a heavier toll.
When at Schweinfurt many planes were lost,
The US airforce cancelled daylight raids.
The ghosts of Hamburg were, in part, avenged.

Commander Harris pressed relentlessly
For more resources to complete the task
Of bombing till admission of defeat.
For him the cost in human suffering
Was weighed against the lives he thought redeemed,
Saved from campaigns, like that of Passchendaele.

But Albert Speer, by building factories
Much further to the east on rural sites,
Or underground, frustrated Allied plans
To weaken gravely German industry.
Nor did the German population flinch.
Immured to horror, docile, dutiful,
They served their leaders, careless of what end;
And though the scars of Hamburg's torment healed,
Fires of purgation smouldered on, concealed.

24 Allied Advances

With Sicily won, and Mussolini held
By anti-Fascists of Badoglio,
The time was ripe to land in Italy.
Churchill, especially, wanted to compel
The Italian nation to forsake the war,
And Allied arms to win the prize of Rome.
He feared, of course, that Adolf Hitler's doubts
Of Italy's commitment to the war
Would strengthen his resolve to hold a line
Within the south of the peninsula.
Though an audacious plan to capture Rome

Might well have shaken his intransigence,
The Allied Chiefs of Staff would not endorse
Invasion on the coast of Italy
Beyond the range of land-based aeroplanes.

Montgomery crossed to occupy the 'toe',
And led his army through Calabria,
As Allied forces took Salerno beach
With strong support from battleships and planes.
The new Italian government could not solve
Its hard dilemma: how it could appease
Its German masters and their enemy.
Capitulation was the painful choice,
And Hitler, quick to guess at treachery,
Gave orders to disarm Italian troops,
Who long had fought as allies of the Reich
In African campaigns and Sicily.
As German troops were transferred further south
To occupy new lines from sea to sea,
So fresh divisions crossed the Brenner Pass.
Salerno beach was ringed with German fire,
When Kesselring advanced and boldly strove
To push the Allies off the mainland shore.
Once more the guns of battleships turned back
The surge of *Panzers* and the grenadiers.
Meanwhile commandos seized Taranto port
And British forces closed on Foggia,
Whose aerodromes would give the Allies scope
To bomb fresh targets, deep within the Reich.
Yet Germans held the mountainous terrain,
And hardened troops of Kesselring now stood
Along the Gustav line protecting Rome.

At Paestum temples and Cassino's walls,
In frescoed churches and by wayside shrines,
In peasant homes, and where the harmless herds
Of goats and cattle roamed the burnished hills,
The agony of war would not abate.

Kursk was the Wehrmacht's last offensive plan
To seize control along the eastern front.
Henceforth, the Soviet army, millions strong,
Would call the tune in claiming back the land
Lost for two years to foreign tyranny,
Where *Einsatzgruppen* terrorised the Jews
And hung the brave, unyielding partisans.
Though Leningrad's ordeal was not relieved,
Yet to the Dnieper'stream the war returned,
And, by the Autumn, bridgeheads had been made
Beyond the western banks. Kiev was freed -
Where once Guderian had wished to fly
Ukrainian flags beside the swastika,
Proclaiming thus the Wehrmacht's destined role
As liberator from the Marxist yoke.
Manteuffel made a brilliant counter-stroke,
But nothing now could stop the Russian flood,
Except a swift withdrawal, and a stand
Upon a shortened, strong defensive line,
A strategy that Hitler would not brook.

MacArthur planned the seizure of Rabaul,
Japan's headquarters in the southern isles,
By fighting through the archipelago
To Papua and then to Bougainville.
Flamethrowers' searing jets and napalm bombs

Drove desperate Japanese from isle to isle,
To jungle hideouts where they slowly died,
Cut off from help of men or sustenance.
New landing strips and bases made each step
A launching pad to stage the next assault.
In mid Pacific, Admiral Nimetz strove
To close his fleet upon the Philippines,
Taking some isles and bypassing the rest.
Marines on reef and beach at Tarawa
Were killed by murderous fire from pill-boxes;
But bold survivors, set on swift revenge,
Hurled back the Japanese, who later charged
With helpless cries of 'banzai' to their deaths.

A different set of islands gripped the mind
Of Winston Churchill: Cos, Leros and Rhodes,
Held by Italian troops, but now at risk,
Since Mussolini's fall, from German arms.
Churchill pressed strongly for a British force
To seize the islands, hoping to persuade
The nearby Turks to join the Allied cause.
Once more the name 'Gallipoli' was raised
To cast a doubt on Churchill's eastern schemes.
Eisenhower declined to give assent;
So British operations were too weak,
When Germans landed from the sea and air.
Just as the Trojans gained a brief success
In driving the Achaians to their ships,
So now, against the tide of war, was won
A sudden victory in Homeric seas,
Before the brutal sack of Germany.

The monster 'Tirpitz', moored in Kaafjord,
Awaiting there her prey of Allied ships,
Had not succumbed to British bombing raids.
But midget submarines alone might reach
The claustral vantage-point at which she lay.
Two passed beyond the fjord's winding neck,
Through nets and mines, though several times enmeshed,
And lodged two tons of charge against her hull.
Explosions crippled her, but Grendel-like,
She menaced still the Russian convoy route.
The intrepid men who'd manned the submarines,
Defying all the weighted odds of war,
Were rescued by the damaged warship's crew.
But *Tirpitz*" coup de grace from Lancasters
Capsized her in the depths of Tromso Fjord.

Only the *'Scharnhorst'* now remained a threat
To Allied convoys in the northern seas.
South of Bear Island, she was held at bay
By four destroyers, till the 'Duke of York'
Could join action with her heavy guns.
Torpedoes struck the battlecruiser first,
Then shells from 'Duke of York' at six miles range.
When 'Scharnhorst' sank, two thousand men were
     drowned,
Though British warships rescued those they found.

25 The Teheran Conference

With Axis' power now seemingly eclipsed,
A conference was held within Iran,
Beneath the Elburz high volcanic peaks.
If all three Allies stayed of one accord,
Then victory was assured, but, if they split,
The German army still had strength to fight -
As Frederick did when the Czarina died -
And keep in thralldom half a continent.

Who were these men, the 'Big Three' potentates,
Controlling armies of the greatest power
That history could recall, debating now
The future of the war-encompassed world?
Most sedulous in many arts of war
Was Winston Churchill, British Premier.
In that grave crisis on the fall of France,

When Germans stood in sight of English shores,
And barges filled the ports of northern France
To ferry the triumphant Wehrmacht there,
When German aircraft flew by night and day
To terrorise the British populace,
Then Churchill's voice, undaunted, had evoked
The half-awakened islanders' resolve
To fight or die in liberty's defence,
To summon up defiance, and the will
To persevere whatever be the cost.
In government he respected others' views,
Yet made decisions unequivocally.
He argued with his colleagues, unrestrained,
Probing their answers, questioning their plans,
Testing the limits of habitual means,
And raising issues no-one had foreseen -
Bold enterprises on a foreign shore,
New weapons that the boffins should invent,
Encouragement, or threats, to neutral powers,
Reluctance of his generals to attack,
Domestic matters not on Party lines,
The sloth of civil servants, and his thoughts
On how to organise the post-war world.
But rarely were the judgments overruled
Of Cabinet or united Chiefs of Staff.
His mastery of language won the hearts
Of all who heard his broadcast rhetoric.
Yet many did not like him. They recalled
How harsh he'd been when hungry workers struck,
Or how he'd quit the Liberals when they failed,
How adamant he was to save the Raj.
But all forgave him in those darkest days

When island Britain stood alone in arms.
His was the greatness of that solemn time,
And his the voice of Britain's finest hour.

Less loved by far was Georgia's man of steel
For his control of Russia in the war.
The Soviet people could not disregard
How he had built a godless 'workers State':
The death of millions on the peasant farms,
And fear of secret police, the lack of goods,
The dull monotony, the fulsome praise
Of greater tyranny than forbears knew
Beneath the decadence of Tsarist rule.
Cunning, ambitious, secretive and cruel,
Stalin was now Supremo in a war
For life and death of all his countrymen.
German invasion first unbalanced him,
But he regained his old tenacity.
He worked intensely, stationed near the front,
Controlling armies, formulating plans,
Appointing generals, shooting those who failed,
Ensuring that the commissars were there
To keep the soldiers loyal. No strategy
That he did not confirm; and, all the while,
He kept the State intact: collective farms,
Administration, services, supplies;
Above all, weapons and enlisted men -
Even from the far Siberian lands
Which faced the threat of Japanese attack.
Just as he'd struggled violently before
Against autocracy, so now with those,
The foreign enemy, who dared invade

The land of Russia and the Soviet State
Which he, Josef Dzugashvili, had made,
He persevered with cold and passionate hate.

The third was Roosevelt, a crippled man,
Confined to wheelchairs, yet the strongest one
As leader of the great democracy -
A modern Titan State, rebuilt anew
From that depression suffered recently,
When millions could not work. He was the man
Who took it on himself to cure those ills,
By government help, by fresh expenditure
To prime the pump, by lands reforrested,
New roads and aerodromes and dams,
Employment for the young, and easy loans.
He saw how much America preferred
To isolate herself from foreign wars;
How Woodrow Wilson's hopes were nullified
When Congress would not ratify his plans.
And yet he knew, despite the nation's will,
The world required America to play
A greater role in its new tragedy.
He recognised, in Churchill, one who stood,
Like Roosevelt himself, for liberty.
And so he led peacetime America
To countervail the growth of German power
By help to Britain, when she fought alone.
Likewise, he saw Japan's rapacity -
Her war in China, cruelty in Nanking,
And menaces to Western colonies
In south-east Asia and the Philippines.
His oil embargo forced upon Japan

The crucial choice of compromise or war.
Though he did not foresee the deadly blow
Of Yamamoto's planes at Oahu,
He welcomed the American response.
Wisely he said that Hitler should be first
To be defeated by the Allied powers,
Despite the arguments of Admiral King,
MacArthur, Nimetz, and those other men
Who bore the brunt of Japanese assault.
With consummate ease, the chair-bound Roosevelt
Controlled his party, and the means of power -
Appointments, money, Congressmen's regard,
And, of course, American people's votes,
Which offered him four terms as President.
Paralysis did not impede his will,
Nor stunt ambition, nor indeed reduce
His sense of duty to affairs of State.
He undertook, with Congress's consent,
The perilous journey to the conference -
Stalin would go no further than Teheran -
As once before his courage was displayed,
When, on a British battleship, he'd met
The English Monarch and, as Head of State,
Had stood upright, supported by his son.

The foremost question still was where to use
Their overwhelming power to most effect.
Churchill and Roosevelt did not concur
On when and how a second front should come.
Both now believed the Channel must be crossed
To bring the Wehrmacht to contest its hold
On northern France and entry to the Reich;

But British experts, led by Alanbrooke,
Saw much to gain in southern theatres,
For every German soldier there engaged
Would be diverted from the front in France.
Stalin's opinion was that 'Overlord' -
The Channel crossing - must not be delayed.
He promised, if no later than the Spring,
To launch the Russian armies' new campaign.
The Wehrmacht then would lie upon the rack
Which Hitler's war had made for Germany.

The Allied leaders recognised the role
Of Balkan partisans. Churchill believed
Substantial aid should go to Tito's force.
Stalin was cautious, prescient of the fact
That Tito was a rival Communist,
Unwilling to acknowledge Soviet power
Within the bounds of Jugoslavia.
It was agreed, however, to support,
With arms and agents, his guerilla war.
What then would Turkey do, if she observed
How Hitler's empire was in sharp decline?
What offers should be made of planes and aid,
Constructing aerodromes, or giving help
If neighbouring Bulgaria were fought?
Only Churchill vehemently spoke
Of winning Turkey to the Allied cause.
Stalin was sceptical, Roosevelt unmoved.
They thought of little but the crucial plan
To open up a second front in France.

Later discussions ranged beyond the field

Of how to end the Nazi tyranny.
Stalin announced that, when the task was done,
He would direct the might of Russian arms
Towards the east, against the 'Rising Sun',
Until Japan were similarly crushed.
What Stalin said of Poland gave less hope
Of harmony between the Allied powers.
Churchill proposed that Poland, as it were,
Should move towards the west by ceding land,
And from the Germans take a like extent.
The Russian leader based his country's claim
On ethnic reasons and the loss of land
When Poles invaded in the civil war.
The Polish problem would remain a thorn
To aggravate the wartime partnership.
Stalin spoke of vengeance for those crimes
Committed by the Germans in his land.
Never again must Germany invade
The Motherland of Russia, come what may!
For what had been destroyed his price was great:
Fifty thousand officers put to death,
The German people forced to till the ground,
Their State dismembered, industry removed.
Churchill was much offended by this plan:
War criminals alone should be arraigned
And Prussia dealt with harshly for its part
In Germany's aggression in two wars.
A new confederation, not unlike
The Habsburg Empire, was his own response
On how to reconstruct the German State.
All these ideas were openly discussed;
They raised deep questions, later to be faced

With victories won, and changing attitudes.

Just as the first triumvirate had claimed
To rule the Roman empire with the sword,
So now these three, possessed of half the world,
Proclaimed that they would beat the Fascist powers,
And settle once again the bounds of States.
Each one discounted his contentious cause -
The maintenance of British colonies,
Extension of the Marxist Soviets,
The USA's financial dominance.
Yet all acknowledged how united force
Alone could bring dictatorship to bay.
The end was evident: to rid the world
Of monstrous wickedness in mighty States;
The chosen means, the new triumvirate's.

26 The Siege of Leningrad

Nine hundred days - since Hitler had withheld
His northern armies close to Leningrad,
And told von Leeb to send his tanks away
To reinforce the crucial Moscow front -
The city on the Neva was besieged.
The Finns would not advance beyond the line

Which marked their border when the war began.
How then could German arms seize Leningrad,
Without a battle fought at heavy cost
In fighting street by street? Hitler preferred
The prize of Moscow and the rich Ukraine;
'Stop at artillery range', von Leeb was told.
They did not want three million mouths to feed.
Were Leningrad to yield, it would be razed,
Its people left to die in frozen wastes
Beyond the reach of Communism's rule,
Outside that city where its acolytes
Had stormed the Winter Palace long before.

Voroshilov's army held the front
From Lake Ladoga to the Finland Gulf,
But citizens enrolled, though ill-equipped,
To re-inforce the city's inner lines.
Thousands of women laboured to defend
The long perimeter with hurried works,
Like busy ants, in columns to and fro,
Digging long ditches to oppose the tanks,
Or hammering stakes, or building pyramids
In concrete rows, like blunted teeth of war.
Soviet warships in the western Gulf
Fired shells on German lines, and even guns
From one old battleship were brought ashore
To fire their salvoes from a muddy crest.
Before the trap had closed, the Russians moved
Machinery and workers to the east,
But soon the Moscow line was overrun,
And then the station at the town, Mga,
Then Schlusselburg on Lake Ladoga's shore,

Which barred the door on every route by land.
Supplies must come to Tikhvin, then by boat
Along the Volkhov River and by lake.
Within the city rations were reduced.

Germans had reached the Neva, whence they saw
The golden spire upon the Admiralty;
And, to the south, at Alexandroskaya,
They held the terminus for city trams.
Their guns, sporadically, sent swarms of shells
That killed at random people in the streets -
Women shopping, children still at play -
Or gutted factories, where workers strove
For Party targets now, at last, with will.
Incendiaries fell on warehouses of food,
Reducing even more the numbered days.

Onset of Winter did not bring relief,
Though German troops now suffered in the snow
For lack of proper clothing. Ice grew thick,
And on the lake the ships no longer brought
Their precious cargoes from the eastern shore.
Sledges crossed at first with small supplies,
Then lorry convoys came with food and fuel,
Unceasing columns, careless of the risk
Of blazing headlights, for more drivers died
When surface cracks engulfed them in the lake
Than from the diving Stukas' trail of bombs.
Exhausted drivers, haunted by the eyes
Of hungry men at Osinovets port,
Now struggled to complete two trips a day.
Starvation had begun. A million mouths
Could not be fed from frozen lorry loads.

Then Tikhvin fell, and trains no longer ran
To Novaya Ladogo on the lake.
As Leningraders died, the work began
To build a road far eastwards from the port.
Through forest pines and freezing glades of swamp,
A track was laid, of timber crudely cut,
Until, at last, the vital link was made
From rail to lake. On frozen bark and ice,
The endless lorries drove through bitter nights
And fleeting, sunless days.

Death in fearsome numbers walked the streets,
Where once the nobles trod, of Petersburg -
On Nevsky Prospekt and the Palace Square,
At Winter Palace and St Isaac's dome,
Still golden in the pallor of the time,
By the Bronze Horseman and the Kazan Church.
People lay where life deserted them,
Deep in snow, like gentle shrouds of peace.
Others, with sledges, dragged with painful steps
The bodies of their loved ones, wrapped in rags,
Often a swaddled baby briefly mourned
With frozen tears of grieving Leningrad.

Not all could long withstand the slow ordeal
Of hunger, cold and imminence of death,
Untouched by weakness and the claims of flesh.
Some stole, or cheated, or ignored the fate
Of those whose dwindling rations they could seize -
The elderly or weak who'd lived too long.
Yet most were proud to share their common fate,
Beyond the thought of Party Commissars,

Who forced a bare equality on all -
With extra rations for selected groups -
Even beyond that Russian fortitude
Which braved for centuries a slavish State.
Touched by humanity - perhaps by God -
They worked for all, and measured out their food,
Sustained by hope, by life's persistency.
"From the black dust, from death and ashes' place,
The garden will arise as once before.
So it will be. I believe in miracles.
You gave me that belief, my Leningrad."[15]

When Lake Ladoga thawed, ships sailed again,
Though, as supplies increased, the grasp of death
Reached out to take the famine's aftermath.
Yet men returned to clear the city streets,
Enduring still the cruel, erratic toll
From German guns and bombs unheralded.
Workshops opened, children went to school,
As Spring infused the life of Leningrad.
Again, on Nevsky Prospekt, plied the trams.

As Stalin's generals learnt to shift attacks
To points of weakness in the German line,
The scales of war tipped irrevocably.
Yet Hitler would not let his northern wing
Withdraw beside the Baltic littoral,
For fear that eastern Prussia would be lost.
With fierce attacks, the Soviet army fought
To drive the German spearhead from the lake.
Assaults from either side, at last, released
'The Corridor of Death' from German hands.

The siege had ended; Leningrad alone
Had faced the fate of medieval towns:
Months of isolation and the death,
By famine and disease, of multitudes.
Yet in black dust, where death and ashes hid,
The garden of St Peter grew unbid.

27 Monte Cassino

Allied advance was slow in Italy:
Across the hills and rocky mountain spine
Soldiers laboured, stopped by clinging mud,
Or transverse rivers swollen by the rain.
In villages and towns the roads were blocked
By German demolitions, which destroyed
The street facades to make up tumbled heaps
Of dirty stones and yellow stucco dust.
Bulldozers heaved the rubble to the side,
And flattened paths by roofless, ruined homes.
Men were surprised by cunning booby-traps,
Or lost a limb from stepping on a mine,
Though tenuous routes were marked with coloured tape
And notices proclaiming sudden death.
Through vacant windows, sniper bullets flew
To kill an officer or leading man
Who turned a corner first, or raised his head

Before his men broke cover at a run.
Though under fire, the sappers built pontoons -
Flimsy for infantry, sturdier for tanks -
Like Irish navvies, labouring with spades
To smooth the banks, whilst German marksmen aimed,
And neatly shot a few unfortunates.
At major obstacles, like mountain crests,
The Wehrmacht waited, till the Allied plans
Were well matured to launch a grand attack,
And then withdrew to hold another line.

As Autumn tinged the trees and unkempt vines,
And soaked the fields where mules and cattle lay,
Slaughtered by retreating soldiery,
The Allied hopes of occupying Rome
Before the Winter foundered in the rain.
So Alanbrooke proposed another plan -
Invasion from the sea at Anzio,
To outflank German lines and join hands
With Allied spearheads driving from the south
To cut off enemy units in retreat.

The German army, ordered to stand fast
While south of Rome, and hold the Allies there -
Indefinitely, by Hitler's express will -
Prepared to man a new defensive line,
Which crossed the rugged hills and Apennines
From where the Garigliano reached the sea,
Until it met the Adriatic coast.
The Führer ordered 'fight for every yard'.
Accordingly, with German thoroughness,
They fortified the winding Gustav Line:

Each pass concealed a well-positioned gun;
Houses were strong-points, roads and pathways mined;
Each knoll a covert observation post;
Each farm a lager, hiding Tiger tanks
Or training *Nebelwerfers* on a point
Of Allied troops' advance; each bridge was blown;
Each ford made hazardous by hidden guns.
Reserves stood ready for an Allied breach,
To counter it with ardent promptitude.

The ex-Luftwaffe general, Kesselring,
Had studied hard to close the door on Rome
And keep the north of Italy intact.
The Gustav Line now locked and barred the way.
Its pivot was Cassino, where there stood,
Upon a spur, the ancient monastery.
The road to Rome, Route 6, ran down below,
Beneath precipitous hills and through the town,
Commanded by the German guns above.
In this defile the war in Italy
Would blaze like tinder in a narrow stove.

Yet first the Winter tested soldiers' nerves,
As armies shivered in the driven snow
That froze on crevasses and windy peaks
Above the shining threads of silver streams.
German paratroops, American G.I.s,
British survivors of the desert war,
French from Morocco, General Anders' Poles,
New Zealanders, and Gurkhas from the East:
Most were no more the youthful innocents
Of early battles, shocked by sudden death,

But hardened veterans, whose wary eyes
Regarded coolly each day's chance of life,
Of death, of wounding, glory or disgrace.
They oiled their guns and honed their bayonets well,
Knowing the outcome of a shot or stab
Depended on the instant circumstance.
They knew the urgent questions at the start:
"How far would creeping barrages advance?
What was the boundary for some platoon?
Should they proceed beyond a captured wood?
What time would ammunition be obtained?
Were rations quite enough for several days?"[16]
They knew the quiet, preceding an attack,
Before the roar of guns that blasted shells
Above their heads into oblivion,
When faces were remembered from the past
Of unreal families, wives of long ago,
Children unseen, and ageing parents dead.

It proved impossible to cross the hills
And steep ravines, advancing under fire,
To outflank Monte Cassino from the north,
And so the first attack was soon repulsed,
With heavy casualties; and yet it drew
The eyes of Germans off the western shore,
Where, from the sea, a new assault would come.

And thus, at Anzio, the troops debarked
With little opposition for some days.
The road to Rome was open, but ignored.
No Rommel, nor a Patton, seized the chance
Of sudden glory offered briefly there.

They did as even Hannibal had done,
Neglecting, after Cannae, to advance
And gather up the greatest prize of all.
Whilst Kesselring had brilliantly prepared
His new reserves, entrained from further north -
Each unit knew what special routes to use
And promptly could deploy for any threat -
The Allied leaders dallied cautiously:
No break-out from the bridgehead was prepared
Till all was rendered absolutely safe.
Both men and trucks accumulated there.
When Churchill heard of this, he was enraged:
"We should have hurled a wildcat on the shore;
But all we'd got was but a stranded whale!"[17]
And when, at last, some inland probes were made,
German defence was more than adequate.
The bridgehead was sealed off; a cresting wave
Had fallen on the sand and seeped away.
Hitler was enthused by this success.
If such a landing were to be repulsed,
What precedent would all the world observe!
How would the Allies dare to land in France
Against the fortified Atlantic Wall?
What would the Russians think of second fronts?
He ordered thus a drive to reach the coast.

From distant heights artillery disgorged
A flux of steel on beaches crammed with men.
Then columns, led by *Panzers*, filled the roads,
With clinging troops upon the Tiger tanks.
But Allied marksmen picked them off like flies,
And others, at the trenches, only died

245

In vain attempts upon the bayonet frise;
While off-shore salvoes hit the armour, too,
And struck the waiting infantry reserves.
The counter stroke was spoiled, so Kesselring
Acknowledging defeat, withdrew once more
His shattered remnants to the starting line.

Though Hitler fumed and ordered fresh attacks,
His generals knew the bridgehead was secured.
Yet still they might contain it, if the Line
That stretched across the Apennines were held.
And stalemate there in Italy could balk
The Allied plans to threaten Germany.
Success or failure turned upon the hinge
Of granite rock at Mount Cassino's spur.
Hermann Goering's Wehrmacht paratroops
Lay patiently in stony dugouts there,
Defending now what saintly Benedict
Had built against the violence of his times.

Freyberg's New Zealanders, of desert fame,
Began a new attack against the Hill.
Although the German general had forborne -
From some religious conscience not yet lost
Amidst the overweening claims of war -
From sending his rough paratroopers in
To occupy Cassino monastery,
Freyberg himself, observing how the walls
Could sweep his men with close-directed fire,
Demanded that the monastery be bombed.
Monks and holy treasures had been sent,
By German order, down below the Hill,

And warning leaflets fell from Allied planes.
At Alexander's order bombers came,
Diverted from strategic tasks afar,
On factories at Milan, or in the Reich,
And smote apart the venerated stones.
No longer bound by scruples, German troops
Found excellent cover on the ruined crest,
Where rubble lay on centuries of prayer.

Before the next attack upon the Hill,
British gunners pulverised the ground
With myriads of shells, and once again
The Allied aircraft dropped their tons of bombs
Within the precincts, now where Germans hid.
Earth shook as from the hammer blows of Thor;
Dark clouds of smoke obscured the wintry sun.
Could life outlive such paroxysmal blows,
Stunning each sense, confounding nerve and brain?
Yet, clinging to the earth, survivors stayed,
Their dead and wounded laid within the crypt,
Spirit undaunted, ready to endure
The next ordeal, an infantry attack,
Outflanking movements, even, at the last,
What every soldier feared, encirclement.

Whilst battle raged within Cassino town,
Through which the crucial Roman highway ran,
New Zealanders and Gurkhas struggled up
The coarse terrain of Monastery Hill.
Each yard of progress made from rock to rock
Came under fire from quick-repeating guns,
Small arms or rifles. Then, with cover found,

The bursts of mortar fire tormented still
The gasping figures crouched behind a stone,
Or in a crater on the pock-marked slopes.

Meanwhile the ruined streets inside the town
Echoed the storm that raged so close above.
A yellow fog of smoke-screens, tinged with dust,
Filtered within the broken, roofless homes,
Where companies of soldiers waited long
In preparation for the next assault:
Waiting till a distant, crackling voice
Came through the earphones, saying 'hold' or 'move',
With time to plug a freshly bleeding wound,
Or close the eyelids of a comrade lost;
Waiting for the sharp, laconic words
That sent some men, obedient, to die;
Waiting to cross a street, with bayonets fixed,
And lob grenades through empty window frames.
This grenadier, now blinded or convulsed,
Perhaps was one they'd heard across the street
Last night in warfare's momentary lapse,
Singing their favourite song from Africa,
Which Desert Rats had shared with Rommel's men;
Or one who'd whispered over no-man's land
To Tommies he'd forgotten how to hate -
His old opponents in the noble art
Of killing men for some outmoded cause.

A Gurkha company on slopes above
Had reached a prominence called Hangman's Hill.
Elsewhere they faltered, handicapped by rain
That fell in torrents, turning slopes to mud,

And by relentless wounding German fire.
The Gurkhas stayed, high on their threatened perch.
Under a Red Cross flag, some orderlies,
Led by a doctor, climbed to Hangman's Hill.
A German post, observing, sent them on
To seek permission from a near H.Q.,
From where they went to bring the wounded down.
A second trip was made, one more refused;
But no-one fired from Monastery Hill,
When, for the third time, stretchers-bearers climbed.
A few days later Freyberg ordered down
The brave survivors, hungry, tired and cold.

On Monte Trecchio the British looked
Across the Rapido valley at the town,
Its ruined buildings like some aged teeth,
And at the cratered slopes that rose behind,
Towards the crown of rubble on the crest.
Artillery was trained on Highway 6,
To enfilade the road which brought supplies
To long beleagured German paratroops.
Few trucks drove down by day, but in the night
The sound of movement echoed through the hills,
And British sentries heard familiar words:
German orders, challenges and oaths.
And as each sunset tinged the tarmac strip,
An ambulance, which flaunted on its roof
The Red Cross banner, drove beneath the Hill,
Stopped briefly and returned, beneath the guns
Of men who feared some enemy deceit.
Mount Trecchio itself was under fire,
Which raked its slopes at frequent intervals.

Binoculars were hooded to avoid
The beams of sun that gave their post away
And brought a sudden hail of German shells.

Alexander redeployed his force:
Americans were stationed in the south,
French, under General Juin, on their right,
The British and Canadians facing down
The Liri valley and the road to Rome,
And, in the north, beside Cassino town,
The valiant Poles, whose task would be to reach
Cassino's peak across the perilous hills.
The Germans now were weaker than before,
From casualties and Kesselring's command
To hold reserves against the threat to Rome
From Anzio, or from a further bid
To land beyond the Tiber's estuary.

A massive barrage signalled the assault.
Quickly the French made headway in the south,
Their mountain troops advancing hill by hill,
Until they reached the Liri's winding stream
And, turning westwards, drove the Germans back
Towards the Allied bridgehead. By their stroke,
A first great breach was opened in the Line.
Then British gunfire carpeted the land
In morning mist below Cassino Hill,
As infantry crept forward, forced to ground
By chattering *Schmeissers*, till a wireless call
Brought answering fire that silenced every one.
Through olive groves and woodland they advanced,
Until delayed upon a shallow ridge

By side machine gun fire from German tanks,
Where British Shermans stood opposing them.
Foot soldiers, short of cover, lay confused,
Frustrated, till a British Fusilier
Ran forward where the leading Tiger stood
And, as its guns were turning, fired one shot,
A Piat round, which blew the tank apart.
Knocked down by blast, he stood once more and fired.
A second tank withdrew; the way was clear.
Now eagerly they pressed through standing corn,
Until, at last, the fatal road was reached,
The way to Rome for which the toll was paid
In sacred stones and yet more precious lives.

Though first repulsed, the Poles were not deterred
By scathing fire that thinned their forward lines
As they traversed each valley floor and height,
Taking each post by storm or hand grenade.
They clambered up the final barren yards
And found, upon the summit - emptiness!
The Germans had withdrawn, leaving there
Amongst the ruins on the holy hill
That peace which had so long attended it.
As for the Poles, of them it would be said:
They died for freedom, gave their souls to God,
Their bodies to the earth of Italy,
But, to their native land, their Polish hearts.

From Anzio a break-out had begun,
With two objectives: firstly, to engulf
The Wehrmacht as it left the Gustav Line,
And, secondly, to take the capital,
Erstwhile the seat of Fascist government,

But still the Holy City to the world.
Allied power, on land and in the air,
Was now too strong for Kesselring to match.
His troops drew back, and though they made a stand
At Terracina and the Alban hills,
Could not contain the American advance.

In London, Winston Churchill, overjoyed
To hear Cassino's capture, strongly urged
That Allied forces should ensure they caught
The greatest number of the German force,
The key to which was sealing off Route 6;
But token units only were despatched
By General Clark to where the highway ran.
The town of Valmontone was not seized,
And Germans hurried through to form new lines
Prepared upon the northern side of Rome.
Clark had his own reward, and lead his men
To rapturous welcome in the Roman streets,
From those who'd welcomed Mussolini there,
Like 'blocks and stones and worse than senseless things'[18].
Yet Rome was taken, with slight damage done
To ancient buildings and great works of art.
For, unlike Hitler, Kesselring decreed
That Rome would not be fought for street by street.

An Allied army, seven nations strong,
Had turned the key and heaved aside the door
Of Hitler's line, defended at all cost.
But German soldiers shared the honour there,
For, on Cassino's slopes, they had not flinched
Before the might of air power, and the thrust

Of four successive infantry attacks.
Whence such intransigence? Was it their oath -
Obedience to Fuhrer to the death -
Or was it pride as soldiers, or their bond
To one another as *'ein Kamerad'*,
Or was it love of Fatherland and home,
Or duty to oneself as absolute?
Yet, in the cruel nobility of war,
At Mount Cassino every nation found
That same devotion on a common ground.

28 Tito's Partisans

Exploding bombs on Belgrade's stricken streets
Had mocked the Führer's arrogant pretence
That Nazi soldiers needed to restore
The peace and order of the Balkan States.
To intervene against the stubborn Greeks
And save the Duce's forces from defeat
Were cause enough. Nor had he brooked delay,
Whilst German troops stood poised along the Bug,
Prepared for blitzkrieg on the Russian steppes.
Though young King Peter flew to English shores,
His army was defeated, and the vice
Of Nazi government tightened on that land
Where for so long the hated Turks had ruled.
Pride had not fled the hearts of Jugoslavs.
Around Mihailovic an army grew
Of Serbian peasants loyal to the king,
Fighting from the hills a war of stealth.

Contemptuous of Slavs, the Wehrmacht killed
A hundred for each German soldier lost.
With peasant families shot, their houses burned,
And villages erased in vacant fields,
Mihailovic gave way, like Charles de Gaulle,
And held his army impotent in camps.

Not so the fierce resistance of those men
Embittered by an ancient poverty
And new inspired by Communist ideals.
Uncertain, till the flames of war had lit
The skies of Russia, where their loyalties lay,
The partisans of Tito now took arms.
No cruelty would deter them; they would fight
To drive invaders from their native soil
And free the land from exploitation's toll,
To see a new society built with work,
Unfettered by false claims on surplus wealth.
Their leader, Tito, organised their zeal
With party discipline and firm control
Of scattered units in the western hills.
Sabotage of trains, of bridges, roads,
Sudden attacks upon outnumbered men -
Stragglers, gun-posts, foraging patrols -
Ambushes, sniping, blowing up of dumps:
By such guerilla war the German foe
Was harassed without pause, until he chose
To hold the strong-points only - junctions, towns
And places fortified - whilst Tito's men
Took refuge in the hills and won support
From Bosnian peasants, who supplied their food.

In reprisal hostages were killed,
Including Cetniks of Mihailovic.
The partisans killed prisoners in response,
With gun or knife as circumstance required.
A cruel dilemma faced Mihailovic:
Should Communists, opponents of the king,
Hold all to ransom, letting Cetniks die,
For their own callous ends? He compromised;
If he was not molested in the hills,
He would inform the Wehrmacht in return
Of partisan encampments. Thus there grew
A bitter breach within the Jugoslavs.

Italy's invasion brought to light
The Balkan struggle and its new import,
As Allied armies on the further shore
Attacked the common Fascist enemy.
Eager for fresh offensives, Churchill saw
The scope of Slav resistance, and foretold
That more divisions forced to intervene
Meant fewer for the Wehrmacht to dispose
Against the Allied fronts. Italian troops
Might even turn, in Jugoslavia,
Upon their allies, for the Axis cause
Had brought disaster to the Duce's arms
In every theatre where Italians fought.
But whom should Britain help - Mihailovic,
And Cetniks who acknowledged still their king,
Or Tito's rebels, zealous to achieve
A Marxist government under Moscow's sway?
At Churchill's orders men were sent to judge
The state of play within the Balkan war.

They dropped by night in rebel-held domain,
And signalled back to London what they'd learned.
For Winston Churchill, one decisive end -
To wipe out Nazi rule in every land -
O'errode all others; hence he did not flinch
At firm alliance with the Soviets,
And did not now condone the Cetnik cause,
For all his due respect for monarchy.
Tito alone fought unreservedly;
Therefore to him was proferred Churchill's hand.

Five times Wehrmacht offensives took their crop
Of partisan guerillas. Limestone hills,
As gaunt as hungry flesh, gave scant support.
Yet in the caves, in gorges deep with trees,
The rebels hid, accumulating guns,
Nursing their wounded, formulating plans.
Many times they broke encirclement -
As at Drvar, when German guns had fired
Upon the cave where Tito was ensconced,
Who climbed a cleft before the soldiers came.
They shot the Drvar villagers instead,
Whose rotting bodies lay untended there.
Each time the rebels infiltrated through,
By fording rivers, hiding until night,
Scaling the icy crags above a pass,
And using cover like a hunted beast,
Before regrouping for a rapid march
To safer zones. Often the bravest died;
Those like Sava Kovacevic, shot down
Beside a German strong-point in the hills,
Who'd charged Italian tanks with furious hate,

And shouted his commands from mountain tops
To Montenegrin peasants like himself -
Heroic, violent, rash, immoderate -
And now a crumpled body by the road.

Others, like Djilas, facing constant death,
Fought on as Communists, but in their dreams
Recalled their native images of Christ.
Tito himself, who when the war began
Commanded those who wavered to be shot,
Had trained in Moscow, yet remained less loyal
To Stalin's will than to his country's needs.
Resolute and rational, always sure
To keep his army safe in Party hands,
He never lost compassion for his men,
Hating to see the wounded left in caves,
Even with the lives of all at stake.

Along the Dalmatian coast, a base at Vis
Brought British help by plane or submarine.
Here Tito met to reconsider plans,
Watching across a strip of azure sea
The iron-grey hills, which hid the crimes of war
And horrors of an internecine strife,
Where Croat Ustasi destroyed with fire
The villages of Orthodox belief,
Where Cetniks slaughtered Moslems in return,
And Axis forces fought the partisans
With mutual cruelty. As war returned
To ancient savagery, the throats were slit
Of peasants, children, hostages alike.
Others were shot, machine-gunned on their knees,

Or clubbed with rifle butts, or drowned in streams.
Yet rules of conflict, made in time of peace,
Were not ignored by every soldier there.
Mihailovic helped Allied troops escape;
Safe passes were observed when Djilas went
To parley with some German officers;
And British agents - Deakin and MacLean
And Randolph Churchill, Winston's daring son -
Tried hard to end the strife till war was won.

29 The Defence of India

Too far across the broad Pacific seas
The Japanese perimeter now stretched.
Could Nippon troops defend their sprawling realm?
Yet, on the Chinese mainland, they advanced,
Threatening airfields built by Chiang Kai-Shek,
Where U.S. planes that flew across 'the Hump'
Brought to his armies manifold supplies.
And further west, in Burma, plans were laid
For Kawabe to launch a grand assault
On Britain's army, stationed in the hills
Beyond the Chindwin on the Imphal plain.
Success would clear the route to India,
Where disaffected millions might rebel
And hail the empire of the Rising Sun,
Once liberated from the British Raj.
Then, too, the Japanese could reach the source

Of those supplies that succoured Chiang Kai-Shek,
For U.S. flights to bases in Yunnan
Began from Burmese airfields near Ledo.
Hopes of glory hung on victory there:
To set aggressive war once more ablaze,
And on the ruined empires of the West
Create a vast dominion of Shinto,
From Hindustan to China's ancient wall,
Ruled by the *samurais'* avenging sword.

The British Fourteenth Army under Slim
Had been rebuilt, though humbled by defeat.
The Arakan offensive was renewed,
And, in the jungle, Japanese patrols
Now met a skilled, tenacious enemy.
Even before he knew Kawabe's plan,
Commander Slim proposed to bring about
A major conflict, hoping to destroy
Kawabe's force before the British moved
To occupy the colony again.
To fight a battle on the Chindwin's banks
Endangered his supply from India;
Therefore he chose an orderly retreat
To draw the Japanese upon Imphal,
Where terrain and supply lines favoured him.
For, like Montgomery, he preferred to fight
On ground of his own choosing, even if,
Within the interim, he must endure
The taunts of weakness.

On native boats and rafts of fresh-cut logs
Kawabe's soldiers crossed the Chindwin flood.

Across the valley, climbing to the hills,
Into the jungle, thick with teak and pine,
His infantry outflanked the scattered posts
Of British units ready to withdraw.
With bayonet and grenade on jungle paths,
Or clearings where the bamboo clusters hid
A crouching soldier or a bleeding corpse,
A hundred petty actions took their toll
By killing first the foolhardy and brave,
And burdening with wounded those unscathed.
Surrounded road-blocks waited for relief.
Would fresh reserves from Imphal get to them
Before they glimpsed below them on the road
The barrels of Kawabe's mobile guns,
Hawled up by mules from Chindwin's muddy banks?
'Advance through the hills, like a ball of fire!'[19]
Kawabe's troops were ordered at the start.
Those who faltered met dishonoured death
Beneath the sword blow of an officer.
Phlegmatic British yielded post by post,
Withdrawing slowly, fighting off attacks
With bayonet, kukri, bullet and grenade,
Indians, English, Gurkhas side by side.

North of Imphal, beyond the Somra Hills,
General Sato threatened to engulf
The British base, Kohima, on the route
To where the railroad lay at Dimapur,
The door to India, through which supplies
Reached Fourteenth Army. Eastwards railtracks ran
To Ledo's airfields, vital for 'the Hump'.
Were Dimapur to fall to Japanese,

The British host in Burma would be lost,
Strangled at source, and left to wither there,
Like monsoon forest in the tropic heat
Awaiting rain that nevermore would come.
Succour to China from the hardy crews
Who flew Dakotas unremittingly
Would be withdrawn. All Asia then would see
The threatening shadow from the Rising Sun.
Slim's forces could not garrison both towns:
He chose to reinforce Kohima ridge.
Had General Sato seized this golden chance
To send his major force across the hills,
Skirting the road, and enter Dimapur,
He would have been the toast of Tokio.
But Sato was no Rommel: one brigade
Was sent to cut the road. His army then
Invested, from all sides, Kohima town.

Upon the ridge the British held a line
In earshot of the leading enemy.
With clubs and knives they fought them, hand to hand,
Or charged machine-gun posts behind grenades,
Or listened, at the dead of night, for steps,
And comforted the wounded where they lay
Protected by a single line of men
From frenzied butchery. Supplies were short,
Especially water from the only spring;
So aircraft flew through automatic fire
At tree-top height to drop inflated tires.
Upon the Governor's bungalow and land,
Where once a gentle lawn and garden grew
Of rhododendron ringed around with pine,

The shells descended, burning timber black;
Defiantly one chimney stood intact.
Grenades were lobbed across the tennis court.

Often at night a fervent whisper came
In imitation of a British voice,
'Hey, Johnny, let me through, the Japs are here'[20].
No answer came, nor any shot returned
When snipers in the trees fired down below.
At heavy cost the British troops had learned
To recognise these tricks to make them shoot.
No more did they reveal where whole platoons
Lay hid in dark; they waited now to hear
The mortar shells that presaged an attack.
Then only, on fixed lines, a hail of steel
Was fired along a boundary or hedge,
And Bren guns clattered at each moving form,
And boxes of grenades were emptied fast
By hasty fingers, clawing at the pins.
Buildings caught fire, escaping men were shot,
Some blazing still and screaming in the mud.
Unburied bodies lay profusely there.
Within the British lines the wounded men,
Unable to be sorted from the dead,
Had visits from the padre, and from those
Who crawled with food and tea to front-line troops
To fill the mess tins thrust with muddy hands.
Surrounded for ten days, Kohima fought,
Before fresh troops broke through from Dimapur.
But even when the walking wounded left,
The Nippon snipers shot a handful dead.

Whilst Slim controlled, with cool and rational skill
Defensive conflict on the Imphal plain,
Planning a counterstroke when time was ripe,
A rash, offensive leader had resolved
To take the battle to the Japanese.
Orde Wingate had impressed Churchill himself
With plans to fight behind the enemy,
Concealed in jungle and supplied by air.
His men, the Chindits, trained to long survive
The fearful hardships of a jungle war -
Exhaustion, ambush, shortages, disease -
Were flown to bases near the town, Indaw.
Not all the square-winged gliders safely reached
The landing strips, rough cut in forest glades;
Some crashed on hillsides with their towing planes,
Or broke apart on tree stumps, or capsized,
Spilling out men and mules in death or pain.
But Chindit operations soon began,
Building an airstrip, marching to attack
Supply dumps, railways, roads, with two designs:
To handicap Kawabe as he fought
Across the Chindwin in the western hills,
And ease the way for Stilwell's Chinese force
To reach Myitkyina and safeguard the road
Projected to be built into Yunnan.

Through dank and tawny forest, dark by day
Beneath a patchwork canopy of leaves,
Amid the mingled sounds of wild fowl, grouse,
Of cautious deer and clumsy buffaloes,
Wingate's columns stubbornly patrolled,
Fearful of a leopard's sudden spring

And vipers hidden in the jungle grass.
Collecting units from their rearward troops,
The Japanese attacked the Chindit camps,
But hundreds fell to kukri and grenade.
Thirty Zeros, diving on 'Broadway' base,
To their amazement met a Spitfire flight,
Which, stationed on the strip, shot down fifteen.

But, fast upon this victory, Orde Wingate -
Creative, ruthless, ready to ignore
Superior orders to attain his ends,
Committed to his men, as they to him -
Crashed on a forest hillside near Imphal.
His inspiration, burning strong, was doused;
But, under his successor, Chindit men,
Who stung the Japanese with frequent raids
On their interior lines and army camps,
Confirmed what Slim had earlier believed:
That man for man the British could outfight
Kawabe's army, and no longer fear
That only Nippon soldiers could endure
The brutal dangers of a jungle war.

Upon Imphal Kawabe's army closed,
Through mountain country, where each wooded ridge
Hid his platoons or light artillery,
Along the spokes of roads towards the hub,
Outflanking road-blocks, rushing them at night;
Past Mao Sonsang, Litan, Potsangbam,
(Called 'Pots and Pans' by British infantry).
Then with a sudden hook on jungle tracks,
They cut the vital path to Bishenpur

Descending from the railhead at Silchar.
Three Nippon soldiers crept past British guards
Above the gorge at Milestone 51
To set explosives on the hanging bridge.
One jumped, the others died when it blew up.
In tree-filled nullahs high on knife-edge crests,
Foot-soldiers met in contest to the death.
Along the roads and tangled, slimy paths,
Tanks clambered forward, often with a man
Exposed above the turret, or on foot,
To guide the way, though vulnerable to fire.

Within Imphal, Lieutenant-General Scoones
Sat in Headquarters, playing spider king,
Reading reports from every compass point,
Successes, set-backs, cries to reinforce,
Demands for ammunition or for planes,
Appeals to move the wounded: every one
Requiring his decision urgently.
Thousands of minor actions slowly stemmed
The frantic drive of ardent Japanese.
Despite their losses, often without hope,
They flung themselves upon unyielding troops.
For British soldiers under Slim's command
No longer did the word 'invincible'
Make of their enemy a dreaded foe.
He could be stopped, outfought and often killed,
Like any other troops, though he alone
Would not surrender, and, when wounded, lay
In wait for soldiers taking him for dead.

Along Kohima ridge, above the town,
On wooded slopes made slippery by rain,
Hidden in bunkers, Japanese remained.
Slim did not hurry; he would reinforce,
With troops from India now freely sent
By rail to Dimapur. Had he not seen
The waves of conquest rise, and wash against
The walls of Hindustan, in these cruel hills
Where Naga tribesmen lived, outside of time
In harsh simplicity? Now at full flood
The tide of war would ebb. A counterstroke,
Conceived before, was pregnant in his mind,
Well nourished by the passion of defeat,
Swelling whilst the furious battle raged
To hold the line Kohima to Imphal.
Gurkhas, Punjabis, British, all could feel
The pulse of battle seething in their blood,
As high on Garrison hill they gathered strength
To drive their foe beyond the facing ridge.

With heavy casualties, the first attacks
Upon the high extremities were held.
Regrouping in the centre, they advanced,
Above the Governor's ruined residence,
Towards Jail hill and Kuki Piquet crest.
Maelstroms of shells and bombs from Hurricanes
Made scant impression on the Japanese,
Fast in their bunkers, waiting for the call
To man the loophole guns and fling grenades.
Charging uphill, slipping on muddy banks,
Reduced by sniper and machine-gun fire,
Some British soldiers reached the bunker mouths.

They signalled back for tanks, which churned their way
To point-blank distance, and with solid shot
Smashed open concrete walls. No Japanese
Raised flags of white or held their arms aloft.
Pole charges thrust through loopholes, bayonets,
Grenades and kukris slaughtered those alive.
From Naga village down to Big Tree hill,
Along Kohima ridge, the Japs withdrew.
No counter movements flung the British back,
For Sato's men, exhausted in defeat,
Were now disorganised. Only the will
To follow every order held at bay
Disintegration and the rapid loss
Of all they'd won beyond the Chindwin stream.

This was not war to reinstate the power
Of British landlords and imperial sway,
Of great monopolies by land and sea,
Of moneylenders, Indian and Chinese,
Who'd ruined Burmese peasants with their loans.
For this was conflict 'gainst a brutal caste,
Whose cruelties o'erstepped the bounds of war
And brought men to their knees, like animals -
Chinese civilians slaughtered in Nanking,
Wounded soldiers crudely bayoneted,
Allied prisoners overworked to death,
Weakened by beatings, hunger or disease -
A caste, misnamed 'bushido' warriors,
Whose sad misrule destroyed the writ of law
Throughout East Asia and their native land
And mocked their claim to 'co-prosperity'.
To put an end to their atrocities,

The Fourteenth Army's men of varied race
Had fought and died beneath the British flag
In Burmese forests and on Imphal plain.
'When you go home, tell them of us and say,
For their tomorrow, we gave our today.'[21]

30 The Normandy Invasion

The western shores of France would witness now
A clash of arms decisive in the war.
Plans to invade the long Atlantic Wall
Were now complete. A million Allied soldiers,
Brought by sea from southern English ports,
Would land in Normandy. For beaches there
Were not so fortified as near Calais,
Where Wehrmacht soldiers watched the hazy line
Of English cliff-tops, white against the sky,
And searched the narrow sea for hostile ships.
Indeed, the British, masters of deceit,
Elaborated schemes to feign attack,
With decoy camps and military gear,
Built in the eastern counties opposite.

Hitler himself had glimpsed the real intent
To land in Normandy; not so his Staff,
Whose expert judgment weighed the evidence
Of maps, logistics, distances and time.
They would ensure an army was retained
In Pas de Calais, even when the blow
Was struck on Norman beaches far away.
Allied aircraft reinforced the trick,
By flying missions northwards of the Seine
To bomb communications and supplies
As heavily as over Normandy.

Rommel, however, ordered to prepare
A strategy against the second front,
Strengthened defences everywhere he could.
Along the coast from Cherbourg to Le Havre
Gun sitings were improved, beach obstacles
Of wire and steel enlarged, and minefields laid
At sea for ships and on the treacherous sand.
His enemy, Montgomery, in command
Of Allied armies set to land in France,
Insisted on a wide attacking front:
Of British and Canadians to the east,
Americans as far as Cotentin.
'Crocodiles' with flails for exploding mines,
Amphibious tanks, conventional armour,
Rations, arms and men: all were assembled,
Awaiting word to send them into France.
At Eisenhower's command they would depart.

Rain, wind and heavy waves foreboded ill,
For landings on an open beach required

A steady sea and air supremacy.
Already men were sealed in hulls of ships,
Communication strictly monitored,
The southern coast a war exclusion zone;
Already coded poems had been sent
To French Resistance groups in Normandy;
Already men were seasick in the boats.
But Eisenhower enjoined a day's delay -
Any more would miss the favourable tide
And risk the loss of crucial secrecy.

Then, suddenly, the fickle weather changed.
With brighter skies, but still in heavy seas,
The vast armada left its friendly coast
To face a continent of German arms.
Were this to fail, the Nazis would be free
To hurl against the Russians in the east
A re-united Wehrmacht, undeterred
By ancient fears of war on double fronts.
All those embarked, bound up in coops of steel
That tossed like apples on unresting sea,
Knew this significance. In such a task
Their personal trepidation had no place,
Which eased the fear of battle wounds and death.
Though some were eager to set foot ashore
And meet an enemy, whose name alone
Had long confronted them, others who'd fought
In Italy, North Africa or France
Were circumspect, recalling now the fierce,
Unyielding fire of German arms, friends lost,
The slow discomfort of the battlefield,
And sudden havoc, fraught with blood and pain.

Against the moonlit sky they watched the ranks
Of droning aircraft, turning soon to bomb
The German installations on the coast.
Already there the flash and smoke of shells
Coloured the Summer night with Vulcan shades,
As, eight miles from the shore, the naval guns
Discharged their carillons of thunderous fire.

Deep-down in concrete bunkers Germans lay,
Surprised, bewildered. Was this not a time
When weather forecasts ruled invasion out?
Was this a hoax to draw across the Seine
The Fifteenth Army, waiting to the north?
Rommel himself was home in Germany,
Asking the Führer vainly for command
Of all the *Panzers* held in Normandy,
And bringing to his wife a birthday gift -
Parisian shoes - the last she would receive.
Von Rundstedt, in command in northern France,
Believed in deep defence, with tank reserves
To strike an Allied bridgehead, once contained;
But Rommel thought the *Panzers* should respond
With swift decisive thrusts against the shore
To drive invaders back into the sea.
Yet neither plan would Hitler authorise.
So Wehrmacht soldiers, dedicated, brave,
Would be betrayed by such uncertainties.

Meanwhile, by night, the airborne troops had struck.
Landing by glider, only yards adrift,
The British seized the bridges on the Orne,
And batteries at Merville, placed to fire

In enfilade along the landing beach.
Guarding thus the precious bridging points
Against a German thrust across the Dives,
They waited, resolute, for prompt relief
From forces due to land near Ouistreham.
Westwards, past the dunes of 'Utah' beach,
The American drop was scattered by the wind.
Men drowned at sea; some fell in flooded land.
Survivors fought alone for many hours,
Deprived of leadership and heavy arms.

Yet 'gainst severe attack, St Mere Eglise,
A vital cross-roads, was securely held.
At Pointe du Hoc, the perilous cliffs were scaled
By US Rangers, ordered to destroy
A battery that fired on 'Omaha'.

In early daylight, grey beneath the cloud,
The British and Canadians touched land.
On 'Gold', 'Juno' and 'Sword', their troops debarked,
Along with 'crocodiles' to clear the mines
And engineers to cut through steel and wire.
Men sank offshore, beset by heavy kit,
And German fire killed others on the beach.
The wounded crawled beneath a dune or wall,
Or lay neglected, bleeding in the sand.
But German soldiers were outnumbered there,
And shaken by bombardments earlier.
The esplanade was seized, and progress made
A few miles inland, half the way to Caen.
Only a brief attack by Panzer troops
Towards Lion-sur-Mer posed any threat

To split the bridgehead; so, when Germans saw
New flights of gliders land, and Firefly tanks
Advancing in their path, they hastened back.
Would Rommel have fought on, despite such odds?

At 'Omaha' Americans were launched
Too far from shore in pitching landing craft.
Their engineers, cut down by withering fire,
Could not destroy beach obstacles and mines.
Unwisely US planners had refused
The offer made of British armour flails,
Nor had bombardment from the sea and air
Made much impression on the concrete line
Of German placements on the louring cliffs.
A field division, training near the sea,
Had reinforced the ailing units there.
Well-sited *Spandaus* fired at landing ramps,
As metal doors unfurled, disgorging men,
Who struggled forward, waist-deep in the tide.
Showers of bullets hit them as they ran,
Breaking limbs and ripping open flesh,
Till heaps of bodies lay in torment there,
Dead and dying, maimed, eviscerate,
Shallow wavelets mingling with their blood.
Lighters, chockful with ammunition stores,
Exploded in great galaxies of fire.
Flame-throwing soldiers, canisters alight,
Were burnt like torches, writhing in the sea,
Anticipating thus their victims' pain.
Survivors hid behind beach obstacles,
Or, flattened on the sand, expected death.

The bravest ran for shelter by the road,
Imploring other troops to follow them.

As one by one they gathered, clustered there,
Noting the flash of guns, and taking stock,
They fired, most carefully, at pill-box slots,
Then dashed for cover on the bushy slopes,
Blew gaps with bangalores, and crawling on,
Flung hand-grenades above the parapets,
Where Germans crouched, besieged. Upon the beach,
Amidst the carnage and the wounded cries,
While still the *Spandaus* rattled on the sand
And bursting shells brought swift oblivion,
Fresh soldiers came, crowding the seething waves
And racing on past scenes of agony
To reinforce their comrades at the front.
Now paths were made through minefields near the dead,
Or where the limbless lay, who'd climbed the slopes
In disregard of danger in their zeal.

Not every German there who'd left his gun,
Or quit a pill-box, shaken by grenades,
And raised his hands aloft, escaped the wrath
Of hasty or deliberate rifle shots.
By dusk, all knew that 'Omaha' was won -
Three thousand deaths to gain a narrow beach!
Would war in France revert to what it was
When General Pershing led his young recruits
Against the bloody line of Hindenburg?

On 'Utah' beach the casualties were light,
And soon the hardy paratroops regrouped,

Except those dropped beyond the Merderet.
A bitter fight for Carentan was won,
And General Collins ordered an advance
To cross the Cotentin from east to west
And seal off Cherbourg, vital as a port
Through which the Allied bridgehead could be fed.
By Führer order no retreat was made
To shorten the perimeter defence.
Along the banks and lanes of the bocage
The anxious German units, thinly spread,
Could not withstand a rapid, massed attack.
The Cherbourg garrison, immured in stone,
Survived bombardment from the sea and air;
And when the port equipment was destroyed,
They hoisted high the flag of their defeat.
For many weeks the Allies could not use
Cherbourg's facilities; but 'Mulberry',
Their mobile harbour, met the huge demands
Of armed invasion's quick voracity.

The British took Bayeux, where Charles de Gaulle
Proclaimed once more the sovereignty of France.
Not all the French acknowledged his renown,
Or liked the narrow path he trod between
Subservience and allied parity.
But soon the crowds who pressed to hear him speak -
A voice of national freedom long denied -
Would recognise his proud austerity.
Meanwhile, they welcomed, though with some reserve,
Invaders from the Anglo-Saxon shores.
The French would suffer, if the Wehrmacht won,
Yet few complained of those already dead,

Of villages and towns now desolate,
And bloated cattle rotting in the fields.

Eastwards the bridgehead narrowed to the coast.
Montgomery had planned to capture Caen
Within a day of landing, and to win
Carpiquet airfield for the RAF,
But Rommel knew how vital Caen would be
To move his army westwards to the front;
Nor would he let the British armour free
To roam the plain extending to Falaise
And threaten thence a dash towards the Seine.
In front of Caen his tanks and eighty-eights
Repelled a strong Canadian attack,
Envenomed by the memory of Dieppe.
A Summer storm of great ferocity
Delayed the Allied build-up, and destroyed
More shipping than the enemy had done.
The battle faltered; Allies were constrained
Within their bridgehead, short of airfield space,
Congested on the beaches, and unsure
Of whether Rommel's *Panzers* might attack.

'*Das Reich*' division, based in Montauban,
Composed of SS troops, especially loyal
To Hitler and his ideology,
Was ordered to drive north to Normandy
And reinforce the *Panzer* forces there.
The French Resistance hindered its advance
With ambushes throughout the Auvergne hills.
Reprisals on civilians were invoked:
At Brive and Tulle, French hostages were hung

On lamp-posts in the streets. Then, past Limoges,
At Oradour-sur-Glane, the men were shot
And all the other villagers condemned
To death by burning in the local church.
'Das Reich' arrived in Normandy too late
To tip the scales of conflict; their delay
Contributed to Germany's defeat.
And, with impartial justice, some died there,
Unshriven for their hand in such a crime,
Whose barbarism made at Oradour
So many martyrs in the cause of France.

Montgomery misjudged his army's power
To make advances inland without pause.
For many soldiers, landing under fire
And holding bridgeheads were sufficient tasks.
Only the boldest saw, beyond the sand,
The spoils of fresh campaigns. A second time
The spirit must be roused, and limbs impelled,
And mind directed to a certain end,
A distant wood, a village or a hill,
With German guns concealed at vantage points.
At Villers-Bocage, where the British hoped
To send an armoured column south of Caen,
One German Tiger, firing as it drove,
Destroyed a line of half-trucks by the road.
Others outgunned the British Cromwells there,
Whilst in the town the German infantry
Regained possession, fighting street by street.

To counter this repulse, Montgomery planned
A new attack, called 'Epsom', which would cross

The Odon and the Orne to threaten Caen,
And force the German armour to engage.
But enemy defences were prepared:
For camouflage concealed their forward posts,
Where snipers could remain; a mile behind,
Extensive wire and mines protected tanks
And dug-in infantry; well to the rear,
The main position, built on higher ground,
Held batteries of *Nebelwerfer* guns
That fired three dozen mortar shells at once.

A huge bombardment, lasting several hours,
Made small impression on this deep defence.
With heavy casualties, the British won
A narrow footing on the Odon's banks,
But at Hill One-one-two the mortar fire
Made of the gentle slopes a pitted swamp
Of mud and slaughter, held by neither side.
'Epsom' had failed, yet Rommel was condemned
To use his armour piecemeal, as a shield,
Precluding its deployment in attack.
For Wehrmacht forces fought with one constraint
That nullified their prowess in the field -
Allied air-power ruled the skies of France.

Few aircraft of the Luftwaffe appeared
To challenge Spitfires, Mustangs or Typhoons,
Or shoot the bombers down whose sorties flew
With such dire impact over German troops.
Tigers and Panthers, masters of the lists
Against the Cromwells, Churchills, Valentines,
Whose guns and plating were deficient still,

Themselves became the sacrificial prey
Of fighters' bombs and rockets of Typhoons.
By daylight, also, infantry were strafed
By cannons or machine guns as they marched,
Or struck by bombers, flying tree-top high.
Henceforth the Wehrmacht travelled after dark,
Preferably on cloudy, moonless nights,
Hiding by day in woods or villages,
Dug in and camouflaged, erasing trails
Before they faced another dawn attack.

Initiative had passed from German hands.
Yet Winston Churchill, eager for results,
Still questioned his Commander's strategy,
And feared a stalemate, like the one he'd seen
Along the British salient at Ypres.
Were German soldiers proving once again
That only by attrition would they yield?
Would war in France become a second time
A dreadful siege with fearsome casualties?
Only Alanbrook, Montgomery's friend,
Did not dispute his protege's intent.
He saw the logic of a plan that gave
The crucial break-out to Americans,
While British soldiers undertook to bear
The weight of Rommel's *Panzers* in the east.
Who better than the men that Patton led
To break through the bocage and reach the Seine,
Outflanking by their speed the Boche defence?

And were not stubborn Tommies at their best
In holding ground against whatever odds?

Now Eisenhower agreed that Caen must fall
To heavy bombing. Harris was opposed:
He did not want his strategy delayed
Of breaking the morale of Germany
By mass destruction of civilian life.
His protest was dismissed; the bombers came -
Inhabitants were warned - and shattered Caen.
Only the Abbays rose above the dust
Of grey, historic stones and homes destroyed.
The lessons of Cassino were not learnt:
Tanks could not move through rubbled masonry;
In southern outskirts Germans could defend
The broken ruins, fighting yard by yard.
Carpiquet was won, but aircraft parks
Still lay within the range of hostile fire.

Montgomery's next objective was Falaise,
The town on which his strategy was hinged.
From there, towards the sea, the British front
Would draw the German armour on itself,
While, from Coutances, Americans would wheel
To drive across the wheatland of the Beauce
And reach the Seine, thus cutting off retreat
For every German left in Normandy.
Beside the bridges seized by airborne troops
Over the river Orne and Caen canal,
The armour gathered - Cromwells and Fireflies -
O'erseen by Germans, perched at Colombelles,
High on the rims of factory chimney stacks.
Uneasy silence lay upon the fields
Where front-line troops would presently converge

To light the tinder boundaries of war.
Then waves of bombers cast their heavy shades
Across the starting lines of British tanks,
The spearhead of the 'Goodwood' ground attack;
And minutes later spurts of smoke arose,
Like black and sulphurous vapour from the earth,
In front of where the Bourguebus ridge defined
The southern margin of the German lines.
Artillery and heavy naval guns
Added their tempo to the ceaseless roar
That hung above the Norman countryside.

Then tanks rolled forward, captains now exposed
To sniper fire from nests beside the road
And *Panzerfausts* that blew the turrets off
Or wreathed the chassis round with petrol flames,
Through orchards, where distended cattle lay,
Past pink-bloomed hedges, and on sunken lanes
Where one skilled shot could block the narrow way
With queues of armour, frozen on their tracks.
On either flank the infantry advanced,
Beside the orchards, green with early fruit,
Through growing wheat, where raking *Spandau* fire
Gave little ease. The corridor was sealed,
With guards who dug themselves in limy soil,
Equipped with anti-tank *Piats* and Brens.

A copse might shelter German eighty-eights,
Finding their range on slow-approaching tanks,
A farmhouse a platoon with *Panzerfausts*,
A hamlet one whole company of men,
Disposed amongst the vacant cottage rooms,

Where stone protected well, and guns could fire
From chosen look-out points on roof or wall.
In villages the belfry towers were climbed
By nimble snipers, trained to shoot at sight
The officers who led the first assault;
And hull-down *Panzers*, draped in foliage,
Levelled their long and slow-traversing guns.

As British soldiers waited, resolute,
Their comrades skirted round defensive posts,
Called up a creeping barrage in support
Or, with good luck, a well-directed strike
By fighter-bombers, guided from the ground.
Once more attacks went in, but oftentimes,
Till Germans quit their bastions, were held.
And then, again, a mile or so behind,
Re-sited guns within a farm or cot
Required another carefully planned assault
With several more predicted casualties,
Like those already lying in the corn,
Whose shallow helmets, hung on rifle-butts,
Were tilted, as in homage to the dead.

Astride the Falaise road on Bourguebus ridge -
Called 'Buggerbus' by British infantry -
An SS unit overlooked the plain.
Long range eighty-eights with other guns,
And *Nebelwerfers*, fortified the slopes.
Artillery and Tigers in reserve
Commanded the approaches to the ridge.
Frequently, as Fireflies lurched across
The railway line embanked south-east of Caen,

They burst in flames from armour-piercing shells.
No infantry could reach the German guns.

A violent Summer storm then intervened.
Where, just before, the green abundant plain
Stood rich with crops and ripening orchard fruit,
Now foison turned awry to flattened wheat
And trees uprooted. Bodies - once of men -
Devoid of limbs, or crumpled, black with fire,
Lay in the debris, near their smashed machines -
Like broken toys in nurseries of the gods.
Was Normandy to be another Somme,
A few miles won for thousands maimed and dead?
How could the Germans, bombed and strafed by day,
Disturbed at night, outnumbered on the ground,
Watching the Allies' steady growth of power,
Remain so long defiant of their will?

To some, especially RAF Command,
The answer was deficient leadership.
Montgomery's reputation now had sunk
Below the nadir of the 'Epsom' plan.
Why had so many bombers been misused
To gain the paltry fields of Normandy,
Destroying Caen, instead of German towns?
How could the Russians fight so many Huns,
When this invasion stalled against far less?
Were British soldiers 'led by donkeys' still,
As once their fathers were in Picardy?

Whilst doubts were cast in London and in France,
The German High Command did not rejoice

At 'Goodwood''s bafflement. To them it spoke
Of plugging broken lines with precious tanks,
Of desperate moves by weary infantry,
Of no reserves, of warfare without hope,
The only prospects one of slow retreat,
Or swift collapse in face of crushing power.
Foreseeing 'Goodwood', Rommel had transferred
The weight of *Panzer* forces south of Caen,
Stripping the armour from his western front.
He did not know Montgomery's strategy -
Nor did the press in London and New York -
To which the German army now conformed.
Though 'Goodwood''s target was to reach Falaise,
Its second purpose had been well achieved.
Though hardy British Tommies were not quick
To seize new ground or rout the enemy,
They'd well endured the unrelenting fight
Against the hard testudo of defence
That Rommel's tanks had raised in Normandy.

Towards St Lo Americans advanced
Through miles of bocage, chequered with small fields
Of subdivided pasture, fringed with banks
On which the sturdy hedgerows formed a screen.
Dug-in machine guns, single *Panzerfausts*
And rifle units targeted the gaps -
At corner gates, where cattle once debouched,
Or where artillery had smashed a hedge,
Or engineers had blasted passages.
Surmounting banks, the Shermans were exposed,
While on the narrow lanes, a burning wreck
Could long encapsulate a line of tanks.

Thus, once again, the infantry were called
To bear the fardels of the grim assault.
So field by field, preceded by the bombs
Of Thunderbolts or Mustangs, soldiers crawled,
Or charged abruptly, or lay in repose
As Germans mortars rivetted the ground
And *Spandaus* rattled, sixty shots a time.

Down exits deeply cut beneath the banks,
The Germans moved in orderly retreat
To man another well-protected line
With undiminished, passive fortitude,
Now not so much for Hitler, but for pride,
As *Kamerads*, and in obedience.
Each time, however, dead and wounded stayed -
Young grenadiers and hardened officers -
Not far from where the US conscripts fell,
Who suffered likewise for those meagre yards
Of farms on lease from Norman peasantry.

Meanwhile, upon a staff car near Bernay,
A Spitfire's cannons struck a sharper blow
Than that which fell with hammer strokes on Caen.
For Rommel, wounded, no more would be free
To quarrel with his old adversary.

31 The Marianas

Across the vast Pacific, US power
Had reached maturity. Only such force
Could contemplate a plan for two attacks:
The first, by Nimitz, on the ocean route,
Past scattered islands, bearing on Japan;
The second, by MacArthur, on a trail
That led, through tropic jungle, to his goal,
The Philippines, and his avowed return.
The Marshall Isles were won, then Tarawa;
Next Kwajalein and Eniwetok fell,
And devastating raids were made on Truk,
A major base for Hirohito's fleet.

The outer ring of Japanese defence
Was overrun. An inner ring must hold
Along the line of Mariana Isles,
The Palaus and New Guinea, to protect
The home possessions and the vital oil
Which met the needs of war economy.
No longer could the Japanese assume
That martial spirit, training and their code
Would still suffice. Aggression, and the will
To prove their race superior to all,
Had driven them to victory. Now they saw
The face of stark, dishonourable defeat;
For in defence they lacked resourcefulness.
Each soldier fought with undiminished zeal,
Prepared to die to save the Emperor's cause,
But planned retreat had never been foreseen.
Men ran in panic, or, more often, charged
To certain death against a line of guns.
For suicide could countermand disgrace;
Such was their bleak philosophy of life.

Outnumbered now, the army did not move
Its far-flung bases to consolidate.
MacArthur leapfrogged, leaving some to fall,
Like ripened apples rotting in the grass.
The Imperial navy could no more protect
The garrisons and merchant navy fleet
That brought supplies to ports within Japan
And recent conquests, now dependencies.
So US submarines found rich rewards
In hunting tankers or bulk cargo ships
On course for Yokohama or Kobe,

Or Singapore or Indonesian ports.
But Admiral Ozawa hoped to bring
The Americans to one decisive match,
For he retained the confidence to strike
With battleships and carriers and planes -
The Zero fighters famed at Oahu -
And win a victory greater than Togo's
Against the Russian fleet at Tsushima,
When Asia humbled European pride.
Yet one foreboding fact eluded him:
That in the fleet of US carriers
New flights of Hellcats occupied the decks.

Whilst army forces constantly advanced
Along New Guinea, seizing Biak Isle,
The navy planned to break the inner ring
With landings in the Marianas chain,
The isles of Saipan, Tinian and Guam,
The last of these owned by America,
Until it fell to enemy attack.
Japan had gained the rest from Germany,
When all the latter's colonies were lost.
Three purposes were claimed for Nimetz' plan:
To use the Marianas as a base
For launching the invasion of Japan;
To fly from there new Superfortresses
To devastate the archipelago -
For Chinese airfields, built by Chiang Kai-Shek,
Were currently at risk from land attacks -
Thirdly, the US navy hoped to lure
Ozawa's fleet, quiescent for so long,
From where it lay at Tawitawi Isle.

Admiral Spruance, like Ozawa, saw
That one decisive battle might ensure
Command at sea, until the war was won.
For if Ozawa overreached himself,
He might incur a fatal penalty.

Heavy bombing weakened Saipan's troops,
And naval shelling pulverised the shore,
Though pill-boxes survived, and beaches lay
Exposed to gunfire from the hills behind
And enfilades from points on either flank.
At Tarawa the lesson had been learnt
To land Marines in amphtrac carriers,
Preceded by amphibians, duly armed
To clear a passage through the beach defence.
But, even now, too many Japanese
Survived the first bombardment, and lay down
Incessant mortars, rifle fire and shells
That stopped invading vehicles on shore
And left Marines to shelter where they could,
In debris, shell holes, ditches, stumps of trees.
And yet, like stain, the beachhead slowly grew,
With each assault on bunker or pill-box,
Until the beach defenders were destroyed.
Then stretcher-bearers bore the wounded off,
And graves were dug to bury dead Marines
Before the tractors levelled out the sand.

When news of Saipan reached Ozawa's fleet,
He cancelled plans to help defend Biak,
And sailed due east in two divided groups:
In front a decoy, followed by a force

Of six great carriers, equipped with planes
Whose lack of armour suited them to fly
Much further than their US counterparts.
Ozawa thus intended to surprise
The larger force of Admiral Spruance' fleet
By air attacks whilst out of US range.
Reports by submarines informed Spruance
Of close impending conflict, yet he chose,
Against advice, to keep his carriers back
To guard the transports landing at Saipan -
His primary role, indeed, to save the troops
Entrusted with the Marianas' task.
Already at Guam his planes had struck
The aerodrome Ozawa hoped to use
To reinforce his aerial attack.
For only aircraft stationed on Guam
Could bring the Japanese to parity;
Nor did Ozawa know of losses there.

Across the empty ocean flew the swarms
Of fighter-bombers, eager to avenge
Defeat at Midway, and revive again
The fires of victory for their Emperor-god.
Yet few had fought in battles earlier.
These now were ardent youths, too briefly trained
And careless of their lightly-armoured planes.
American radar warned of their approach.

As Hellcat fighters rose to challenge them,
Fighter-directors on the ships below
Gave every plane precise intelligence -
Enemy range and speed and altitude,

Cloud cover, sun and visibility.
An officer well-versed in Japanese
Could hear upon the flagship, 'Lexington',
The enemy controller, high above,
Orbiting his task force unaware
That, as he spoke, his words were overheard.
Veteran pilots manned the new Hellcats,
Who knew the Zero's climbing rate and turn,
And lack of armour at the pilot's back.
In level flight and speed of dive and climb,
In armour, guns and airborne radar sets,
The Zero was outmatched. Like wounded birds
The stricken fighters fell, their burning engines
Doused within the sea, or blowing up
In billows of black smoke. And even those
That reached their target seldom landed hits.
Protective fire surrounded every ship.
A new device brought down a dozen planes -
A shell that burst while only proximate.
Nor did the Japanese who turned for home
All find their carrier base, for submarines
Had sunk the 'Taiho', largest in the fleet -
From which Ozawa took his admiral's flag -
And also 'Shokaku', an ancient ship,
Severely damaged in the Coral Sea.

Four times in all fresh waves of aircraft flew
To strike a further blow at Spruance' force.
Each time the Hellcats shot most from the skies
And chased survivors from the battle zone.
Now was the moment for a swift response -
An air attack against the Imperial fleet

Before it could disperse or run for home.
Yet US spotters could not track it down
Beyond the broad horizon of the sea;
Until, at last, a plane from 'Enterprise'
Discovered it far distant in the west.
Three hours of daylight meant return by night,
Landing in darkness, tired and short of fuel;
But doubt nor fear did not impede resolve.
This was the long-awaited chance to crush
The vital sea power needed to defend
The tenuous empire of the Rising Sun.

Off carriers' decks two hundred aircraft rose.
A radio message came from their command:
New bearings meant an extra sixty miles
To reach the enemy. Crews and pilots
Heard the relayed news; their chatter died,
As each reviewed his lonely enterprise.
Small chance remained that many would return.
The empty ocean, darker than the night,
Would be their landing ground.

Over the target time was limited.
Bombs and torpedoes sank one carrier;
Three others and one battleship were hit,
And, once again, the obsolete Zeros fell,
Like flotsam from the skies. The Hellcats turned,
And through the night flew back towards their fleet.

With fuel-gauge empty, many aircrews heard,
Despairingly, their engine's final cough.
Although at risk from Nippon submarines,

The expectant fleet turned searchlights at the sky,
Set running lights, and lit the landing strips.
Night fighters rose to guide their comrades back,
As star shells lit the moonless arch of sky.
Intensive search saved many more next day.
Though eighty planes had crashed, most men were found;
The ocean took its tithe of forty-nine.

Upon Saipan a Japanese attack,
Too late delivered, suffered heavily
From US guns that wrecked advancing tanks.
Now, rapidly, Marines o'erwhelmed the south,
Except where forests hid their desperate foes,
Invulnerable to all but scorching flame
And hand grenades. Across the centre,
By Mount Tapotchau, success was harder.
From Death Valley's densely pitted hills
Machine-guns poured cross-fire upon the plain,
Until, out-flanked, each gun-post was destroyed.
General Saito, when his line collapsed,
Ordered a final suicide attack,
A *gyokusai*, 'seven lives for one'.
Five thousand men, armed only with grenades,
Or bayonets fixed on poles, or sharpened sticks,
Streamed down a gulch between the US lines,
Shouting, killing, absolute for death,
Until the frontal fire of heavy guns,
Carbines and pistols, brought them down in droves.

Others died, less willingly, from fear:
Civilian families, counselled to expect
Mayhem and rape from foreign soldiery,

Jumped from the cliffs, or blew themselves apart,
Or ran beyond the shallow surf and drowned.
The inner ring was costly still in blood.

The isles of Guam and Tinian fell likewise
To sudden landings and persistent fire,
As Nippon soldiers chose the *Kodo-ha* -
The 'imperial way' - preferring death to shame.
Their shattered bodies, bulldozed in the earth,
Became a dismal sacrifice to war.
Then aerodromes were built for fighter planes,
And runways lengthened to facilitate
The coming of the Superfortresses.
One day from Tinian, a single one
Would fly to see a full atonement done.

32 The Stauffenberg Plot

Within the Reich the German people toiled,
Adjured by Goebbels to make common cause
Against the enemies besetting them
On every front, especially in the air,
Where Allied bombers flew by day and night.
For total war had come to Germany.
Women no longer stayed within the home;
They also worked to make the things of war.

Foreigners, too, from countries occupied,
Worked - some as slaves - in place of German men,
Who all, with few exceptions, fought in arms,
In French bocage and hills of Italy,
Or far on Russian steppes in Summer dust,
Or desperately outnumbered in the air
Above the battlefields and burning towns,
Or deep in submarines. Obedient
To State authority, inert in moral sense,
Most Germans salved their consciousness of wrong,
Though rumour told of heinous secret crimes,
Like genocide and vile experiments
Promoting so-called racial purity,
And, from the days of peace, things were recalled
That seemed to have foreshadowed such events.
But still, in some, the flame of conscience burned.

Before the war the Munich settlement
Dissolved a plot to purge the Nazi State;
For who could draw the sword against the man
Who'd stopped the nation on the brink of war
And gained new land with foreigners' consent?
Yet all were not deceived. New plans were made
By Wehrmacht officers, by bureaucrats,
Within trade union cells and church enclaves,
Within the parties banished underground -
The Communists and Social Democrats -
And in those honest homes that had not lost
Their reason and their native dignity.

Gradually the work of secret police
Uncovered those committed to rebel:

Patriots, Christians, liberals, socialists,
The White Rose movement and 'Red Orchestra',
The plotters in the *Abwehr*, and the men
Who met in Kreisau at von Moltke's home;
Though Axel von dem Bussche even went
To Hitler's quarters with a hidden bomb
Upon his person ready to explode -
Only to find his meeting was postponed.

Too often plots were made but not fulfilled.
Within the Wehrmacht many officers
Were disillusioned by the use of power
To terrorise civilians in those lands
That they had conquered; yet would not rebel
Against a leader blessed with victory.
And even in defeat, they would not choose
To break their solemn oath to Hitler's will.
Only a handful, conscious of their task,
Knew that the evils of the Nazi State
Demanded action, greater in its scope
Than personal honour or a soldier's code.
They saw the nation grievously misled,
Its name besmirched, its values desecrate,
And thus resolved to render up their lives
To this one end: to strike the tyrant down.

Their plan contained a clever irony:
The plotters would subvert the very force -
The army in reserve - that was designed
For home security! With Hitler dead,
They would arrest the Party leadership,
Citing its intent to seize control

Of army and the State for personal ends,
Regardless of the German people's will.
A Wehrmacht officer contrived the plot,
Claus Schenk von Stauffenberg, who in his youth
Had faith in Hitler's nationalistic aims.
But war in Russia taught him to detest
The *Einsatzgruppen*, and the racial hate
That made the Wehrmacht agent of those crimes
That would for ever stain his country's name.
He realised then that Hitler would destroy
All that the Germans had once coveted
Of Christian values. Severely wounded
In north Africa - losing an arm and eye -
He was promoted soon to Chief of Staff
Within the army held in home reserve.
Certain of his country's pressing need,
Von Stauffenberg became the vital force
That animated all the hopes and plans
Of other soldiers troubled still by doubt.
Although his post in Berlin was the key
To activate the army in reserve,
Yet now he chose, despite his handicaps,
To undertake the one decisive role:
Von Stauffenberg himself would place a bomb
Near Adolf Hitler at a conference.

At this time in the war the Führer stayed
Within his 'Wolf's Lair', built at Rastenburg,
Deep in a Prussian glade of gloomy pines,
Not far behind the German eastern front.
There he conferred with Wehrmacht officers,
Surrounded by three lines of barbed wire fence,

By mines, pill-boxes, chosen SS guards.
Increasingly myopic, fearful, harsh,
He lived as a recluse, fond of his dogs.
Yet, charismatic still, he could inspire
Despairing generals, looking to retreat,
With fresh assurance and the will to fight.

Von Stauffenberg was summoned to attend.
His rank and purpose took him swiftly past
The sentries on each gate at Rastenburg.
Within a changing-room, he armed the fuse
On one small bomb. A wire that held the pin
Would soon dissolve - ten minutes would suffice.
As Stauffenberg, with Keitel by his side,
Walked with his case along the compound path,
Within the building Hitler sat at work,
Examining the latest army maps.
Around the table stood some officers.
Windows were open in the Summer heat.
On entering, von Stauffenberg took care
To warn the guard of an expected call.
The Fuhrer shook his hand without a word,
But scrutinising him. The case was placed
Beneath the table near where Hitler sat.
A little later Stauffenberg had left,
Whilst muttering a brief apology.

With deafening crack and bluish-yellow flame,
The bomb exploded in the midday quiet.
Dark plumes of smoke rose up, and shards of glass;
Wood, fibreboard and paper swirled about.
Voices called for doctors; the wounded screamed;
Some ran with shredded clothing, hair in flames.

Upon a stretcher, veiled by Hitler's cloak,
They carried out a body from the room.

With two co-plotters, Stauffenberg observed
What he believed was Adolf Hitler's death.
His staff car passed one barrier with ease.
The second one was closed; he asked the guard
To telephone the officer in charge.
As yet the name of Stauffenberg was safe.
He passed the gate, and reached the aerodrome.
Slowly the Heinkel flew towards Rangsdorf
Over the ripened wheat of Prussian farms.

Meanwhile a message gave ambivalent news
To plotters in a Bendlerstrasse room:
The bomb exploded - Hitler is not dead!
For though some men had died, he had survived,
Protected by an oaken table leg,
Or - so Hitler thought - by destiny.
Confusion reigned upon the Bendlerstrasse.
Should 'Valkyrie' - the plan to use reserves -
Be implemented whilst the Führer lived?
Would officers obey the new commands?
Would some find out who was responsible?
Could Fellgiebel at Rastenburg succeed
In sealing off communications there?
All was uncertain. Who could end their doubts?

Eventually the orders were dispatched.
Troops in reserve began to move against
The Nazi Party leaders and SS.
Arrests were made, and buildings occupied.
Even in Paris, Stulpnagel's response

Was swift arrest of Nazi leaders there.
Rommel considered opening up the front
To Allied forces, and a general peace.
Yet by the time that Stauffenberg arrived,
The tide was turning. Himmler had been charged
To oversee the foiling of the plot.
Then contact was restored with Rastenburg.

This time came messages for other ears -
For army centres, Party officers.
In Berlin, Major Otto Remer called
At Goebbel's house to verify 'Valkyrie'.
Goebbels rang Rastenburg, where Hitler's voice
Was easily recognised. Remer was told
To take command of soldiers in Berlin.
For Remer all that mattered were commands -
A Fuhrer order was the word of God!
He acted quickly: soon the plotters saw
A ring of troops assembled down below,
Machine guns trained on doorways to the street.
General Fromm, who'd vacillated much,
Waiting to see the fateful balance fall,
Now took control, arresting in his turn
The chief conspirators. Others soon vowed
Unbroken loyalty to the Führer's name.
Von Stauffenberg proclaimed he was alone,
That others had but followed his command,
But Fromm ignored him. Olbricht, Haeften, Mertz,
And Stauffenberg were taken under guard.
Outside, the glare of headlights lit the square.
A firing squad of NCOs was formed,
And one by one the four conspirers fell.

But, as he died, von Stauffenberg cried out,
'Long live the sacred land of Germany.'[22]

Elsewhere the plot was stifled ruthlessly -
In Prague, Vienna, Paris, army chiefs
Had acted swiftly on the hopeful news
That Hitler might be dead. Now, once again,
The SS and the Party bureaucrats
Resumed control and tried to settle scores.
The wounded Rommel, home to convalesce,
Was ordered to stand trial or kill himself.
He chose the latter; Hitler dare not claim
That such a German hero had rebelled.
A witch-hunt followed; army cadres were purged,
Civilians tainted by a rumoured word
Were promptly sent to concentration camps.
Many, like von Trott and Schlabrendorff,
For fear their families would be victimised,
Refused to flee, and waited for arrest.

Roland Freisler, judge in the People's Court -
Whom Hitler named 'Vishinsky of the Reich' -
Refused to hear their valiant defence,
And shouted at them 'rabble', 'traitors', 'pigs'.
Yet some cried out that murder had been done,
And told of how they'd followed God's command
To kill the tyrant, even treasonably.
Despite their torture, and the crude contempt
Of Freisler and his chosen audience,
The prisoners stood unbowed, released from crime,
Content in conscience, seeing in their fate
The prelude of the national tragedy.
Suspended on meat-hooks by coils of wire,

They hung in anguish, filmed for Hitler's sight;
Though military cadets, when called to watch
The gruesome record in their cinema,
Walked out in protest, saving meagre scraps
Of German honour, and the Wehrmacht's pride.

Failure of von Stauffenberg's attempt
Was verily the Fuhrer's last success.
Though slightly wounded, he believed afresh
That destiny had chosen him to raise
The German nation far from this nadir
Of treachery and military defeat.
Henceforth the Wehrmacht would be well policed
By Party officers and Himmler's men.
Now, also, for the Prussian landed class
Who'd ruled the army since the *Kaiserreich*,
And in the former war denied due rank
To Corporal Hitler as an officer,
The time of vengeful reckoning had come.
No one would now be trusted; all must yield
To Hitler's judgment, even in defeat.

The Allies had declined the overtures
Of honest men, like Bonhoeffer and Trott,
Who strove with good intent to rid the Reich
Of Nazi crimes, and lay foundations yet
Of freedom and a democratic State.
For Churchill feared that Stalin would renege,
If any hint of peace talks reached his ears.
The door was closed; no German voice was heard.
Ten righteous men were not identified.
But as von Tresckow eloquently said,

'Integrity begins with sacrifice;
Those of our circle put on Nessus' robe.
Coute que coute the effort must be made,
For all that matters now is not our plight,
But that we take this step in history's light.'[23]

33 Bagration

In Moscow cynics told a Russian joke:
'What is an old believer?', one man asks.
'Someone who thinks the second front will come'.
Yet when, at last, in Normandy it came,
The Russians staged, as they had always pledged,
A new offensive on the eastern front,
Designed to test the German war machine,
Confronted now with what it dreaded most -
War on two fronts, the old endemic fear.

A hero of the army of the Tsar
That drove Napoleon from Russian soil
Gave Soviet strategy its latest name:
'Bagration' was a plan for four assaults
Upon the German line that stretched afar
From Finland lakes to western Ukraine steppes.

The main attack - more than a million men -
Would aim to seize the huge Minsk salient,
Where Busch's army felt itself secure,
The last remaining force on Russian land.
Secondary moves in Finland and Ukraine
Would drive towards the Baltic and Warsaw,
Whilst in the south, Roumania would face
A Soviet army hoping to pre-empt
Ploesti's oilfields, crucial for the Reich.
Deception measures, similar to those
Which long misled defence of Normandy -
Misinformation, air reconnaissance,
And dummy weapons - gave the Germans cause
To expect attack upon their southern flank.

But on the central front the trap was sprung,
With Soviet forces seemingly inert -
Digging trenches, resting forward troops -
Till suddenly the covert partisans
Disrupted telephones and transport links,
And Russian aircraft launched a mass of raids,
Unhindered by the dwindling Luftwaffe,
Whose fighters were deployed within the Reich
Against incessant bombing from the west.
Without a barrage heralding attack,
The Russian infantry, at dead of night,
Surged in their thousands forward from their lines,
Supported by artillery and tanks,
An overwhelming tide of savage men,
The hated host imagination feared
Of Asian hordes at threshholds of the Reich.
Yet these were trained for modern ways of war,
Imbibed in bitter schoolrooms of defeat:

In night attacks a path was lit by flares,
And searchlight beams dedazzled German troops;
Plough tanks drove passages through zones of mines,
And wooden causeways led through marshy land.
Just as the Wehrmacht, on this very day,
Had raced ahead in Russia without pause,
Regardless of the pockets in their rear,
So Zhukov now insisted on advance.
His troops were not reliant on supplies;
Raw vegetables collected on the march,
Dry crusts of bread, and straw for horses
Pulled off empty roofs were food enough.
Nor would Soviet soldiers disobey
An order to attack, however rash,
When in the rear a Party Commissar
Awaited, with a bullet, those who fled.
Progress was rapid, hastened by the use
Of US lorries, sent in multitudes,
Which now transported Russian infantry.

Minsk was recaptured, and behind the front,
Surrounded Germans handed over arms.
The march of bondage eastwards soon began,
Each painful step obliterating more
The memories of Fatherland and home,
Of friends and families few would see again.
Through Berlin, Hamburg, Munich, Nuremburg,
Adorned with glowing emblems of the Reich,
These hollow-eyed war veterans had stepped
In distant days of meretricious fame.
Though some amongst the endless, captive line
Recalled, with irony, how they'd opposed
The Nazi State, as secret Communists,

And hoped for some more comradely response
From captors of a proletarian State.
By Stalin's order Communists were shot
For fighting for the Reich despite their creed.

As Russian troops raced forty miles a day,
The salient at Minsk was overrun.
Then new offensives shook the Axis lines:
The Finns once more fought bravely to defend
Karelian lakelands from their Soviet foe;
The Baltic States were battleground again
For mighty foreign armies, trampling down
Their fragile culture on the littoral;
Whilst war-struck Poland saw the Bug traversed
By Soviet arms, as three long years before,
Raped by the Germans, she had seen them pass
To spoliate her neighbours' vaster land.
Red armies, also, lined the Vistula,
And threatened to engulf the Balkan States.
Roumania had seen her borders breached,
And, wakening to the import of her choice
To follow Nazi arms against the Slavs,
Abruptly staged a royalist coup d'etat,
Arrested Antonescu, and changed sides.
Ploesti's vital oil would flow no more
To fuel the Reich's declining war machine.
Hungary, too, a German satellite,
Awaited an invasion from the east.
Such great advances won by Stalin's arms
Presaged catastrophe for Hitler's State,
Though little did the Russian armies know
The cost in blood of Nazidom's death-throe.

34 Victory in Normandy

Within the stony ruins of St Lo
American soldiers waited silently,
Listening for the drone of heavy planes,
Whose bombing raid would presage their attack.
Cloud cover hid the targets; bombs fell short,
And slaughtered many, helpless to object.
But further south, the narrow bombing zone
Where Panzer Lehr were leagured in defence,
Was peppered with three thousand tons of bombs,
Which cratered every yard. Equipment lay
Amidst the carnage, strewn in scattered heaps.
Veteran soldiers ran dementedly,
Until the drumfire of the US guns
Completed there the havoc of the bombs

With high explosive blasts and shards of steel.
But shaken by their self-inflicted loss,
The US infantry was slow to move.
In foxholes and in strongpoints German troops
Still fought courageously, however few.

Yet here the die was cast by strategy.
Montgomery's plan to threaten, to the east,
A British break-out driving to the Seine,
Had drawn the Wehrmacht forces to that flank.
Rommel had placed his *Panzers* and reserves
To stop offensives there along the Orne,
And left a thin and discontinuous line
Across the bocage of west Normandy.
Omar Bradley knew this was his chance
To crack the crust of opposition there.
His Shermans stood behind the infantry,
Leashed up like sleeping hounds against the time
When from their lair the Germans would be prised,
While Patton's army waited to exploit,
With rapid movement, enemy collapse.
Already air supremacy was won,
Proscribing all mobility by day
To any kind of Wehrmacht fighting force.

Though bocage country had for long delayed
The US armour, stalled in chequered fields
By sturdy banks of tanglewood and hedge,
Now new-equipped with sharpened forks of steel,
Recast from rusting German obstacles
Of Omaha's and Utah's beach defence,
The Shermans soon began to carve their way,

Unhindered, through the fields of Normandy.
Whilst German tanks - outnumbered heavily -
Were forced to move by night on narrow roads,
Americans outflanked them in the fields
And roamed immune from aerial attack.
With gathering momentum, Bradley's force
Advanced due south to close upon Avranches.
From there, across a single bridge, there passed
A mass of soldiers, vehicles and tanks,
Which threatened to encircle what remained
Of German arms in western Normandy.
Bradley, however, cautiously pursued
The Allied blueprint. Ports in Brittany -
St Malo, St Nazaire, Brest, Lorient -
Were still assessed as vital for supplies,
Though German sabotage could cripple them.
Even as the French Resistance rose
Against the Wehrmacht trapped in pockets there,
The US army sent their columns west,
Instead of eastwards, where the time was ripe
To gather up the sheaves of German arms.

Over London flying-bombs now fell -
V1 ramjets, nicknamed 'doodle-bugs' -
And once again the hardy Londoners
Obeyed the wailing siren calls to hide
In shelters made of iron, or underground.
Some heard the pulsing drone abruptly stop
And woke to the expectancy of death.
With heaps of rubble suburb streets were marred,
And busy shoppers died in Knightsbridge stores.
One early Summer morning, near Whitehall,

A V1 fell on guardsmen as they sang
'*Te Deum*' in their chapel near the Park.
The Fuhrer claimed that he would win the war
By forcing Britain to negotiate.
Churchill's response was, as before, to ask
That Londoners should stoically accept,
Like servicemen, the dangers of the time,
And not expect a change of strategy,
With premature attempts to land in France
Where 'doodle-bugs' were launched. Skilled defences
Limited the threat: guns ringed the capital
And fighters learned to shoot the bombs in flight.
Observers plotted where they fell to ground,
And German agents were then misinformed.
Though casualties were high and nerves on edge,
The Londoners endured most patiently.

Montgomery, meanwhile, reinforced his flank
On Caumont ridge; and British troops struck south
To seize Mount Pincon, struggling up its slopes
Against the shelling every move invoked,
Leaving the dead, like winnowed chaff, behind.
Each stone-built farmhouse threatened the advance,
Each copse might hide a gun, each field of corn
A grenadier with shouldered *Panzerfaust*,
Each tuft a *Schuemine*, blowing off a foot.
The Suisse Normande of scattered hills and trees,
With winding lanes and shallow Summer streams,
And hamlets hard to find on army maps -
Whose names made little sense by radio -
No infantry, nor armour, could traverse
Without due fear of heavy casualties.

What gratitude those weary soldiers felt,
On foot, or cramped in confines of a tank
Which smelt of apples, cordite, sweat and flesh,
On hearing overhead the scream of planes -
When Spitfires or Typhoons fired cannon shells,
Or bombs, or rockets, down on German posts,
Annihilating gun or mortar crews,
Tiger or Panther tanks, whatever stood
So resolute against a ground attack.
Such air potential made the outcome sure:
However bravely Wehrmacht soldiers fought,
They could not match a rocket-firing plane,
Or hide, in battle, tanks of forty tons.

Beside Route One-five-eight, across the plain,
Canadian armour drove throughout the night,
In one unbroken line, south to Falaise,
Tanks nose to tail, and edging through the dark
With sudden lurches on a cratered road,
Ill-lit from time to time by hostile fire
From anti-tank guns or from *Panzerfausts*.
Now reinforced by Polish army tanks,
They crossed the rolling fields of yellow wheat,
Past unknown hamlets - Tilly, Gramesnil, Mines -
Until, at Quesnay Wood, a strong redoubt
Of SS *Panzers* stopped with withering fire
Their progress to Falaise.

Regardless of advice from High Command,
Hitler now ordered one bold counter-stroke,
Of German armour, westwards to the coast,
Through Mortain to Avranches, to cut the road

Supplying General Patton's southern force.
The vision of the Führer even saw
The rolling up of Allied forces there
And victory in the west. Von Kluge knew
This was a hopeless dream, but, fearful that
His earlier sympathy towards the plot
Of Claus von Stauffenberg might be revealed,
He did not risk opposing Hitler's will.
From all along the threatened German front
He stripped the armour. Unbeknown to him,
His plan was sent from Ultra intercept
To Bradley's staff. The US general
Made of this threat an opportunity.
The desperate drive of *Panzers* reached as far
As nine miles from Avranches, but under fire
From corridors of guns, and helpless to
Evade the searching planes, they halted there.
Above a quilted pattern of bocage,
The Typhoon pilots looked for trails of dust
That traced indelibly the paths of tanks;
Then swooped exultantly to fire their swarm
Of hissing rockets, watching for the puffs
Of blackened smoke that marked a crippled tank,
Before they climbed towards the pristine sky.
On Norman farms and orchards, empty now,
Except for bloated, upturned carcasses,
The smoking wrecks of vaunted Tigers lay
And new, long-barrelled Panthers, masters once
Of Allied armour on all battlefields.

The Wehrmacht's chance to form a further line,
Perhaps along the Seine, was almost lost.

General Model, his *Panzer* arm destroyed,
With ammunition seriously short,
As new Commander, ordered a retreat.
The German pocket westwards from Falaise
Must be withdrawn. Encirclement was now
Montgomery's aim; so Patton's army,
Almost unopposed, raced on to Argentan.
At Conde, British drove the Wehrmacht back,
And near Falaise Canadians and Poles
Converged upon the German bottleneck.
No longer just by night would frenzied troops
Make haste to circumvent the Allied trap.

At sunrise desperate units crossed the fields,
Or rode on wagons, lorries, tanks,
Astride gun limbers, or on bicycles,
In long disordered columns down the lanes
That once had seen their conquering advance.
Precision shelling by the British guns
Took heavy toll of unprotected troops.
With eagle eyes, Typhoons and Spitfires roamed,
Diving to launch two thousand pounds of bombs,
Or rockets, or with cannon fire to strafe
At tree-top height those targets named as 'soft'.
As wrecks and bodies hampered the retreat,
So, hour by hour, the execution grew.
Debris blocked a bridge across the Dives;
Burning trucks made roads impassable;
And horses lay, in tangled traces, dead.

Some German tanks broke loose across the fields,
But, hit by bombs or rockets, blazed alone,

Like warning beacons on a sea-girt wreck.
Columns of troops were bombed, vanguard and rear,
To block their movement; then the fighters flew
From end to end with shrieking cannon shells,
Until the frantic men and animals
Lay dead or maimed, contorted like the damned.
Some Germans waved white flags - to no avail.
To whom could they surrender but themselves?
For Omar Bradley held his troopers back,
For fear that now the flood of soldiery,
Emboldened to escape encirclement,
Might inundate a premature attack.
He chose to let the fighter-bombers strike,
And watch in safety as the Germans bled.

But soon Montgomery ordered, from the north
Advances by Canadians and Poles
To close the trap along the Norman lane
Between Chambois and Trun at St Lambert.
A reckoning time had come for German arms,
As raging soldiers fought with no constraint,
Not always now for *Volk* and Fatherland,
But finally in hope of 'Heim ins Reich'.
Against such fury Allied troops were slow
To clear each copse or farmyard, house or barn.

Some SS *Panzers*, having broken out
Beyond the closing circle of pursuit,
Returned to help their countrymen escape.
Thus Polish Sherman tanks, who'd bravely fought
To close the gap behind the German mass,
Now found themselves upon a transverse ridge,

Besieged by their retreating enemy.
But as escaping Germans came in range,
A sharp cacophony of Sherman guns
Struck down the men who rode upon the trucks,
Unwounded and the wounded all alike,
And maddened horses trapped in harnesses.
Survivors jumped in ditches, others ran,
White flags aloft, towards the Polish tanks,
Drawing upon themselves the SS guns,
Which mercilessly shot their comrades down.

At last St Lambert fell. The ring was closed,
And with it the campaign in Normandy.
Those Germans who'd escaped beyong Falaise
Did not forget the might of Allied arms.
Though Wehrmacht troops had fought tenaciously,
Especially when surrounded or alone,
Though quick to counter enemy attack,
Though technically proficient, better led
And armed with more effective weaponry,
They had been soundly beaten in the field
By amateurs conscripted into arms -
British tommies, American GIs -
Who'd driven from the soil of Normandy
The last remaining German grenadier.
Deception plans, resistance by the French,
The weight of numbers and materiel,
The use of massive air power unopposed:
All these played major parts; but none so much,
Wherever common soldiers had to fight -
On landing beaches, bocage, woodland, plain,
In sunken lanes implanted deep with mines,

In empty farms prepared with booby traps,
In thin-skinned tanks confronting eighty-eights -
As love that moved them, time and time again,
To offer up their lives and not complain.

35 The Warsaw Rising

In London exiled Poles proclaimed their rights
To govern their unhappy countrymen.
By radio and agents they conversed
With patriots still struggling in Warsaw
To keep alive the flame of Polish life.
A secret army - *Armja Krajowa* -
Was well established, many thousands strong,
Supplied with arms by British aircraft drops

And centred on Warsaw. A plan was made,
That as the Wehrmacht moved in full retreat,
Uprisings would exact a heavy toll,
And yet anticipate the Bolshevists,
Whose claims to liberate were viewed with doubt.
Had Stalin not agreed with Ribbentrop
To share the spoils of Poland's cruel demise?
Nor would the former landowners submit
To any kind of communist reform;
Nor others welcome Russian mastery,
When national pride had been so long suppressed.

Upon the Vistula's opposing bank
The Germans held the suburb of Praga
Against the threat of Soviet attack.
Stalin's triumphant army had now lost
The impetus that carried it so far.
Supply lines ran far back beyond the Bug,
Soldiers were tired, and opposition hard,
As Germany's own borders were approached.
Manteuffel's *Panzers* gave a sharp riposte
To Russian spearheads on East Prussian land.
Yet in Warsaw and London who could know
That Zhukov would not cross the Vistula;
That for long weeks the Soviets would pause,
Until they judged their arms preponderant.
When Poles within the capital observed
How heavy were the German casualties,
Then saw their columns cross Kierbedzia bridge,
Their hopes rose up: their city would be free!

Between the armies, Warsaw held its breath.
Rebellion now might claim the seat of power.
The exiled Government urged them to this end;
And Russians broadcast similar appeals.
But even as the Polish leaders met
Within a factory by the ruined streets,
Fresh Wehrmacht units, *Panzer* and SS,
Marched back across the city, on their way
To fortify the eastern front again.
A new commander, Heinz Guderian,
Recalled from his disgrace, would strive to hold
The bridges of Warsaw.

From ruined homes in Wola, Zoliborz,
In Mokotow and on Napoleon Square,
Rebels with hand-guns stealthily emerged.
As shots rang out, and roof-top mortars fired,
They charged the German strongpoints everywhere -
In barracks, depots, offices of police.
From passers-by the cries of wounded came,
Some caught in cross-fire, cut by shattered glass,
Or struck by masonry. The Vistula
And Old Town held the key. Could they be seized?
But all three bridges were defended well;
Not one was taken, nor strategic points.
Separate districts, now in rebel hands,
Like Zoliborz, could not communicate.
With desperate messages, young children ran
Through burning streets of dust.

German response was swift and violent.
Himmler himself, Head of Security,

Took personal charge of this rebellion,
He who had said ten thousand Poles might die
To build one tank ditch for the German Reich.
Though Wehrmacht troops were present, special squads
Of convict soldiers under loose control
Were utilised at first - Russian traitors,
Men released from jail, Ukrainians who
Hated every Pole. As they advanced
By killing, looting, rape, so house to house
The Poles confronted them. Prisoners were shot,
Or, under fire, built German barricades.
Civilians died in thousands in Warsaw -
Women, children, aged men and youths,
The latter shot cold-bloodedly in groups
For fear of their recruitment by the Poles.
Yet snipers from the *Armja Krajowa*,
Some wearing stolen SS uniforms,
With armbands of the national red and white,
Took heavy vengeance on the convict force.
Polish flags at windows flew in hope
Of those who'd seen their city gutted twice.
Surely the Allies would convey some help
With sustenance across the Vistula,
Or planes from London dropping food and arms?
Would not their comrades, trained and armed abroad,
Be parachuted on Pilsudski Square?

Such dreams had little substance. Stalin knew
An army without tanks, or heavy guns,
Could not dispute a Wehrmacht counterstroke.
What would he gain by intervention now?
They could not offer bridges to Warsaw;

His armies had been checked; they needed rest.
He would not welcome Polish patriots,
Opposed to revolution, in Warsaw;
And so he branded them 'adventurers',
Who, for their own ends, sacrificed the lives
Of helpless people, otherwise content
To wait for liberation by his troops.
In Lublin he had Polish Communists,
Who called themselves a National Government.
As for the British, they could only send
A score of bombers from their nearest base
In far-off Italy. Three reached Warsaw
And dropped a few supplies. Churchill had tried
To make Stalin agree that British planes
Should land on Soviet fields. At which request,
The 'Bear' had merely growled.

At Himmler's instance, Hitler intervened.
Warsaw, the ancient Polish obstacle
To Aryan expansion in the east,
Must be subdued, and block by block erased,
Its people slaughtered, never to impede
The destined march of German 'Kulturmensch'.
So Wehrmacht units reinforced the bands
Of crude irregulars. Heavy weapons
Closed upon the streets - tanks, artillery,
Mortars, eighty-eights, even the giant
'Karl' morser battery, and new 'Goliaths' -
Automatic tanks that carried bombs
To blow apart a post, or barricade.

First, Stuka bombers dived on central blocks
Held by insurgents; then the shelling came,
Intensified by mortar rocket fire.
Collapsing buildings blocked the narrow streets;
Tanks could not pass nor turn. Like Stalingrad,
Warsaw became a conflict hand-to-hand,
Of Wehrmacht infantry and desperate Poles.
As house by house the fated city burned,
The cellars wracked by petrol-driven flames,
All hope of Allied help was cast away.
An AK paper wrote, ironically,
'For living, we, the Poles, apologise,
For hindering the Germans' eastward drive,
And now the Russians progress to the west;
For damaging the Allies' unity.
We beg the whole world's pardon that we live;
But we shall fight, if needs be, all alone.'[24]

Yet strangely, as the Germans slowly gripped
The dying city in a ring of iron,
The attitude of Stalin mollified.
American bombers landed in Ukraine,
Dropping supplies en route above Warsaw,
Though few within the Poles' perimeter.
A Soviet Polish army was allowed
To fight its way to Praga, and across
The Poniatowski bridge into Warsaw;
But Russian soldiers offered them no help.
Though Germans were retreating from Praga,
And blew the bridges on the Vistula,
The Soviet Poles withdrew with heavy loss.
Stalin had made his gesture of support.

The Germans also knew the world could watch
The mismatched battleground within Warsaw,
And note the crimes of Wehrmacht and SS.
As armoured columns drove down central streets
To isolate the rebels, and their guns
Bombarded strongholds in the narrow lanes,
They tried to send civilians to the rear,
And treated Polish prisoners honourably.
Commander Bach-Zelewski, once in charge
Of *Einsatzgruppen* on the eastern front,
Now took it on himself to recognise
The *Armja Krajowa* as combatants,
With rights denied to partisans or spies -
No doubt in mind of future war-crime trials.

The Polish leader, Komorowski, knew
Resistance now was hopeless. Terms were made
For prisoners and for citizens to leave.
As soldiers gathered, laying down their arms,
Their faces drawn from lack of sleep and food,
The wounded dressed with blood-stained bandages,
They stood and sang the national anthem there:
'Not yet is Poland lost'; and as they marched
To their captivity, some German troops,
On guard with lowered arms, saluted them.

Flames of the Jewish ghetto were recalled,
As now the rest of Warsaw shared its fate.
No city suffered more for its defiance:
Two hundred thousand citizens had died.
The banks along the Vistula were clear

For Germans and for Russians once again
To gratify their ancient enmities.
No longer would the valiant Poles protest
And stem the ancient feud of east and west.

36 The Liberation of Paris

In Paris women still contrived to look
As pretty and as chic as years before,
In spite of shortages, and empty shops,
And rickshaw taxis and the German signs
That cluttered every public thoroughfare.
No longer were the field-grey soldiers seen
In cafes on the sunlit boulevards.
Detachments marched in strict conformity,
And sentries stood alert at entrances.
A second time the wind of war approached,
Though now the flags that trembled in the breeze

At Concorde, Quai d'Orsay, Hotel de Ville,
Were not the tricolor, but swastikas.

The shattered Wehrmacht could not hold a line
In front of Paris, nor along the Seine.
Now Patton's army drove them through the Beauce,
Past Chartres cathedral, high above the plain,
Still sentinel, despite the claims of war,
To Christ's dominion in the land of France.
Each side of Paris crossings were soon made.

Was Paris now to burn, like Stalingrad?
The Allied generals did not want to fight
To liberate the capital of France.
Were they to be the execrated names,
Destroyers of the ancient citadel?
Beyond the boulevards, the narrow lanes,
Like those of Warsaw, favoured the defence.
Were Allied shells and bombs to turn these streets -
As they had done so recently at Caen -
To smoking rubble? What would victory bring -
Three million people hungering for food?
At such a prospect, Eisenhower recoiled.
Instead he planned a broad encirclement,
Leaving the city still in German hands,
Until the Wehrmacht garrison complied
With Allied terms for laying down their arms.

De Gaulle, however, saw things differently.
Accepted now as leader of the French
By Churchill and by Roosevelt, he knew
That, here in France, not all would welcome him.

Communists, especially, hoped to seize
The reins of power from Vichy's failing hands,
And make of France, no longer occupied,
A workers' State, as Communards had done
In Paris when the Prussian war was lost.
Accordingly de Gaulle sent agents there
To plan for his arrival, and to spoil
The instigation of a *coup d'etat.*
Within the city, groups of patriots,
Restrained for years, awaited calls to arms,
And hearing how the Allies had progressed,
Grew, like the Poles, impatient to proclaim
That they themselves had saved their capital
By driving the oppressor from their midst.
All work was stopped by public services.
No buses ran, and vacant streets were still.

But then, above the Prefecture of Police,
The long forbidden tricolor was raised.
Around the city others now appeared,
Until the hated swastika became
The mark of where the German garrisons
Maintained control in isolated parts.
Shooting broke out, as police and others fought
Against collaborators or patrols.
Paris, once more, saw hasty barricades -
Like those which faced the guns of Cavaignac -
From furniture and ripped-up cobblestones
And damaged vehicles of trade or war,
Manned by men whose hand-guns would defy
A Tiger tank or field artillery.
General von Choltitz, German Commandant,

Though angered by the rising, feared as much
The Führer's call to burn the city down.
For even he, a Prussian officer,
Bound by his oath of strict obedience,
Flinched at the thought that Paris would be razed
By his express command. A truce was made -
Brokered by a Swedish diplomat -
But neither side could easily restrain
Reprisals born of long engendered hate.

In any case, de Gaulle had other plans:
An armoured group, commanded by Leclerc,
Was eager now to enter Paris first.
Americans would follow with due force.
When Eisenhower approved, advance began.
Leclerc well knew the fate of Paris turned
On minutes won or lost. He sent ahead,
Commanded by a farmer from the Sarthe,
A force of Sherman tanks. As twilight fell,
They passed Porte d'Italie and crossed the Seine.
No guns were fired; few people recognised
That these were Frenchmen, once again in arms.
They reached Hotel de Ville, now wreathed in flags,
And greeted there their bold compatriots,
Fresh from the turmoil of the barricades.
Von Choltitz would not cravenly comply;
His soldiers fought around Les Invalides,
The Ecole Militaire and Quai d'Orsay,
Whilst German snipers in the Tuileries,
Amidst the formal flowers and quincunxes,
Shot many Frenchmen dead. Then he surrendered:
Paris, at last, was free.

Next day, at Montparnasse, de Gaulle arrived,
Triumphant from his progress through the land.
He must return, before all other tasks,
To occupy the Ministry of War.
Its empty rooms, unutilised for years,
Remained as they had been when Paul Reynaud,
Alongside Charles de Gaulle, had quitted them.
Then, calling at the Prefecture of Police,
He went, at last, to meet the partisans.
Despite their protests, he would not proclaim
The French Republic to th'expectant crowds:
It had not died; it need not be revived.
Instead he told how Paris was reborn:
'Abused and broken, martyred, but now free!
Paris, now freed by her own citizens,
Assisted by the proper arms of France,
Supported by the whole of fighting France,
That is by France herself, eternal France!'[25]
He did not mention what the Allies did,
But there were other times for gratitude.

A sea of people stood along the route,
At every window, even on the roofs,
Applauding, cheering, waving tricolors,
As, from the Arc de Triomphe, slowly walked
Along the Champs Elysees, Charles de Gaulle,
One step ahead of other officers.
Upon the *parvis* outside Notre Dame,
Another crowd awaited silently
De Gaulle's arrival for the service there.
As he approached the portal, shots were fired.
In panic, people flung themselves to ground,

But not de Gaulle, who, looking straight ahead,
Proceeded quietly into Notre Dame.
Through war and peace his courage would remain.
By his integrity France lived again.

37 Arnhem

Across the plains of France the Allies drove,
Whilst, in the south, a second landing came
And hastened northwards, fast along the Rhone,
Since German opposition there was light.
Tumultuous crowds in Brussels welcomed back
The British who had crossed the Dyle Canal
Four years before. It seemed to Eisenhower,
And all who saw defeated Wehrmacht troops
Withdrawing through the towns with wounded men
And salvaged weaponry, that even as
The shades of Autumn fell, victory had come.
One bold and powerful thrust might end the war,
And whilst the Soviet armies were delayed
For lack of strength to cross the Vistula,
The Siegfried Line might rupture, and present
The prize of Germany to Allied arms.

But still the lorry convoys ran at length
From Normandy to Belgium and Lorraine.
No port yet served the growing need for oil
And guns and food for armies at the front.
Though Antwerp had been taken, on the Scheldt
The Germans held the gateway to the sea.
Elsewhere in Holland launching pads were built
For V2 rockets, targeted to land
On Antwerp and the London area.
Invulnerable to aircraft and to guns,
They brought a final blitz to bear on those
Accustomed to a lottery of death.
Thus V2 bases were a further goal
Of Allied forces on the continent.

Montgomery planned a fresh initiative.
If Bradley's armies halted their advance,
The British in the west could be supplied
To mount a swift offensive to the Ruhr
And capture the industrial heartland there.
The plan belied his reputation gained
For cautious strategy and measured speed,
For massive build-ups, lengthy barrages,
And pegging out the ground at every step.
This time he would convey an airborne force
To capture crossing points on major streams
That flowed across the line of their advance,
Making a path for soldiers on the ground
To hasten north and reach the Zuyder Zee.
Then, wheeling east, they would present a front
Along the line Zwolle-Deventer-Arnhem.
Outflanking by this means the Siegfried Line,

They'd fall upon the Ruhr and seal it off;
Whilst driving northwards, Bradley's army, too,
Would reinforce the Ruhr encirclement.
All would depend on timing the attack
To hold the crucial bridges long enough,
Before the Wehrmacht's certain counterstroke.
Unverified reports of *Panzer* troops
Abroad in Holland did not shake the faith
Of those who saw this moment opportune
To win the war before the Winter came.

General Student, whose elite paratroops
Had fought so hard to take the isle of Crete,
Now in command along the Meuse canal,
Was startled by the sound of many planes,
And saw, above the gables of the town,
A vast armada flying to the north -
Gliders, tugs, Dakota carriers,
Full, he well knew, of Allied paratroops.

Most landed safely at their dropping zones,
And soon the bridge at Eindhoven was held.
Grave also was secured, across the Maas,
But, on the Waal, Nijmegen bridge remained,
Like that at Arnhem, still in German hands.
Americans took Groesbeek to the east,
For from that ridge artillery could fire
In range of bridging points across the Waal.
Beside the concrete road that ran due north,
The British tanks awaited the command
To drive across the German-held terrain,

Towards Eindhoven and the 'corridor',
Defended by the vanguard paratroops.

'Red berets' of the British airborne force
Descended west of Arnhem, to avoid
The polder land beside the central bridge.
Whilst some remained to hold the dropping zones,
One parachute brigade formed up to march,
And in the suburbs sometimes were delayed
By kindly Dutch, who welcomed them with tea.

General Model, just recently relieved
As officer commanding in the West,
Was stationed now, by chance, in Arnhem town,
And quickly took command of its defence.
Two SS units, back from Normandy,
Refitting now in Holland, were nearby.
Without delay they closed with British troops,
Outgunning them with heavy weaponry.
Meanwhile, south of the Maas, a German force
Moved rapidly towards the Arnhem bridge,
Seizing the southern pylon, just in time
To stop the British rushing from the north.
Opposing forces stood at either end.
Which one would be the first to reinforce?
On this event, the tide of war would turn.

Across their starting line the British tanks
Rolled forward, one by one, along the road
That stretched beside the saturated earth.
In cypress woods the German gun crews lay,
Behind their *Panzerfausts* and eighty-eights.

But, as the tanks in single column left,
A rolling barrage fell on either side,
From British field-guns firing in support;
And Typhoon fighters skimmed above the trees,
Their rocket fire directed from the ground
To immolate defensive strong-points there.
Though tanks were lost, the column quickly reached
Eindhoven bridge, and soon had passed beyond.
At Zon they were delayed at the canal,
For reconstruction of the crossing there.

In parkland at Nijmegen near the Waal,
A regiment of US paratroops
At daylight launched their storm-boats in the flood.
Though many fell, exposed to heavy fire,
The rest, unbroken, won a slender hold,
And pressed courageously towards the bridge.
Two British tanks, meanwhile, had been destroyed
By Germans perched on girders high above,
As they had stormed the southern bridge approach.
Others raced on, through half a mile of fire,
And gained the northern end as, from the west,
The remnant US paratroops emerged.
So Arnhem's highway lay ahead of them.

That final bridge across the Neder Rijn
Was now the crucible. Soon after dusk
A British unit tried to storm across,
Devoid of cover, from the northern bank.
Like hapless lions they fell before the guns.
Some German half-tracks, similarly brave,
Soon smouldered fiercely on the cluttered span.

But Germans now had infiltrated through
Between the British troops who held the bridge
And those who formed the two perimeters
At Oosterbeek and Wolfheze dropping zone.

In tall Dutch houses by the bridge approach
The paratroops fought on phlegmatically
With rifles, mortars, *Piats* and hand-guns
Against artillery and Tiger tanks,
Whose fire demolished buildings floor by floor.
Phosphorous shells ignited in their midst,
Impelling them to move from house to house,
Until they were entrapped within a school,
Above a cellar where the wounded lay
Attended by an heroic Arnhem wife.
As casualties increased, the doctors said
To Colonel Frost, the officer in charge,
Surrender them or see them burned alive.
An armistice was made, and Red Cross flags
Accompanied the wounded as they left
In British jeeps that Germans commandeered.
The shooting was resumed. All contact now
Was lost with other troops.

Later waves of parachutists came,
Delayed by fog at English aerodromes.
South of the bridge the eager Poles had dropped
With heavy losses from the German flak;
And struggled yet to reach the ferry boats,
Till Germans overran the northern bank,
Ensuring that no further help would come.

Meanwhile the British troops near Oosterbeek
Were undergoing concentrated fire
From SS *Panzers* and artillery.
Wireless transmission did not operate;
No aircraft could be called to lay down fire.
Supplies were failing; dead and wounded grew,
But still they made, though unavailingly,
Attempts to reach their comrades at the bridge.

In dire extremity, like those of old
Who'd fought at Maldon or on Hastings hill,
With 'heart the greater as our might grows less'[26],
Each fought with a sustained ferocity,
Discovering within himself reserves
Of physical endurance, with no thought
Of personal life, discomfort, pain or death.
Each measured out his action to the need
To feed the bullets in and aim with care,
To load the mortars - ducking as they fired -
To dress each wound and cover up the dead,
And comfort dying men in each brief pause
Between the German rounds of 'mortar hates'.
In such adversity the British lost
Their coarse disguise of common soldiery.
Foul language was not heard; men were polite.
They helped each other, heedless of themselves.
No resentment clung to their mistakes.
Amidst the savagery of bloody war,
With dirt and hunger, thirst and lack of sleep,
In shell-holes, ditches, wrecks and ruined homes,
They lived a life uniquely civilised,
Nearer to death, yet nearer still to God.

For Frost's survivors nemesis had come.
Phospherous shells drove soldiers from the school.
No longer could the road-block there be held.
Forlornly now they saw the Germans cross
The blackened bridge so long denied to them.
So Wehrmacht troops traversed the Neder Rijn
Three hours before Nijmegen bridge was reached
By British units driving from the south.
Continued fighting meant that all would die,
Including wounded burnt in caustic flames.
As they emerged, beneath surrender flags,
The German soldiers stood applauding them,
And, to their captives, offered cigarettes.

On polderland the road to Arnhem lay,
Low-lying, wet and criss-crossed by canals.
Tanks of the Guards Division, in a line,
Made silhouettes against the vacant sky
As they advanced along the narrow dyke.
The German guns could target them at will
With armour-piercing shells from nearby farms.
Fearing that the verges there were mined,
The lorries in support kept to the road,
So traffic jams developed frequently.
Germans, now advancing from the north,
Formed anti-tank screens on the road at Elst.
As contact with the R.A.F. was lost,
The Typhoons overhead could not attack.
So infantry were ordered to proceed
Along a minor road through Oosterhout;
But unaware how desperate was the plight
Of those 'Red berets' still beyond the Rijn,

They fought too cautiously. Yet messages
From paratroops had come. One briefly said:
'No ammunition left. God save the King'.
Few soldiers from relieving forces crossed
The Neder Rijn to reinforce them there.
Supplies of every kind were running out,
And those dropped from the air, with heavy loss
Of planes and pilots, flying very low,
Fell mainly into waiting German hands,
Beyond the lines of British paratroops.
They watched, within their small perimeter,
Like hungry dogs, caged up, while others fed.

The order came, at last, for their retreat.
In heavy rain and wind, at dead of night,
The fit, and walking wounded, slipped away
Across the river on some makeshift boats,
Leaving the crippled manning weapons still
To misinform the Germans of their plight.
Three-quarters of the British airborne force,
Who'd dropped at Arnhem near the Neder Rijn,
Could not recross the river where they'd fought
So gallantly to seize the single way.
Their rites of passage stopped at Arnhem bridge.
They stayed as prisoners, proud in their defeat,
Or lay in graves of fertile polderland.

Had Montgomery planned a bridge too far,
Or had the weather jeopardised success
By hampering the later airborne waves?
Was German strength enhanced by circumstance -
Two SS units, stationed to refit -

Or was a treacherous Dutchman to be blamed?
Why was the bridge at Nijmegen not crossed
With more despatch to hasten on relief?
The paratroops, wherever they were dropped,
Had fought with valour unsurpassable.
Would those at Arnhem have preferred to risk
A dropping zone much closer to the bridge,
Despite the polderland and heavier flak?
And why were British infantry so slow
To bring relief between the Waal and Rijn?
The order had been given 'at all costs',
But not relayed to soldiers at the front.

A catalogue of errors and mischance
Had proved Montgomery wrong. Yet if possessed
Of greater force by land and in the air
He might have won. But that preponderance
Lay with America, whose high command
Was loath to find, for Britishers, the means
To make a major thrust to end the war.
Was Patton, who had fought his way to Metz,
Whose troops confronted now the Siegfried Line,
Prepared to stand impatiently aside?
If British forces entered Germany,
And raced to beat the Russians to Berlin,
What would the New York papers say of this?
Nor was Dwight Eisenhower a strategist,
For all his diplomatic skill and charm.
He had not called upon sufficient power
To make Montgomery's daring plan prevail.
He still preferred to marshall Allied force
At every point on his extended front,

Closing all his armies on the Rhine,
And testing where the enemy proved weak.
As Grant had done within the 'Wilderness',
He fought his battles measured by success
In casualties inflicted on the foe,
And did not really want a British march,
Like Sherman's to the sea in Georgia.

A salient had been won, but not enough
To cross the Rhine and swing the armies east.
Now much of Holland stayed in German hands,
Its population facing Winter blight,
When some would starve. Still V2 bases fired
On Londoners, and killed in Antwerp's port,
More Belgians there than Allied servicemen.
On Walcheren Isle a bitter conflict raged,
Until, at last, the estuary was free
For Allied ships to navigate the Scheldt.
Another year of death would be endured,
And millions more would answer its command.
The British graves in Holland laid no claim
To precedence in honour or respect,
And yet a certain pride would linger there
With those who lay at Arnhem, now at rest,
Who gave their lives to hasten war's arrest.

38 The Battle of Leyte Gulf

One hope remained for warlords of Japan,
As from the Marianas US power
Spread westwards to the inner fastnesses
Of Nippon empire: the Imperial fleet
Was still formidable. Two battleships,
The giants, 'Yamato' and the 'Musashi',
Outgunned the largest in the US fleet.
Supplied with oil from Indonesia,
Most ships were stationed close to Singapore,
For US submarines took heavy toll
Of any traffic northwards to Japan.
The parallel advance by sea and land
Of Nimitz and MacArthur posed a threat
Of desperate urgency. Their paths converged

Upon the Philippines. Were these to fall
No oil would reach Japan. Her forces too,
Across the seas, on every fighting front,
Would be immobilised. The die was cast.
Just as Imperial navy manuals said:
The battle is the means of victory
And all must bow to what the battle needs.

Ironically the US navy, too,
Looked to a final clash of major fleets;
For since the 'infamous day' three years before,
It had amassed, in every class of ship,
Unrivalled numbers. Admiral King preferred
To concentrate against Formosa next,
But when the isle of Leyte was perceived,
By air attack, to be ill-garrisoned,
Nimitz and MacArthur both agreed
On prompt invasion of the Philippines.
The navy would transport MacArthur's force
To Leyte Gulf, from which they'd seize Luzon.
Aware of this, the Japanese now planned
A naval action, daring in its scope.
A pincer movement would attack the ships
That brought the landing force to Leyte Gulf;
Whilst, further north, a group of carriers
Would act as decoys, drawing far away
The major ships of Admiral Halsey's fleet.
Japanese naval experts still had faith
That battleships could dominate the sea,
And yet they knew Americans believed
That victory rested now with sea-borne planes.
And so, like hunters choosing favoured baits,

They sacrificed a fleet of carriers.
As transports landed men by Leyte Gulf,
Guarded by Kinkaid's fleet, off Luzon Isle
The powerful ships of Halsey's carrier group
Perused the sea with radar and air scouts.
Kurita's force, approaching from the west,
Was spotted first by US submarines,
Who sank two cruisers, and then signalled back
Kurita's northbound route. He planned to pass
San Bernardino Strait, and rendezvous
With Nishimuro's group, which would traverse -
As once Magellan fatally had done -
The Surigao Strait, to meet Kurita
Near to Leyte Gulf; but Halsey's planes
Swept fast across the brilliant inland sea
To intercept Kurita's battlefleet.
When aircraft based on Luzon intervened,
Once more the Hellcats proved superior
In rate of climb and dive and armourplate -
Though one survivor bombed the 'Princeton''s decks
And later fires forced her abandonment -
Then ships alone could not defend themselves
Against the Hellcats' systematic dives
With air-torpedoes, bombs and cannon-fire.
'Musashi', hit at least two dozen times,
Her bow submerged and engine room defunct,
Rolled ponderously to port, and sank forthwith.
With other ships on fire, Kurita turned
To get beyond the range of Halsey's planes.

Yet now deception plans began to work:
Halsey had seen no Nippon carriers,

Until reports came in from scouting planes
Of such a force, far north and steaming south.
It was, indeed, Ozawa's decoy fleet,
Whose carriers were ill-equipped with planes -
For many had been lost in earlier sweeps
By US aircraft off the China coast -
But served as well for bait. Since Halsey knew
That Kinkaid would defend Surigao Strait
And that Kurita's force had turned away,
He saw the chance of glorious victory.
Did he not now recall how Spruance failed
To seize the moment offered at Saipan
To concentrate against Ozawa's fleet?
Had Admiral Nimitz not himself prescribed
That to destroy the Nippon battlefleet
Took precedence above all other tasks?
But Halsey did not know Kurita chose
To turn again and sail for Leyte Gulf.

Motor torpedo boats were first to sight
The southern pincer, Nishimura's group.
Across the Strait of Surigao was set
A line of Kinkaid's ships - some veterans
Of when Pearl Harbour burned - which opened fire
With armour-piercing shells. The 'T' was capped;
And Nishimura ran into the trap.
In fifteen minutes his main ships were sunk.

Despite this classic victory, Kinkaid heard,
To his dismay, of Kurita's descent
On Leyte's beaches, crowded now with men.
For Halsey's fleet was several hours away,

Engaged against Ozawa's carriers.
Though strikes by planes and then by battleships
Annihilated all Ozawa's force,
Such losses might be doubly redeemed,
If Kurita could gather the reward.

Protection of the disembarking troops
Lay with Commander Sprague's depleted force -
Destroyers and converted merchantmen.
Despite his losses, Kurita retained
The strongest ships that flew the Rising Sun,
Foremost of these the flagship, 'Yamato'.
To intercept this mighty Juggernaut,
Commander Sprague sent three destroyers back -
A contest of gross inequality
Which saw all three inevitably sunk.
Then fighter-planes from merchantmen attacked,
Though poorly armed with general purpose bombs,
Or even on 'dry-runs' with empty racks.
Now driven close inshore at Leyte Gulf,
The unprotected transports lay exposed
To gunfire from the Nippon battlefleet.

But then the gods of warfare intervened
To favour Sprague for his temerity.
Kurita thought he faced a US fleet.
He had no news of how Ozawa fared,
But knew that Nishimura was destroyed.
He'd heard Kinkaid appeal for extra help,
And seen the fresh attacks by US planes
Ordered by Halsey from his distant fleet.
He did not know that Halsey and Kinkaid

Could not arrive in time to intercede.
Thus deluded, Kurita withdrew,
Casting away his country's golden chance
For one great victory in the naval war.
Command was lost. 'Yamato' turned about,
Too wary of an aerial attack.
Americans rubbed their eyes in disbelief
At enemy warships hastening away.

The Imperial navy played one final scene
Of fitting drama in its tragedy.
For months it had prepared young volunteers
To turn their aircraft into guided bombs
And crash on US ships. The wind divine
That shattered Kublai Khan was thus invoked
To name these warriors. By friend and foe,
The men who sacrificed their lives for 'On' -
Their gratitude to family and Japan -
Were called the 'kamikaze'. Some foresaw
A blissful afterlife; all coveted
Heroic death for causes won or lost.
So now, as Admiral Kurita steamed back
To pass again San Bernardino Strait,
In groups of three the 'kamikaze' flew,
Till each in turn, in solitary flight,
Dived down, and held in steady sight ahead
A conning-tower, or bridge, or wireless mast.
Though many fell to ships' defensive fire,
The rest flew on, like hawks towards a lure,
To die amidst the havoc of their foes
In splintered steel and acrid petrol flames.
Thus was the carrier, 'St Lo', destroyed,

As, through her deck, one suicidal plane
Ignited the torpedo stores below.
Henceforth the name of 'kamikaze' grew
To trouble all Americans at war.
Would such a will to conquer or to die
Make of the Japanese a race apart,
Unable to surrender in their pride,
And ready for interminable war?

Once Leyte Gulf was won and landings made,
The conquest of the island was ensured,
Though Japanese resistance cost those dear
Who had the task of occupying it.
Still very few surrendered; so again
The gory work of flame and bayonet
Completed what the bullet left undone.
To capture Luzon was a greater step
That waited on accretion of reserves.

Yet, more important, naval victory
Offered command of all the western seas.
Henceforth the oil of Indonesia
Would rarely reach the islands of Japan.
The ring was closing fast, but still one doubt
Beset all those habituated now
To martial ardour of the Japanese.
Would their resolve to fight at any cost
To save the sacred homeland from assault,
Subvert the war to endless sacrifice
And force the Allies to an armistice?

39 The Battle of the Bulge

As Winter came the war in Europe slowed.
On every front the battlefield congealed
For shortage of reserves, or war supplies,
Which Russia and America contained,
But could not bring sufficiently to hand
For want of transport. In western Russia
Railways must be built; whilst Antwerp port,
Enduring still bombardment by V2s,
Needed refurbishment. In Italy,
The Winter mud impeded Allied arms,
Reduced perforce by transference of men
To other theatres, notably to France.

The German Führer, enervated now
By paranoia, fear and injury,
Yet had not lost his wilful recklessness,
And still retained the charismatic power

To quash the doubts attendant on defeat
With hope of victory, though irrational.
Ignoring what he knew of Allied strength,
He planned a sudden onslaught in the west
To split the Allied front in the Ardennes.
For mindful of success with '*Sichelschnitt*' -
The strategy that broke the might of France -
He saw again the *Panzers'* triumph there:
The thrust of armoured columns through the hills,
Now bleak with Winter boughs and darkened firs,
The burning wrecks of enemy machines,
The entry into stunned and frightened towns,
The Channel coast, and Antwerp's vital port,
And, in conclusion, stalemate in the west.
What then might he achieve: the Russian front
Rendered impregnable, the V2 raids
Continued without pause, command of sea
And air by new electric U-boats
And jet planes? Such was the Führer's dream.

Von Rundstedt knew these aims exceeded far
The means that were available to him.
In vain he tried to limit the attack
To pinching out the Aachen salient
In order to restore the Siegfried Line.
Hitler was contemptuous of this;
And so, with utmost secrecy, was raised,
East of the Ardennes, a powerful force
Of *Panzers* and selected infantry.
No longer were the Allies well informed
By citizens of countries occupied
About the dispositions of their foes,

For now the enemy was cosseted
By provenance in German hinterland.
Thus, in the Eifel, hidden in the woods
That once had marked the bounds of Roman sway,
Selected Wehrmacht units and SS
Assembled for their Führer's masterstroke.

The Allied leaders did not contemplate
Aggressive action by the force they'd seen
Driven so precipitously from France.
They thought of Christmas, and the coming year,
The crossing of the Rhine, and victory,
Then sending home their troops beyond the seas.
They did not know that German infantry,
Who spoke good English, driving captured jeeps,
Had infiltrated through American lines,
And busily were cutting telephones,
Or turning signposts round, or spreading lies,
Such as that General Eisenhower was dead.
American soldiers, thoroughly confused,
Reacted with a systematic check,
Identifying everyone who passed
By means of questions, such as asking names
Of US baseball players, States and towns.
Even General Bradley did not know
The name of Betty Grable's latest spouse!
But Germans who were caught were shot as spies.

Hitler chose, as spearhead on the right,
SS divisions, which would cross the Meuse,
Seize Antwerp, and defend the northern flank.
Eight hundred guns announced the opening phase.

Across the starting line the *Panzers* rolled,
Expectant crews concealing any doubts
Of Wehrmacht strength and enemy response.
Beneath a leaden sky, on snow filled lanes,
The mass of tanks, advancing, easily broke
The thin defensive screen of Bradley's troops,
Though many points were held tenaciously -
Actions on which the final outcome turned.

Near Stavelot lay enormous petrol dumps,
But US engineers set up a screen
Of blazing drums to block the entrance road.
Along this flank the fighting was intense.
Waffen SS, frustrated by delay,
Machine-gunned prisoners in a field of snow.
A few escaped, and told of their ordeal.
Americans henceforth fought bitterly
Whenever SS troops confronted them.
St Vith was held, defended like a rock
On which the *Panzer* tide was forced to split.
On lateral roads and winding steep inclines,
The ponderous armour lost its impetus.
Yet now the skies did not unfurl the scourge
That drove the Germans out of Normandy,
For heavy cloud prevented bombing strikes.
Without air cover could the Allies match,
In combat on the ground, those ardent troops
Who knew this was the final chance to halt
Invasion of their homes and Fatherland?

Model suggested that the '*Schwerpunkt*' change,
With reinforcements on the southern wing,

As it approached Bastogne and Houffalize,
But Hitler would not let what he had called
A turning-point of war be undermined
By taking from his personal bodyguard,
Waffen SS, the torch of leadership.
Since his survival from the army plot,
These special forces, under Himmler's rule,
Had been assigned a new authority.
In Hitler eyes they were a pure elite,
Not tainted, like the Wehrmacht officers,
By doubtful loyalty and a lack of faith
In his own judgment and the Nazi State.
These scruples of internal politics
Precluded now a tactical response
Upon the battlefield, for in the south
Wehrmacht divisions raced through Luxembourg
Towards the winding Meuse. Only Bastogne
Resisted their advance, its garrison
Already reinforced by paratroops
Brought in by lorries, driven hard from Rheims.

Upon this Belgian town five roads converged.
Though German spearheads hastened further west,
Their progress was retarded by the loss
Of Bastogne's vital junctions. Yet the town
Was totally besieged, with all roads cut.
Not since Guadalcanal had US troops
Experienced such close encirclement.
Their blocking forces on the outer roads
Could barely hold the German armour thrusts,
But tanks that reached the town were soon destroyed.
A message sent to General McAuliffe,

Demanding the surrender of Bastogne,
Was answered with the swift reply of 'Nuts!',
Which baffled German efforts to translate.

Allied leaders had been quite deceived
By what, at first, they saw in the Ardennes.
They thought it was a tactical advance,
A spoiling operation, with intent
To draw reserves from Patton near the Saar.
But then events had disillusioned them:
They faced a major German counterstroke,
Which threatened to disrupt their whole command
When Bradley lost all contact with the north.
But there Montgomery acted rapidly.
Ordering British troops to guard the Meuse
At crossing points from Liege to Namur,
He sent liaison officers abroad
To bring him news of how the battle fared.
A wise decision came from Eisenhower:
Within the northern sector, every front
Was placed within Montgomery's command.

The race was on: would Germans cross the Meuse,
And emulate what 'Sichelschnitt' had done
By breaking out across the lowland plains
To reach the coast and split the front in two?
This time their adversaries were more skilled.
For Patton sent, with utmost urgency,
A powerful force from south of the Moselle
To help relieve the Bastogne garrison;
Whilst British forces moved behind the Meuse
To block at any point a German thrust.

Within the Ardennes hills the Allied grip,
From Marche to Stavelot, intensified.
Montgomery made a few withdrawals there,
Whilst gathering a strong offensive force,
Led by General Collins, who had fought
At Cherbourg with intrepid energy.

On Christmas Eve the Germans bombed Bastogne.
Next day it faced a savage tank assault;
But every tank that passed the road-blocks fell
To anti-tank gun fire within the town,
And none escaped of German infantry.
McAuliffe's men had ten shells left per gun,
When Patton brought relief on Boxing Day
By breaking through the close besieging ring.

In desperation Wehrmacht spearheads charged
Towards the Meuse at Dinant and Givet,
Forced by Montgomery's firmness in the north
To veer away from well-defended routes
To Liege and to Antwerp. Four miles short
Of where the Dinant cliffs o'erlook the Meuse,
Whose rushing stream would not be seen again
By soldiers of the Reich, the tanks were stopped.
A violent battle left the woods despoiled
With wrecks and field-grey bodies in the snow.
The Ardennes hills reflected how the war
Had turned from German victory in the Spring
To dire calamity in Winter snow.
Though Allied unity showed signs of strain,
With British boasts to have restored the front,
A speech by Winston Churchill mended all,

By telling how Americans had died
To hold Bastogne and save the Allied line.

At last the weather cleared and aircraft flew.
With memories of the skies in Normandy,
The Wehrmacht soldiers heard the dreaded sound
Of fighter-bombers, diving low to fire
On tanks and trucks retreating hastily
Down narrow roads with crooked bottlenecks.
Air sorties also struck behind the lines,
Where, in the Eifel, railheads, depots, roads
Supplied the *Panzers'* last and frantic bid
To hold the ground so recently regained.
Model once more suggested a campaign
To cut the Allies' Aachen salient,
But Hitler still insisted on offence.
For now he planned a second new attack,
West of the Vosges, the very place indeed
Where Eisenhower had earlier proposed
To order a withdrawal from Alsace -
The anger of de Gaulle had gained reprieve.
But Hitler's plan was soon frustrated there.
No German troops invaded Strasbourg's peace
Beneath the tricolor in Place Kleber
That proved Leclerc had honoured there his pledge.

Deep snowdrifts slowed the Allied infantry,
And ice-bound roads, and mines laid loose in snow,
Delayed the tanks. And yet, at Houffalize,
A narrow defile threatened to entrap
The German armour, harrassed there by planes
And Allied guns with deadly air-burst shells.

Even the Fuhrer recognised defeat.
The *Panzers* hurried back to make a front
Not far from where their start-line had been drawn.
Reserves of armour, vital for defence
Along extensive borders of the Reich,
Had been expended in this one debacle.
Chimeras of success had sealed the fate
Of army, people, Fuhrer, Fatherland.
Once more the pride of Germany recoiled,
Seeing the mighty Wehrmacht lick its wounds.
The weakened beast had turned upon the hunt
And savaged it severely, but in vain.
Yet it would fight - on native soil - again.

40 Victory in Burma

From Chindwin to the Irrawaddy's bend
The Japanese awaited the assault
Of Fourteenth Army. For General Slim,
The victor of Imphal, would countenance
No tardy strategy, but drove his reborn
Soldiers hard, upon Kawabe's heels.
Disorganised and sick, the remnant left
A trail of dead on roads and jungle paths,
Abandoned where they fell, or propped by trees,
Amidst the debris of a forced retreat -
The buckled shells of lorries, wrecks of tanks,
And mud-clogged rifles, splintered boxes, clothes,
The scattered papers, letters, office files
Of men unnerved by war's catastrophe.

But soon Kimura, sent from Tokyio,
Restored the armies on the Burma front,
And set himself to push the British back
Beyond the Chindwin to the Naga Hills.
Slim planned to fight within the Schwebo plain,
In open country suitable for tanks,
Where air and armour could co-operate
And drive the Japanese towards the south,
Till at their backs the Irrawaddy flowed.
But, unlike other generals Slim had faced,
Kimura was not frightened to withdraw.
He would not fight enclosed within the flood
Of curving streams, rather on southern shores.
The British columns therefore only met
A light resistance in the Schwebo plain,
Which proved to Slim Kimura's strategy:
To hold the river crossings and attack
Whatever bridgeheads his opponent made.
Slim knew the problems thus confronting him,
Traversing water under heavy fire:
The mile-wide Irrawaddy's banks and shoals,
With current strong and shores of sand and swamp,
Shortage of boats and dinghies, or pontoons,
And open landings bitterly opposed
By guns concealed in tree-lined river banks,
And enemies now eager to arrest
The shame and hardship of a long retreat.

These tactical demands did not impede
Construction of a brilliant master-plan.
Though Mandalay was foremost as the goal -
A nodal point Kimura had to save -

Slim was aware that, sixty miles due south,
Meiktila was a Japanese redoubt,
Where roads converged and vital airstrips lay,
And crucial as a centre of command.
A secret march, and crossings further south,
Whilst other forces threatened Mandalay,
Might seize Meiktila, cutting off retreat
By Japanese within the river's loop.
Slim had ensured that in the Arakan,
And in the eastern hills where Stilwell fought,
The Japanese would be again attacked,
Unable then to help Kimura's force
In fighting on the Irrawaddy shore.
When time was ripe, he also would engage
The Allied air-power in his two assaults.
Yet on Kimura's error all would rest:
Deploying for defence of Mandalay
Along the Irrawaddy's southern banks,
And in reserve against the bridgeheads there,
Regardless of his vulnerable flank.
Could such a shrewd commander be deceived
For long enough to strike decisively?

On red-dust roads that, when the monsoon came,
Would turn to quagmires ankle-deep in mud,
The British army hastened to approach
The crossing points from Thabeikkyin to Chauk.
Precipitous bends and steeply cambered slopes
Delayed their armour. Fierce encounters, too,
With Japanese, some ordered to their death,
Slowed them the more. But first at Thabeikkyin,
Then at Kyaukmyaung, they crossed the rapid stream.

The major bridgeheads would be further south,
Near Mandalay, and then past Pakokku,
Whence Messervy's corps would strike at Meiktila.

The latter moved along the western hills,
Concealed on jungle routes, supplied by air,
With wireless contact strictly minimised.
A dummy station north of Mandalay
Sent messages in clear to misinform,
And broadcast news leaked 'information' out
Of where the troops of Messervy advanced.
One chance event might wreck deception plans:
An Oscar pilot flying tree-top high
Might spot a column winding through the hills;
A hidden spy might count the passing trucks
And call Kimura's staff by radio;
A prisoner might be tortured to reveal
Some facts pertaining to the British plan.
But Slim ignored such fears, and drew more strength
From how his troops faced all adversities,
Like Major-General Cowan, whose young son
Was killed in the advance on Mandalay.
Hard fighting cleared defensive garrisons
That held the Saingaing Hills. Expectant troops
Closed up upon the Irrawaddy's bank.
The long-awaited time of crossing came.

It would be made where captured maps revealed
A junction point of Japanese commands,
Which did not interlock their boundaries.
Yet tough resistance held them at Myinmu,
Till Japanese survivors chose to drown
By marching in closed ranks beneath the flood.

At night the British launched their meagre boats
To cross a mile of swiftly flowing stream,
Obstructed by half-sunken banks of sand
And freshening wind. Only small arms and
Mortars answered back, for on the southern shore
Air strikes had forced artillery to move,
And now sporadic shells were poorly aimed.
By eight o'clock the further bank was seized.
Later the beach was strafed by air attack,
But Japanese who landed in their rear
Were savagely repulsed by bridgehead troops.
Then suicide attacks, some led by tanks,
Were driven off, with conflict hand-to-hand,
Whilst Hurricanes, called in by radio,
Hit tanks and troops assembled for attack
With rocket fire.

Meanwhile, Messervy's columns further west
Had reached the river, undiscovered still;
For Japanese reports of British troops
In this arena took them for a feint,
Posing as a threat to Yenangyaung,
Whose oil deposits were much coveted.
But crossings now attempted at Nyaungu
Brought near-disaster. One party crossed in
Darkness to the cliffs that overlooked the
Nippons' river bank, shooting two swimmers
Captured near the beach. But others, caught in
Currents and in wind, had drifted helplessly.
Confusion spread as officers were hit;
The boatmen panicked, many soldiers drowned.
The rest retreated to the northern bank.

Downriver at Pagan, a group of Sikhs
Had bravely crossed to reconnoitre there,
And held position, though their comrades failed
To ferry reinforcements to their aid.
As dawn approached, the ancient city stood,
With temple towers of madder red and white
Against the sage green trees and pastel sky,
Now silent, ruined, and blasphemed by war,
Yet noble in transcendence of the time.

The feint attacks at Pakokku and Chauk
Had drawn off the Pagan garrison.
Their allies of the Indian Nationalists
Alone remained, and these surrendered soon,
No more deluded by their masters' boast
To free the Asian subjects of the Raj.
A new attempt to cross began once more
Upstream at Nyaungu, facing on the cliffs.
Again the treacherous current grounded some
On mid-stream shoals, or carried them away;
But, under heavy covering fire, in boats,
Or swimming, wading up the banks, they reached
The other shore - and found no enemy!

Next day were ferried over men and mules,
Tanks, guns and stores, with no opposing fire.
Later a brief attack was driven off,
And Japanese who hid in Nyaungu's caves
Were left to die, entombed in graves of rock,
When British sappers blew the entrance in.
Messervy's force had made the daring step:
The Irrawaddy ran behind them now.

Ahead the prize, Meiktila, to be won!
Yet Slim impressed on Fourteenth Army's men
That foremost in their minds the aim must be
Destruction of the armies of Japan.
If Meiktila were seized, it would become
The anvil for the hammer blow to fall
From Mandalay to crush the Japanese.
The path would then be opened to Rangoon
And Burma freed. But as Messervy crossed
The open plain, at last with armour massed,
Slim was informed that on his eastern flank
Where Chinese had retaken Lashio,
The Allied force would be severely cut
By Chiang Kai-Shek's withdrawal of his troops
To fight the invader in their native land.
Kimura was now free to reinforce
His hard-pressed armies fighting in defence
Of Mandalay on Irrawaddy's shore.
Boldly, too, he drew upon reserves
In Arakan and in the river loop.
Against such concentration was there time
For victory before the monsoon broke
And turned the dusty battlefields to mud?

Slim was resolved: Kimura's destiny
Was nothing short of absolute defeat.
Redoubled efforts drove the British on
To reach Meiktila's manned perimeter,
Which Japanese had reinforced in strength.
Strong-points in houses, guns in rubble-heaps,
Snipers in ruins, met each fresh assault.
In banks of lakes and irrigation streams

Troops hid in bunkers, opening fire point-blank,
And single soldiers, holding each a mine,
Would blow themselves apart to stop a tank.
But fighting hand to hand with bated rage
Across the fields of slaughtered enemy,
The British army took Meiktila town.

Astounded by the news of this event,
Kimura yet reacted rationally.
He could not leave Meiktila in his rear,
His enemy astride the major roads,
His depots and communications lost.
From everywhere in Burma he recalled
Whoever could be spared to fight anew
The battle for the vital garrison.
Even from the lines of Mandalay,
Themselves immersed in violent new assaults,
Some troops withdrew. By air reconnaissance
And keen patrols the British tracked them down.
Before they could converge, they ambushed them;
Road blocks delayed them, aircraft strafed and bombed,
Artillery destroyed their bivouacs.

Those who survived to fight at Meiktila
As often perished on a Gurkha knife.
Yet, at the airfield, vital for supplies,
Determined Japanese encroached so far
That landings were preceded by the task
Of making runways free from hostile fire;
Though still some planes exploded from a hit,
Incinerating men as they arrived.
Only successive infantry attacks,

With bayonet charges, merciless and swift,
Each following a fighter-bomber raid,
Secured at last the field's perimeter.
Meiktila then was permanently safe.

A massive rock, the hill of Mandalay,
Was fortified by ardent Japanese
To dominate the city's northern streets.
In temples and pagodas on its slopes,
They made redoubts, defended to the death.
At heavy cost, a Gurkha unit fought,
With Sten guns and grenades, from post to post;
Until the final stand was overwhelmed,
When, in the cellars, petrol drums were rolled
And set alight by tracer bullet fire.
Fort Dufferin, a second obstacle,
Could not be taken by conventional means -
By scaling ladders on the massive walls,
Or bombing ramparts filled with tons of earth.
But rebel Burmese troops within the fort
Surrendered soon, while Japanese escaped,
Or died in houses, trapped within the town.

Above the fort the Union Jack was raised.
And then the anvil felt the hammer blows,
As British troops spread out, intent to kill
All Japanese who still resisted them.
Kimura would not yet concede defeat;
He drew defensive lines across the map,
And saw them shattered ruthlessly forthwith.
Beset by Burmese, rising in revenge,
And soon outpaced by British mobile groups,

The Japanese reverted in despair
To suicide attacks of slight effect.
Rangoon was won before the monsoon came.

The British had returned; and once again
The seat of Empire flew their monarch's flag.
Yet few of those tired troops, when it unfurled,
Considered as their merited reward
'The white man's burden', British sovereignty.
Their pride lay in themselves, and in their arms,
And in their General, 'Uncle Bill' himself,
Who'd led them from a miserable retreat
To overcome, in combat hand to hand,
Fanatic soldiers, careless of their lives,
Quicker to die for shame of their defeat.
In perilous hills, on morbid jungle trails,
On river crossings rife with accident,
Waiting to hear the sounds of night attack,
Labouring beneath the tropic sun,
Hungry, ill, exhausted, they had fought,
And made the name of soldier their reward.
They were not famous, like the 'desert rats',
Nor honoured, like the Arnhem paratroops,
Nor feted home on leave from fields of France.
They, the 'forgotten army', far away,
Somewhere on distant Asian battlefields,
A motley crowd of mixed belief and race,
Would soon disperse to homes across the world.
United for a moment in their task
To drive the Japanese from Burma's soil,
They had destroyed the dram of evil there
And won renown, less famous, but as rare.

41 The Yalta Conference

Within the womb of mortifying war
There grew, of late, an embryonic peace,
Whose three incongruous midwives -
Churchill, Roosevelt, Stalin - now agreed
A venue for delivering the child.
The Soviet leader once again refused
To travel far from where he oversaw
The Russian armies long extended front.
At Yalta, on the warm Crimean coast,
Between the snow-capped mountains and the shore,
Livadia Palace housed their colloquy,
With guards of sculptured lions, and Russian troops
Patrolling in the park of cypress trees.

For Germany they knew the end was near;
That Hitler's only hope was to foment
Disunity amongst his enemies.
The Allies in the west might fear the loss
Of central Europe to the Soviets,
And contemplate another armistice,
Letting the Germans drive the Russians back
With armies then released from other fronts.
But western leaders held to their resolve
To extirpate the Nazis, root and branch,
With Soviet - or any other - aid.
All still agreed that when the war was won
Dismemberment of Germany ensue.
But what of reparations? Had they not
Caused dire inflation, when imposed before,
And fuelled the hate that Hitler thrived upon?
Only the Russians claimed them as a right,
For they had lost far more in wealth and blood
Than any other Allied combatant.
The matter was referred for later times.
Defeated Germans would, at least, be fed.

Then Roosevelt proceeded to declare
That US troops would only stay two years
To guarantee the European peace.
To which the British premier replied
That, next to Britain, France must stand once more
To play her part as occupying power,
And boast of arms befitting her prestige
Against the day when Germany revived.

Already they had settled on the need
To keep the world secure from fresh disputes.
A new United Nations would be formed
On terms of membership hereby agreed.
Even Marshall Stalin deigned admit
That, whilst the three great powers conjoined by war
Preserved their friendship, nothing in the world
Could harm them - come what may. Yet, though they drank
Warm toasts of comradeship, with heartfelt praise
Of one another's leadership and men,
The Polish question tested their intent.

For now the Russian army had regained
Supplies and troops to renew its advance.
The Vistula was crossed, Warsaw was won,
East Prussia taken - but for Konigsberg
And where, in Courland, Hitler kept a host
To safeguard Baltic waters, still required
For testing new electric submarines.
Deep in Silesia the battle raged
For industries on which the Reich relied
For life-blood of its waning polity.
Thus Poland was no longer held in thrall
By German might and all its hated means.
On ancient streets of Warsaw and Krakow
Red army soldiers marched on cobblestones
Which echoed with the ring of Wehrmacht boots.
Was Poland then once more to be a fief,
In vassalage to this newfangled Czar,
Anointed by unnumbered kulaks' blood,
But new acclaimed in patriotic war?

Britain, especially, could not now desert
The nation she had promised to defend,
For whom she had embarked a second time
On war against the German enemy.
Nor could America deny her faith
In self-determination, and the right
To live within a democratic State.
Stalin insisted that the Lublin Poles -
A Communist committee loyal to him -
Should be proclaimed as government in Warsaw.
The western Allies wanted other Poles,
Including those who'd fled to England's shores,
To play a part in equal measure there.
They recognised the Soviet demand
For Polish friendship, vital to prevent
Another German sortie in the east
Against the oft-invaded Russian land.
Churchill, indeed, supported Stalin's claim
On territory Poland had acquired
By fighting with the Russian emigres
Against the Bolshevists of Lenin's time.
Despite the Polish protests, all agreed
The Curzon Line should mark the boundary,
Whilst, in the west, at Germany's expense,
The frontier would reach the Oder's banks.

Uneasily the three great leaders signed
A declaration on the Polish State.
Suspicion still remained. Could Russia trust
The capitalist powers to give regard
To her security, when they themselves
Had long denounced her claims to represent

A classless workers' State? What of Stalin?
Would not puppet governments be set-up
In Poland and the former Hapsburg lands,
Where shadows fell from Russian bayonets
Of Stalin's army, now invincible?
Were Lublin Poles not Moscow's nominees?

Poland's problems drew in high relief
An underlying conflict of ideas.
As fast as peace approached, the bonds relaxed
That checked the clash of alien beliefs.
The vaunted partnership of East and West
Was now revealed for what it truly was -
A wartime marriage of convenience.

The fight against Japan was then discussed,
For Stalin had already offered help,
Provided that the German war was won.
His terms had hardened, for he did not know
How nearly had the U.S.A. achieved
The making of the first atomic bomb.
Yet Roosevelt was eager to employ
The aid of Russia in the Asian war.
For he deplored the loss of US lives
In struggles to the death on barren isles,
Or blasted by the *kamikaze* planes,
Whose suicides cost fifty men for one.
When Stalin asked for what the Czar had lost
When, long ago, his European fleet
Was sunk by Admiral Togo's cannonade,
The President, surprisingly, agreed.
Port Arthur, Darien and Sakhalin

Would be restored; and in Mongolia
The Soviets would be the major power.
The Kurile Islands were a further prize.
For Nippon soldiers faced Siberia.
Engagement there against a new attack
Would stop their redeployment on those fronts
Where US soldiers would be casualties.
For these pragmatic reasons all declined
To honour what was due to Chiang Kai-Shek.
So China lost all rights in this bazaar,
A country which had fought against Japan
For longer than the sum of all the rest.

Thus did the new triumvirate decide
Upon the fate of millions. Yet they knew
That only dire necessity had caused
Alliance of divergent polities.
Whilst Russia and America had armed,
As Anthony and Caesar's heir had done,
Enough to overawe all other powers.
Britain had reached the limit of her strength,
Though would not reach as low as Lepidus.
Were East and West once more to separate,
Until another Actium were fought,
And one emerged with all imperium?
Were nations, like the Poles, to be proscribed,
Condemned in absence to remain unfree
To keep their masters in brief amity?

42 Iwo Jima

While from the Marianas bombers flew
To carry death to cities of Japan,
The US planners looked for staging posts
To harbour fighter escorts, and to save
The damaged bombers on their homeward flights.
Half-way the isle of Iwo Jima lay,
Equipped already with three aerodromes
For sorties by defending Japanese.
Made of volcanic rock, it stood alone,
A stony fortress, narrow in the south,
Where Suribachi rose above the plain,
Its hollowed summit belching sulphur fumes
Above the bean vines, rotting from neglect,
And empty homes of natives sent away.

General Kuribayashi had been told
To make a stronghold of the 'Sulphur Isle'
Which would inflict horrendous casualties.
How many deaths would US troops endure,
Before they ceased advancing on Japan?
Kuribayashi knew of US strength.
He'd left his sabre back in Tokyo,
Expecting death upon this barren isle.
But he resolved that Iwo Jima's cost
Would set the price of war too high to pay.

Despite the view of many officers,
His troops would not contest the landing beach,
Nor even make an early counterstroke.
Instead the island centre would become
An inner fortress, like an ancient keep,
Bristling with obstacles and sighted guns,
Blockhouses, hidden bunkers, pill-boxes,
And miles of tunnel cut into the rock.
Cave experts fashioned blast-proof entrances
And many exits for retreating troops.
Beneath the ground was stored ten weeks supply
Of food and ammunition. Water came
From cisterns or from wells. On pill-box walls
They painted battle vows - 'Before you die,
Ten enemy for one'[27]. Where once the oaks
And screw-pines grew, and fields of sugarcane,
And lemon grass distilled for flavouring,
Now grey volcanic rock, or concrete walls,
Extended everywhere. Where children once
Had played, the dust now blew; where birds had sung,
The dearth of war condemned the silent land.

Kuribayashi had transformed the isle
From earthly scenes to landscapes of the moon.

US aircraft bombed the island fort
For many weeks before invasion came.
On detailed maps they drew a grid of squares,
And bombed each one with systematic care.
The Japanese were driven underground.
Each bomb that fell convinced them even more
That they must dig yet deeper in the rock,
Sink block-houses in stone, and cover guns
With concrete casemates. Volcanic ash made
Very strong cement. Beneath the camouflage
They lived entombed, sleeping in niches in
The tunnel walls, and writing their last words
In letters home, or lines of haiku verse:
'O let me fall, like scattered petals fall'[28].
Naval bombardment followed for three days.
No ships nor aircraft helped the Japanese.
For Iwo Jima was a soldiers' war.

One day they woke to see beyond the shore
A vast armada, many hundred ships.
As gun-boats neared the beach and opened fire,
Anxious defenders prematurely shot,
And gave away positions of their guns.
A salvo from the warships soon destroyed
Those earmarked by a flash or cannon-smoke.
To deep, black sand the landing craft approached,
Disgorging the Marines, whose heavy packs
Weighed down their steps across the sloping beach.
Some guns remained to enfilade the lines

With slowly chattering rounds that cut men down
And left them dying, staining darker still
The soft warm sand. From Suribachi's slopes
A mass of guns - mortars, artillery
And rocket-firing frames - sent missiles down,
Like Summer storms that stained the rusty earth.
The crowded beach became a slaughterhouse,
In which no hand could stay the fall of death
From skies that shrieked with loud hysteria.
Only the sure response of naval guns,
Precision-aimed to fire a barrage down
On pill-boxes and bunkers now engaged,
Enabled some Marines to crawl ahead,
And struggle up the terraces of sand.

Across the beach steel planking was rolled out
For troops aboard amphibious landing trucks,
And wooden sleds for armoured bulldozers.
Causeways were built beneath relentless fire.
This time no reefs nor jungle stood between
Advancing troops and their antagonists.
On Iwo Jima nothing stood between.
From start to finish every yard was won
By brute assault on unprotecting ground.
No *banzai* charge would offer easy prey;
No friendly planes would decimate the foe.
Each Japanese with *Hachimaki* bands
Would fight till death, and let no comrade live
Who might relent, dishonouring his code.

Already on the beaches surgeons worked
With blunt efficiency in sandy pits
To staunch the flow of dead, and marshall back

To waiting ships the ones with life intact.
They, too, were killed by random mortar bombs,
Or shards of shell, or direct hits that struck,
A second time, the wounded as they lay
In stretchers on the avenues of sand.
From Suribachi's cone, where Vulcan fire
Still burned within and heated every rock,
The Japanese artillery could shoot
On crowded beaches and inland patrols,
Who sought in vain for cover. Its summit
Must be taken; only then could US
Forces overrun the isle.

Defenders were unseen. The dead were found,
Still warm beside their guns, with limbs askew,
Naked from blasts, or hideously burnt.
Each shelf of rock, or cave, each concrete post
Was won by brutal infantry assault,
Though naval guns or tanks might shell ahead
Before Marines advanced for their attack.
With covering fire, the bravest ran alone,
To spray a gun through pill-box apertures,
Or throw grenades or satchel charges in,
Or send a burst of searing yellow flame,
Before the desperate occupants could choose
To stand and fire, or risk a quick escape.
Each unit of Marines lost several men,
As enemy posts were taken one by one.
Advance was measured out in yards, or deaths.
The wounded lay till stretcher parties came,
Whilst bodies were soon buried on the beach
In lines of graves, bulldozed in yielding sand.

A flag was raised on Suribachi's cone,
And everywhere the US soldiers cheered -
On bloody slopes, on beaches, out at sea.
It would, they said, assure to the Marines
Five hundred years of national gratitude.
Meanwhile, the rest of Iwo Jima stayed
Beneath the emblem of the Rising Sun.

No men were wasted in the futile hope
Of driving the invaders to the sea.
Instead the Japanese withdrew in stealth
Towards the rocky fastness of the north,
Exacting casualties at every step,
And leaving snipers hidden in the caves,
Or wounded men still armed with live grenades.
None surrendered, save those nearly dead.
Each strongpoint was defended with cross-fire;
Their ammunition did not flash nor smoke,
Making it hard to pin-point where they hid.
Tunnels had angles, built to stop a blast,
And exits to withdraw a garrison.

No code of *samurais* inspired Marines,
Though some were not averse to other faiths,
Or found a mutual strength in comradeship.
Men fought though wounded; dashed ahead alone
To rout a gun-crew; hold a ridge all night.
They rescued injured soldiers under fire,
And threw themselves in trenches on grenades,
And carried back the body of a friend,
Amidst the shells, for decent burial.
'Uncommon valour there was commonplace'[29].

According to the news from Tokyo,
Americans Marines now occupied
An area 'like the forehead of a cat'.
Kuribayashi was more well-informed,
And moved headquarters northwards to 'the Gorge',
A bleak ravine behind the western cliffs.
He knew no help would come, as he'd foreseen
On leaving in Japan his ritual sword.
He ordered that his regimental flag
Should be destroyed, and as Marines closed in,
In sound of firing, wrote a final verse:
'My body shall not perish in the field,
Unless we are avenged. I will be born
Yet seven times again to take up arms.
My country's future is my sole concern,
When weeds shall cover what lies buried here'[30].
Across the steep ravine loudspeakers called,
In halting Japanese, to lay down arms.
The soldiers of Kyushu would not live
To witness such dishonour. So, at last,
Kuribayashi's fort was blown up.

New bombers flew from Iwo Jima's fields -
B 29s, with gleaming silver wings,
Four tons of bombs and central gun control.
It saved more lives of air-crew than were killed
To gain the island by US Marines.
The question still remained, yet more acute
For what occurred upon the 'Sulphur Isle'.
How many more Kuribayashis stood
Between America and victory?
How many men must still be sacrificed

To save the world from pestilence of war?
Only too well the war-lords of Japan
Had taught their people how to venerate
The shrines of war and glory of their race.
Americans were hated and despised -
Barbarians, who mutilate the dead.
To build an empire, fight in its defence,
To die for 'On', to save the Emperor-god,
Preferring death to shame: for such beliefs
The people of Japan might long endure.
The imperial navy was all but destroyed;
The airforce moribund for lack of oil;
But still the army held vast territories.
Formosa, Okinawa, China lay
Beneath the harsh oppression of its rule.

When Roosevelt, now sick and ailing, heard
Of Iwo Jima's cost, did he repent
Of making unconditional demand
For enemy surrender in the war?
Six thousand men had died for eight square miles,
For one volcano, dormant in the sea.
How many for Honshu, and victory?

43 The Fall of Nazi Germany

Success in the Ardennes had led the way
To German triumphs early in the war.
Just so, defeat in those same wooded hills
Ensured the rapid fall of Hitler's Reich.
On every front the flames of war advanced.
The Western Allies looked towards the Rhine,
Expecting that the Wehrmacht would withdraw
To make a final stand along its banks.
Soviet armies fought on Baltic shores,
On Polish plains and by the Danube's banks;
And where the faltering Duce still contrived

To rule a petty province in the north,
An Allied army threatened to disrupt
The Gothic Line that stretched from sea to sea.

Within the Reich the harassed Germans lived
Beset by fears of foreign soldiery,
Oppressed by secret police, hungry and tired,
Deprived of hope in final victory,
Except when briefly roused by Goebbel's voice
Proclaiming on the radio the news
Of secret weapons and the Führer's will
To rid the world of Jews and Bolshevists.
Hitler himself increasingly withdrew
Within the walls of Berlin's Chancellery,
To brood on his betrayal, how alone
He still sustained the force of Germany,
How armies, led by generals in despair,
Retreated in despite of his command
To save each modicum of national land,
Whatever the expense in German lives.

He now forbad withdrawal to the Rhine;
The Siegfried Line must be the barrier.
Montgomery, once again, proposed a plan
To concentrate the Allies in the north
And punch a hole in Germany's defence.
Failure at Arnhem prejudiced his case,
And US generals claimed a proper share
For their own armies, butting on a line
From Aachen to the mountains of the Vosges.
Eisenhower insisted that they cleared
The western Rhineland of all German troops

Before the river obstacle was crossed.
The Reichswald pine woods, black with Winter rain,
Saw bitter fighting. Many died on mines,
But Churchill tanks left German gun-crews dead
Beside the splintered trees and flattened fern.

Though further south the dams upon the Roer
Were opened to delay the next attack,
Wehrmacht resources were too overstretched.
American units struck at many points.
Preceded by an aerial attack,
Or heavy shelling, infantry advanced
Through villages and towns that could recall
The heady days when Hitler had declared
The Rhineland to be occupied again.
Impassively they watched as weary groups,
Bespattered in their field-grey uniforms,
Defended posts with *Panzerfaust* or gun
For half a day, before survivors left.
They waited then to see the Allies come,
White sheets displayed to signalise defeat.
The Siegfried Line was pierced in every zone,
And Patton's force outflanked it in the south
By crossing the Moselle before Koblenz.

East Prussia reaped the harvest Hitler sowed
When he'd declared the nature of the war
Against the Soviets. Now vengeance burned
For years of savagery, for bitter stories heard,
For millions dead and desecrated lands.
Like debris left to mar the tide's retreat,
Soon murder, rape and pillage had befouled

The Russian progress through the eastern towns.
Families hid in cellars, others fled
In frenzied masses heading for the west.
Desperately the Wehrmacht fought to save
Each river line or outpost, though denied
All air support and fortified defence.
Pockets of troops held out behind the lines,
At Konigsberg and Danzig, at Poznan,
And Breslau where they fought until the end.
But this was not the enemy they'd met
In 'Barbarossa''s great encirclements.
The Soviets had mastered now the arts
Of planning their offensives to exploit
A point of weakness with a tank reserve,
And tactical support by army planes.

Whilst Stalin now relied on Stavka's skill,
Hitler ignored the German General Staff,
Believing it defeatist and disloyal.
With passionate appeals Guderian asked
To rationalise the forces in the east
By staged withdrawals on the Baltic coast,
In Hungary and on the Balkan fronts.
Each time the Führer countermanded him,
For reasons which had lost validity -
To keep the Baltic clear for submarines,
To save the bauxite mines of Hungary,
To bolster Mussolini's puppet State.

Despite American protests, Allied plans
Envisaged that Montgomery would lead
A crossing of the Rhine north of the Ruhr.

As German troops withdrew, they blew each bridge,
But at Remagen demolition failed.
So Bradley's soldiers rushed across the span
And held a bridgehead on the eastern bank.
Such chance of war could not be forfeited;
A new attack developed in the south,
Where fewer Germans watched the upper Rhine
From castle heights and ruined monasteries.

Yet cautious still, Montgomery took his time,
Building a force of overweening power
To leap across the broader-flowing Rhine.
The further shore was pulverized with bombs,
And once again artillery rehearsed
A deafening cacophony of shells,
Before the massive fleet of transport planes
Bestrewed the eastern sky with parachutes,
Like some diaspora of tufted seeds
Infesting native land with foreign growth;
Whilst, on the river, heavy smoke-screens hid
A mass of boats chockful of infantry,
Who soon out-fought bewildered enemies.

Within the shattered cities of the Ruhr,
Where, even now, the wheels of industry
Still turned to feed the appetites of war,
The Wehrmacht had an army group deployed.
Encirclement began from north and south.
By Führer order no attempt was made
To break the ring. For now the Ruhr must hold,
Like Stalingrad, to borrow precious time,
Till secret weapons brought a condign peace.

But Model knew of Germany's true plight;
And when the Ruhr was lost, he killed himself.

Eisenhower told Stalin he'd refrain
From pushing hard to take the capital,
But concentrate on central Germany,
Whilst on his northern flank the ports would fall.
Though rumour now was rife that Hitler meant
To fight in a redoubt within the Alps,
Supported by his dedicated troops
Of Waffen SS, Stalin was content.
He likewise claimed that Berlin was no more
The primary objective of his arms,
Whilst, even as he wrote, his staff prepared
A great offensive on the capital.
Only Winston Churchill raised a voice
Against the aims of western strategy,
In fear of Stalin's post-war policies.
Though earlier, at the Yalta conference,
Churchill himself had met Stalin's demand
For Russia to receive a German zone
Much further west beyond the river Elbe.

Throughout the Winter, Alexander's troops,
Depleted by the needs of other fronts,
Confronting skilled defence by Kesselring,
Had struggled to advance on mountain slopes,
Pitted with snow or glutinous with mud.
Each hillside village meted out delay
With snipers and suspected booby-traps.
But in the Spring, as German troops ran short
Of vital fuel, and lost mobility,

A great attack by allies who had fought
From Sicily and past Cassino's rock -
Americans and British, Indians,
New Zealanders, Canadians and Poles -
Now drove the Wehrmacht back towards the Po.
The Allies' armoured strength could now deploy
Across the river's irrigated plains;
So with the winds of March they swept away
The last Cisalpine shreds of Hitler's Reich.

Only the Fascist rump in Italy
Deplored their ally's fate. They still ignored
What Hitler's hand of friendship had provoked:
The soil profaned with ruined crops and herds,
The broken churches, shattered feudal towns,
Civilians dead and wounded, arms disgraced,
Their ancient land dishonoured to the world.
The Duce tried to make a final stand
Within the Valtellina, but was shot
Beside Lake Como by the partisans.
So in Milan's piazza he was hung,
Head down beside his mistress, who'd remained
More loyal than his gross love had merited;
Both taunted now by mobs who once had hailed
The leader of the new *imperium*.

The final scene of German tragedy
Was fittingly enacted in Berlin.
Enormous Russian armies fought their way
Across the Oder, past the Seelow heights,
And through the city suburbs. Battle raged
For every house and street. Old men and boys,
In shabby clothes, marched wearily to war,

With here and there a shouldered *Panzerfaust*.
Protesters were soon shot, or hung in streets,
The name of 'traitor' fixed on every back.
Bravely they fought, survivors from the Marne
Or Tannenberg or Somme, and boys of twelve,
Whose memories did not reach beyond the time
When every German's honour seemed to lie
In violent war and glories of the *Volk*.

So now they died within the tightening ring
Of ceaseless struggle, fighting house by house,
In mounds of rubble, hiding by the dead,
Deafened by shells and clattering of guns,
In numbed surprise at once familiar scenes:
Now boulevards in ruins, gutted frames
Of monumental buildings, and the smell
Of rotting bodies, cordite, excrement.
In cellars, tunnels, sewers, people hid.
Beneath Anhalter station many drowned
As locks were blasted on Landwehr canal.
Along Kurfurstendamm the broken shops
Were looted even now by sullen youths.
Unter den Linden, shorn of Summer leaves,
Lay silent under barricades of limes.
Potsdamer Platz was littered full with wrecks
Of cars upturned, with debris and the dead.

Behind steel doors and narrow passages,
Guarded by SS men in shiny boots,
The Führer lived beneath the Chancellery.
Only a faithful few remained to hear
His private ramblings and the wild commands
Still issued to imaginary troops.

Some, like Henrici, fought to save their men,
Whilst hoping for a break-out to the west.
Others, like Goebbels, humoured Hitler's dream
Of fresh reserves and sudden victory.
Had he not read to Hitler Carlyle's book
Of how King Frederick heard the timely news
That his most bitter enemy had died -
And then brought word of Roosevelt's demise?
What wild elation filled the bunker then,
As though a President's death could bring to nought
The vast alliance now on German soil,
And stop the headlong rush of Zhukov's arms
Across the river Oder to Berlin!
In Goebbels still a kind of loyalty showed.
Not so in Himmler, Goering and the rest,
Who fled the city, hoping to persuade
The western allies that their main intent
Was stopping Russian Bolshevism come.

As Hitler heard the boom of Russian guns
Behind the empty crackle of the 'phone
That witnessed his defunct authority,
His mistress, Eva Braun, told him her wish
To stay with him until the very end;
A city burgomeister married them.
His final testament denounced the race
That proved too weak for his own destiny;
The eastern peoples had evinced their strength,
And Germany must see itself destroyed.
His hatred for the Jews was unredeemed,
And, even, at his death, he could proclaim
That killing them had been his greatest task.

And then, beside his new-made wife, he died,
Shooting himself by pistol in the head;
Eva Braun had swallowed cyanide.
They burnt the bodies, doused with petrol cans.

Within the lands that Hitler had controlled,
In Poland, and especially in the Reich,
Where once the strains of Bach and Mozart rose
In princely palaces of gold and white,
Unspoken horrors now revealed themselves.
Allied soldiers, long immured to death,
Were sickened by the sights of crowded camps
At Buchenwald and Belsen, Ravensbruck,
Mauthausen, Dachau, Auschwitz, Majdenek,
And many more, where starving inmates rose
On limbs of straw. They met their freedom
Staring from a void, with startled eyes,
Like men accused of some monstrosity.
What long-forgotten deeds, what ancient lives,
Had brought them there beyond the love of Man?
Along the barbed-wire fences, empty towers,
No longer manned, still watched for miscreants.
In Summer heat the cold of death prevailed,
Where mounds of bodies, scarcely humankind,
Were quickly buried, covered deep in lime.
The silent queues of prisoners stood bemused,
Awaiting disinfectant, and the pain
Of reassembling fragments of their lives.
The sick still lay on filthy palliasses,
Dying of typhus, or tuberculous,
With open mouths and cheek bones prominent.
A few, with arms extended, called for food.

Their captors now had fled: the brutish guards,
Who eight feet high on metal hooks had hung
Those prisoners who'd attempted to escape,
Or stole, or answered back, or smiled;
Officials, quietly signing lives away
On numbered lists, with notes of property,
Of jewellery found concealed about the dead,
Of hair shaved off, extracted gold from teeth;
And Commandants, who oversaw their camps,
Like managers of small town abattoirs.
To such pathetic men had power devolved
In that proud land where once the tribes had fought,
Led by Arminius, to humble Rome.

Before the Russian armies thousands fled,
Hoping to find some mercy in the west.
Though German generals sought a separate peace
To end the fighting on the western front
And hold a line against the Soviets,
No compromise was made by Eisenhower.
Americans and Russians on the Elbe
Met at Torgau. Victory was complete.
In Italy an armistice was signed.
Near Luneburg, Montgomery received
Surrender of the Wehrmacht in the north.
At Rheims the Germans finally agreed
To unconditional yielding of their arms.
On every front where German soldiers stood,
The battle ceased. The dust of ruins lay,
In front of them, behind, to right and left,
Upon the dead, upon those more bereft.

44 Hiroshima

Intensive bombing from low altitude
Of cities like Kobe and Nagoya,
Soon set alight the flimsy wooden homes
And crowded blocks of Nippon industry.
Great conflagrations raged in Tokyo,
Devoid of proper means of fire control.
Eighty thousand perished in the flames,
Their bodies piled on bridges, roads or paths,
Some lost in boiling water of canals.
Millions were homeless, as B 29s

Then shifted their attack to smaller towns.
Few ships now reached Japan from foreign shores.
Her merchant navy, drastically reduced
By US submarines and air attack,
No longer brought materials and food
To keep alive her war economy.
Deprived of oil, her aircraft could not fly.
Even her armies, still formidable,
Were scarcely mobile, save by foot or mule.
In Tokyo the Imperial government changed,
As war's misfortunes cast the leaders down.
Yet those in whom unspoken thoughts prevailed
Of seeking peace dared little for the fear
Of public shame or an assassin's knife.
Nor had the Emperor ever shown dissent
From what his government had resolved to do,
Though privately he advocated peace.

Invasion of Okinawa brought again
The awful toll of thousands dead and maimed.
Once more the Japanese, in their redoubts,
Made every yard extravagant in blood.
Civilians died as fast as combatants.
With memories of Okinawa's cost,
US planners faced the crucial task
Of preparation for the final stage:
Invasion of the homeland of Japan.
Prior to a landing on Honshu,
They chose Kyushu for the first assault.
In rugged mountains, armies well supplied,
Fighting to the last embittered man,
Would make invaders pay the fullest price -

More than for Philippines, or other isles
Not sacred to the race of *samurai*.
All able-bodied citizens might fight
In sacrificial combat, like those youths
Who even now as *kamikazes* died.
What then would Honshu cost in US lives?
How many letters home would praise a son
For giving up the fickle flame of life
Upon a wooded hill in far Japan?
How many would return as pensioners,
Without an arm or leg, sightless or deaf,
Ugly with scars, emotionally disturbed?
What sailors would be drowned, or massacred,
By suicide attacks of ship or plane,
As they disturbed the peaceful inland seas
And threatened the dominion of a god?
Were those who lay in graves on Tarawa,
New Guinea, Philippines, Guadalcanal,
Who'd died in thousands for the slender prize
Of Iwo Jima and the Ryukyu Isles,
Who'd lost their lives beneath the blackened sky
When first the Zeros bombed Pearl Harbour's fleet -
Were these no more than foretastes of the feast
That death would dine on, when invasion came
To violate the island of Honshu?

After the war began there was concern
That German science was pre-eminent.
Could physicists, at Nazi instance, make -
Before the war was won - an atom bomb?
Thus Roosevelt and Churchill in response,
Soon authorised co-operative work.

407

A fugitive from Fascist Italy,
Enrico Fermi, learnt how to control
A fission chain reaction. At great cost
Nuclear weapons could now be produced.
Adolf Hitler had not seen their worth,
So German science turned to other schemes.
Then, in the desert, south of Albuquerque,
A nuclear explosion proved success
For Oppenheimer's team of scientists.

Though European war was at an end,
Japan's belligerence and brutal crimes,
Compounded still in China and elsewhere,
Might justify the use of atom bombs.
Yet ancient Dresden's heart and people died,
Immolated by conventional raids,
And gutted cities right across Japan
Yielded abundant harvest of the dead.
What was unique about an atom bomb?
Could Allied lives, and Japanese, be saved
By showing how its cataclysmic might,
Divine in origin, could be excuse
For swift surrender without loss of face?

It fell to Harry Truman to decide,
A task bequeathed by Franklin Roosevelt,
Who died before the Potsdam conference,
Where Stalin was informed - but not impressed -
Of US manufacture of the bomb.
The Russian leader saw the chance for gains
Whatever way a victory was attained.
Nor would he act as broker for a peace,

When Nippon leaders sought his offices.
But Churchill did not hesitate to give
Unqualified support for Truman's choice
To use the bomb to end the Asian war.
He saw it as averting butchery
By manifesting overwhelming power.

From Tinian Island three B 29s
Rose early in the August morning sun
To fly to Hiroshima, built upon
The Ota's delta land and ringed by hills,
And now selected for its major part
In war production and in cantonment.
Despite the leaflets dropped to warn of raids,
Not many left, for most were sanguine still
Their city would be spared. One false alarm -
For just a weather plane - led them to hope
That this was but another August day,
Of brilliant sunshine, mirrored in the gleam
Of estuaries that opened on the sea.

Not every one of Truman's Chiefs of Staff
Approved his will to use such wanton power.
Some, like Admiral Leahy, still affirmed
That bombing and the submarine blockade
Would force a quick surrender on Japan.
They knew the overtures already made
To Moscow for negotiated peace.
Was unconditional victory worth the price
Of lighting now the flames of nuclear war?
But help from Russia would not be required
If at one stroke Japan were impotent.

And how could Truman justify the cost -
Two billion dollars of expenditure -
On one vast project never utilised?
And yet most telling of the arguments
That sent a Superfortress, with one bomb,
Equivalent to twenty thousand tons
Of high explosive trinitrotoluene,
To drop on Hiroshima's populace -
Men, women, children, aged and infirm -
Was that the Nippon soldiers, still in arms
And honour-bound to save the Emperor-god,
Would not surrender, even in defeat.
Only a prodigious new event,
An intervention by divinity,
If goddess Amaterasu herself
Might shatter now their hardened shell of pride.

On board 'Enola Gay', the leading plane,
A naval expert primed the fearsome bomb
Of critical mass of pure uranium.
The fated city, six miles down below,
Gave perfect vision for the bombardier.
As all three planes peeled off to fly away,
A dazzling light, as bright as many suns,
Obliterated all, whilst searing heat
Consumed the core of Hiroshima's life
In deathly silence, till a ponderous knell
Reverberated round the scalded hills
And fled across the slowly darkening sea.
A vast, excrescent cloud rose tumour-like,
To mask the sun and chill the shadowed earth.
Within the city, Death alone remained -

Lord of the scattered bodies, black with burns,
Of twisted frames of steel, of rubble heaps,
Of perished beasts, of ghastly emptiness -
Now absolute and Lord of Life itself.

Two days later Stalin kept his word,
When Russian troops attacked Manchuria
And rapidly advanced past Nomonham,
Where years before the Japanese were held.
Divided counsel ruled in Tokyo:
Some argued now for peace, but army chiefs,
Aware of how their forces were deployed
Across the face of China and elsewhere,
Still advocated war, content to see
The nation perish sooner than their creed.
Were these the *samurai* that Basho knew,
Who'd fought to save the innocent and weak?
Already Hirohito had proposed
The search for peace, when 'Yamato' was sunk
And sea defence reduced to no account.
Now, more boldly, he proclaimed his will
To overrule conciliar dissent.
Saving but his own imperial rights,
Surrender would be made to Allied force.

Meanwhile a second bomb fell on Japan,
Destroying Nagasaki's ancient port.
Thus she surrendered on the Allied terms
That Hirohito's power would be curtailed,
As subject to the occupying power.
In homes throughout the islands people heard,
Unknown before, the *tenno's* high-pitched voice,

411

Obsequious to the Nation of the Gods,
But speaking in the language of the Court,
Which only some could clearly understand,
To end the grievous wounds and massacre:
'We ask: endure the unendurable,
And be the incarnation of Our will.'[31]
Only a few resisted the demand
By leading an abortive armed revolt.
For war itself, in Hiroshima's fire,
Had satisfied its covetous desire.

Sources of Words in Quotation Marks

The demands of metre and context have usually prevented the use of exact quotations. Meaning has been preserved as far as possible.

[1] M. Gilbert, *Finest Hour*, p292

[2] from the Japanese martial song, 'Umi Yukaba'

[3] W. Shakespeare, *The Taming of the Shrew*, Act 5, Sc 2

[4] G.A. Craig, *Germany 1866-1945*, p758

[5] N. Hamilton, *The Making of a General*, pp622-5

[6] K. Douglas, 'Vergissmeinnicht' in *The Terrible Rain*, ed. B. Gardner, pp107-8

[7] ed. D. Flower and J. Reeves, *The War 1939-1945*, p486

[8] ed. J. Noakes and G. Pridham, *Documents on Nazism 1919-1945*, Vol.IV, p320

[9] J. Noakes and G. Pridham, ibid. Vol.III, p1155

[10] J. Keegan, *The Price of Admiralty*, p310

[11] M. Koniev quoted in D. Flower and J. Reeves, ibid. p828

[12] von Mellenthin quoted in D. Flower and J. Reeves, ibid. p828

[13] W.S. Churchill, *Closing the Ring*, p47, vol 5 of *The Second World War*.

[14] J. Terraine, *The Right of the Line*, p548

[15] O. Berggolts in H.E. Salisbury, *The 900 Days: the Siege of Leningrad*, p568

[16] D. Flower and J. Reeves, ibid. p690-691

[17] W.S. Churchill, *Closing the Ring*, p432

[18] W. Shakespeare, *Julius Caesar*, Act I, Sc 1

[19] W.J. Slim, *Defeat into Victory*, p298

[20] D. Flower and J. Reeves, ibid. p794

[21] D. Flower and J. Reeves, ibid. p801

[22] J. Fest, *Plotting Hitler's Death*, trans. B. Little, p278

[23] J. Fest, ibid. pp173, 290

[24] G. Deschner, *Warsaw Rising*, p130

[25] J. Lacouture, *De Gaulle: The Rebel*, trans. P. O'Brian, p575

[26] R. Hamer, *A Choice of Anglo-Saxon Verse*, p69

[27] R.H. Spector, *Eagle Against the Sun*, p495

[28] R.F. Newcomb, *Iwo Jima*, p14

[29] R.H. Spector, ibid. p503

[30] R.F. Newcomb, ibid. p272

[31] D. Flower and J. Reeves, ibid. p1035

Main Works Consulted

Allen T.B., 'The Battle of Midway' in *National Geographic* Vol 195 No 4 April 1999

Allen W.E.D.& Muratoff P., *The Russian Campaigns of 1941-43*, Penguin, 1946

Beevor A., *Stalingrad*, Viking Press, 1998

Belfield E. and Essame H., *The Battle of Normandy*, B.T. Batsford, 1965

Bradley O., *A Soldier's Story*, Henry Holt and Co., New York, 1951

Bryant A., *Triumph in the West*, Collins, 1959

Bryant A., *The Turn of the Tide*, Fontana, 1965

Campbell C., *The World War II Fact Book*, Black Cat, 1985

Cannadine D. (ed.), *The Speeches of Winston Churchill*, Penguin, 1990

Carver M., *El Alamein*, Wordsworth, 1962

Churchill W.S., *The Second World War* (6 vols.), Cassell, 1952

Clark A., *Barbarossa*, Cassell, 1965

Commonwealth War Graves Commission., *Recipients of the Victoria Cross*

Cooper A., *Born Leader*, Independent, 1993

Craig G., *Germany 1866-1945*, OUP, 1978

Deschner G., *Warsaw Rising*, Ballantine, 1972

de Gaulle C., *Memoires de Guerre* (3 vols.), Plon, 1956

Djilas M., *Wartime* (trans. Petrovich M.B.), Secker and Warburg, 1977

Dundas H., *Flying Start*, Hutchinson, 1998

Eisenhower D., *Crusade in Europe*, Doubleday, 1948

Encyclopaedia Britannica (fifteenth edition)

Fadeyev A., *Leningrad in the Days of the Blockade* (trans. Charques R.D.), Greenwood Press, 1971

Fest J., *Hitler*, Weidenfeld and Nicholson,1974

Fest J., *Plotting Hitler's Death*, Weidenfeld & Nicolson, 1996

Flower D. and Reeves J., *The War 1939-1945*

Foot M.R.D., *Resistance*, Granada, 1978

Fraser D., *And We Shall Shock Them*, Hodder & Stoughton, 1983

Gailey H.A., *War in the Pacific*, Presidio Press, 1996

Gardner B. (ed.), *The Terrible Rain*, OUP, 1974

Gibson G., *Enemy Coast Ahead*, 1946

Gilbert M., *Second World War*, Holt McDougal, 1984

Gill H., *The Journey back from Hell*, HarperCollins, 1994

Guderian H., *Panzer Leader*, Penguin, 2009

Goure L., *The Siege of Leningrad*, Stanford UP, 1962

Hamer R., *A Choice of Anglo-Saxon Verse*, Faber & Faber, 1970

Hastings M., *Bomber Command*, Pan Books, 1981

Hastings M., *Das Reich*, Pan Books, 1983

Hastings M., *Overlord: D-Day and the Battle for Normandy 1944*, Michael Joseph, 1984

Hamilton N., *Monty: The Making of a General*, Hamlyn Paperbacks, 1982

Hawes S. and White R.(eds.) *Resistance in Europe 1939-1945*, Viking, 1975

Heilig B., *Why the German Republic Fell*, Robert Schalkenbach Foundation, 1945

Henig R., *The Origins of the Second World War*, Routledge, 1984

Hersey J., *Hiroshima*, Alfred A. Knopf, 1946

Horne A., *The Lonely Leader*, Pan, 1994

Horne A., *To Lose a Battle*, Penguin, 1969

Jones R.V., *Most Secret War*, Penguin, 1978

Keegan J., *The Price of Admiralty*

Kedward H.R., *Occupied France*, Blackwell, 1985

Kiriakopoulos G.C., *Days to Destiny*, Franklin Watts Ltd, 1985

Lacouture J., *De Gaulle* (2 vols. trans. O'Brian P.O.) Harvill, 1991

Laffen J., *British VCs of World War II*, Sutton, 1997

Lapierre D. and Collins L., *Paris Brule-t-il?*, Robert Laffont, 1964

Liddell Hart B.H., *History of the Second World War*, Bookthrift Co, 1971

Liddell Hart B.H., *The Other Side of the Hill*, Cassell, 1951

Maclean F., *Eastern Approaches*, J. Cape, 1949

Matanle I., *World War II*, Colour Library Books, 1989

Masson P. (ed.), *The Second World War* (Larousse), Longmeadow, 1989

Mau H. and Krausnick H., *German History 1933-45*, Oswald Wolff, 1962

Michel H., *Histoire de la Resistance*, 1950

Michel H., *La Defaite de la France*, 1980

Michel H., *La Seconde Guerre Mondiale*, 1972

Montgomery B., *El Alamein to the River Sangro*, Hutchinson, 1948

Montgomery B., *Memoirs of Montgomery of Alamein*, Companion Book Club, 1958

Morgan T., *An Uncertain Hour*, Arbor House, 1990

Natkiel R., *Atlas of World War II*, Military Press, 1985

Newcomb R.F., *Iwo Jima*, Holt, Rinehart and Winston; 1st edition (1965)

Noakes J. and Pridham G.(eds.), *Nazism 1919-45*, Exeter, 1988

Ousby I., *Occupation*, Pimlico, 1999

Overy R., *Why the Allies Won*, Strategy, 1995

Pean P., *Vies et Morts de Jean* Moulin, 1999

Salisbury H.E., *The 900 Days: the Siege of Leningrad*, Da Capo, 2003

Saville-Sneath R.A., *Aircraft Recognition*, Penguin, 1943

Schoenbrun D., *Maquis*, Robert Hale, 1990

Shirer W., *The Rise and Fall of the Third Reich*, Simon & Schuster, 1960

Slim W.J., *Defeat into Victory*, Pan Books, 1999

Spector R.H., *Eagle against the Sun*, Macmillan, 1984

Terraine J., *The Right of the Line*, Hodder & Stoughton, 1985

Tickell J., Odette, Chapman & Hall, 1949

Trevor-Roper H. (intro.), *Hitler's Table Talk*, Enigma Books, 2000

van der Post L., *The Night of the New Moon*, Hogarth Press, 1970

Vercors, *Silence de la Mer*, 1942

von Mellenthin F.W., *Panzer Battles 1939-1945*, University of Oklahoma Press, 1956

Wilmot C., *The Struggle for Europe*, Collins, 1952

Wilmott H.P., *The Great Crusade*, Free Press, 1991

Wood A., *War in Europe 1939-45*, Longman Higher Education, 1987

Wykes A., *The Siege of Leningrad*, Ballantine Books, 1968